STAGE
MANAGEMENT
AND THEATRECRAFT

PLATE I

Mr. Gillie (James Bridie), Garrick Theatre, London

STAGE
MANAGEMENT
AND THEATRECRAFT

A Stage Manager's Handbook

by

HENDRIK BAKER

Line Drawings by
MARGARET WOODWARD

Foreword by
BASIL DEAN, C.B.E.

FOURTH EDITION

LONDON
J. GARNET MILLER LTD

NEW YORK
THEATRE ARTS BOOKS/ROUTLEDGE

FOURTH EDITION
published in 1988 by
J. GARNET MILLER LTD
311 Worcester Road, Malvern, Worcestershire
WR14 1AN
© Copyright   1988 by Hendrik Baker

ISBN O 85343 556 1

Published in the U.S.A. by
Theatre Arts Books
an imprint of Routledge
29 West 35th Street
New York, NY 10001
U.S.A.
ISBN 0-87830-559-9

Library of Congress Catalog Card No. 68-16449

In both countries:
FIRST EDITION 1968
SECOND EDITION 1971

Printed in Great Britain by A. Wheaton & Co Ltd, Exeter

FOREWORD

A letter to the Author from BASIL DEAN, C.B.E.

Dear Hendrik Baker,

This Handbook will prove of immense value, not only to the student contemplating entrance to our profession as a stage manager, but also to the enthusiastic amateur, who need no longer regard the job as appropriate for the least talented member of the troupe, but as one possessing its own especial satisfactions. In my young days I would have jumped for joy to have had such a compendious volume at my elbow, instead of being left to pick up scraps of information as I went along, like a hen ranging the farmyard.

The stage-manager is a key figure in the modern theatre. As the various techniques of stage craft continue to advance, so, too, do his responsibilities for the efficiency of the whole production. The clear and precise terms in which each item of information is set forth in this Handbook is a cogent reminder that an ordered, disciplined mind—' first things first ' is a good adage!—and a refusal to panic in emergency are essential for good stage-management.

This is a notable contribution to the practical literature of the stage. I wish it every success.

Yours sincerely,

Basil Dean.

London, N.W.8
September, 1967

To

DOROTHY ELTON

I never find, when the prompter signals, ' Next,'
Scenes change as fast as in the text.
Counterweights stick; a god who intervenes
Caught in mid air cries out on the machines.
A tuft of trees juts out from the ocean's swell,
And half of Heaven remains in the midst of Hell.
—*La Fontaine.*
Translated by Lee Simonson.

CONTENTS

SCENE DESIGNS

by the author

LINE DRAWINGS AND PLOTS

ACKNOWLEDGEMENTS

The Author and the Publishers are most grateful to Mr. Laurence Atteridge (on behalf of the management of the St. Martin's Theatre, London) for permitting the reproduction of the stage and lighting plans (Figs. 9 and 36) and to Mr. C. J. Bates, A.R.I.B.A., William Holford and Partners for the plan of the Northcott Devon Theatre, Exeter (Fig. 21), and to the Questors Ltd., for Fig. 19.

Thanks are due to the following for permission to reproduce photographs and drawings: Mr. Houston Rogers (Plates 1, 14, 15 and 17); Mr. Angus McBean (Plates 6, 7 and 16); The Swarbrick Studios (Plates 8–13 and 18); the Hall Stage Equipment Company (Plates B, C, E, DD and EE, Figs. 10, 13, 14, 24, 25, 26, 28, 29, 30 and 31); Brunskill and Loveday Ltd. (Plate F); *The Chemist and Druggist* (Plate G); *The Scotsman* for Plates 2, 3, 4 and 5; the National Theatre for Plate Va and Vb; The Architectural Review for Plates H and Z b and for Fig. 54; The Architect's Journal for Plates X, Y, Za, AA and CCa and CCb; to Denys Lasdun, Redhouse and Softley for Plates R and T and for Figs. 57, 59, 60 and 61; to Transworld Airways for Plate BB (5); and to John Reilly Photography, Hinckley, Leics. for assistance in preparing illustrations.

The lighting equipment and colour mediums illustrated in Chapter 8 are obtainable from the Strand Electric and Engineering Co. Ltd. (Figs. 37–43 and 51).

INTRODUCTION

A play begins with an idea. The idea is the source of the author's inspiration which he develops in his story. He creates characters, situations and dialogue and his manuscript is the inspiration for the production. While the author creates the play, others have to convey his ideas for it to be performed. These can be divided into two groups. Artists who are creative and those whose work is interpretative. The author, director and designer work in the field of creative ideas. The director gives his ideas to the artists who, in turn, absorb them creatively by adding something of their own to what he has told them. They are engaged in interpreting the play with others employed behind the scene.

The work of the stage manager embraces something of both groups for he can be described as the link between the creative idea and its translation to practical reality. He unites the work of all individuals and departments engaged in the production of the play. The stage manager is the representative of the producer or manager and is responsible to him for everything connected with the play on the stage side of the proscenium. The producer delegates the preparation of the show to the director and the stage manager carries out the director's instructions so far as these are concerned with the mechanical side of the production. From the first night, the stage manager assumes responsibility for the director and sees that the performance on the first night continues throughout the run of the play. He will have one or more assistants according to the size of the production. The assistant stage manager is his deputy; responsible for maintaining an accurate record of rehearsals and keeping him closely informed on all matters relating to them. The stage manager is in contact with everyone associated in the production and the following list will provide some details so that they are understood when mentioned later in this handbook.

THE PRODUCER OR MANAGER

At the head of a play bill or programme is the presentation. Usually a company presents the play or an individual does so on behalf of a company. He is called the producer and is responsible for the finance and supervision of everything concerned in the production.

THE AUTHOR

He writes the play and according to his contract retains control over its presentation. He may require a specific kind of production i.e. by an established management with a view to a London or New York theatre. He approves the cast and the director. He attends rehearsals and changes in the manuscript are made with his approval.

THE DIRECTOR

He directs the play. He approves the actors, scene designs and costumes and plans the staging of the play for presentation in the theatre. He rehearses the actors and everything created for the performance is under his control.

THE DESIGNER

He designs the settings and costumes for approval by the producer and director. He supervises the construction and painting of the settings and chooses the furnishings required.

GENERAL OR BUSINESS MANAGER

He assists the producer in all matters concerned with the presentation of the play. In particular he attends to contracts and financial details of income and expenditure and provides a detailed analysis of the financial situation in the form of an estimate of box office receipts and budget of production cost.

PRODUCTION MANAGER

He is responsible for organisation of the stage departments and has the specialist's knowledge of the whole field of technical production. With a company presenting a variety of plays from drama to musical productions his duties are exacting and include administration of the stage, electrical, property and wardrobe departments. He is a competent organiser and combines management with technical and artistic skill.

COMPANY MANAGER

He is engaged for a particular production and is the producer's business representative with the play.

PRESS REPRESENTATIVE

He attends to all matters relating to advance and current publicity.

PRODUCTION STAGE STAFF

Master Carpenter. He is in charge of all stage staff and is the senior member of the production staff. He supervises the setting and handling of the scenery and is concerned afterwards in its maintenance.

Property Master. He is responsible for properties and frequently is highly experienced in their manufacture. He assists the designer and his originality finds expression in all kinds of emergencies. He maintains the furniture and properties and is responsible for the provision and handling of articles used during the performance.

Chief Electrician. He obtains the lighting equipment and electrical effects and is responsible for the maintenance of the electrical and engineering equipment in the theatre. During the performance, the lighting equipment is operated under his control. Depending on the size of the production, he may also be responsible for the recording equipment.

Wardrobe Mistress. She assists the costume designer in the preparation of the costumes. Thereafter she is in charge of the wardrobe and is responsible for cleaning and repair. Her staff includes assistants and dressers attached to the artists. When the wardrobe mistress is employed permanently in a theatre, she is often responsible for the cleaners and she is known as the Housekeeper.

In productions with a small number of artists and staff, the stage manager combines the duties of company manager and is described as *company and stage manager*. His first assistant is called the *deputy stage manager* and is in charge of the performance from the prompt corner, with one or more *assistant stage managers* to help him. I have tried here to give information concerning the organisation and technical methods used in the professional theatre. Work in the amateur theatre includes many aspects of the professional stage and although the amateur stage manager will not follow professional custom exactly, I hope he will find the methods described useful in giving him a foundation on which to build. The technical side of the theatre has a long history and many devices used in the past continue to be the best solution to problems found today. The considerable advance in lighting and mechanical reproduction brings a fascinating addition to the work and it is hoped that this book may interest those attracted to it and perhaps encourage some to begin a stage career.

CHAPTER I

THE HISTORY OF THE STAGE

' Good luck to all. Tell Pfutz not to be too long dying'—Telegram from the Duke of Saxe-Meiningen to his company on the opening night of *Julius Caesar*.'

THE GREEK THEATRE

The working space of the theatre is a raised platform upon which the play is performed and it is divided from the audience by an opening called the proscenium arch. Before discussing the mechanism of the stage, it may be of interest to describe briefly the origin and development of the stage from the time when it was simply a flat space with an altar at the foot of a hill. This was the earliest form of Greek theatre, which was later improved by the addition of wooden or stone benches built in a semi-circle behind one another up the hillside around the central viewing area. The Greek name for a spectacle is *thea* and they called the place where the performance was seen the *theatron*, from which we have received our word ' theatre.'

The acting space was called the *orchestra*. There was no scenery and the play was illustrated entirely by the costumes and masks of the players. In due course something more was needed to interest and entertain the audience and a symbol or object significant to the play was placed in a central position on the acting area. The first attempt at scenery had begun. Later a hut was built as a background for the actors, and was also used as a dressing room. It was called the *skene*—from which we get the words ' scene ' and ' scenery.'

The skene had a central door through which the players appeared and this wall and opening were called ' front of the skene.' From this originates the word *proscenium*. It will be seen that the position of our proscenium arch was originally at the back of the acting area of the stage. The central opening had a quality of isolation which, in subsequent periods of history, was used for the exhibition of tableaux, as in the Elizabethan theatre. The open stage with few entrances imposed restrictions on the Greek dramatist who was concerned with making his story convincing to the audience. The skene, which later contained three doors, gave the playwright more freedom in advancing his plot and provided an opportunity for a variety of entrances and exits of his characters. The façade of the skene became the scenic background which was subsequently established as a permanent stone setting in the form of a palace or temple. To indicate a scene, a statue was placed to identify the locality of a temple, and painted panels were inserted between the columns of the façade to illustrate a group of trees or other exterior scene.

Nevertheless, the playwright was restricted in his efforts to portray an interior scene. To overcome this difficulty a tableau was arranged upon a wooden platform on wheels—the wagon stage or *eccyclema*—which at the instant required was rolled into view through the large centre doors of the skene. An early eccyclema was a low semi-circular platform which could be revolved on a pivot and swung out at any of the doors of the skene. The device was perhaps the forerunner of a simple revolving stage. Another method for changing scenes was the *periaktoi*. Three-sided prisms revolving on wooden pegs were mounted flush with the walls on either side of the stage. The three sides were painted with different localities which in turn were revolved towards the audience. The need for concrete illustrations has always been essential in the development of the playwright's dramatic situations. And the stimulation of make-believe was evident in the desire of the early dramatists to obtain every possible scenic assistance to illustrate their plots. Some of the methods achieved were so practical that they have survived today. The eccyclema is the forerunner of our boat-truck and the mechanism devised for the periaktoi is revived in musical plays where part of the scene can be quickly revolved to alternate with something quite different painted on the other side. Later in Greek history, a raised platform was built in front of the skene where the actors were more clearly seen. This was the earliest indication of the stage on which we perform today.

THE GREEK PLAYS

Two influences were responsible for the origin of the Greek theatre and the plays performed there. The dramatic movement in the plays came from religious rites and the plots were developed from the early myths that were symbolic of human experience. The Greeks were highly civilised with a beautiful language, but lacking any historical background, were not far removed from barbarism. They were realists inasmuch as they worshipped humanity, and fate was the only power pre-determining events that controlled them. Their pagan religion included many gods, all of them endowed with human passions, mainly concerned with their own affairs and only sometimes interested in mortals. Wine was drunk often to excess and water was regarded as useful in physical pleasures for swimming and sailing. They liked parades and in the Spring and Autumn, pro-cessions were organised devoted to Dionysus or Bacchus, the god of wine, merriment and fruitfulness.

This popular deity was supposed to live in vineyards and the crowd following the procession wore goat-skins, danced and sang while making sounds like this animal. The goat singer was called a ' tragos-oidos,' and this name developed into the word *tragedy*, meaning a play with an unhappy ending. Likewise the name ' comos ' became *comedy* of which Aristophanes, born in 448 B.C., was the leading dramatist later in Greek history. At the head of the parade were musicians playing the Pipes of Pan. The Greeks, finding the procession tedious after a while, looked for something more entertaining, and Thespis, a young poet among them, stepped forward and gave his lines to one of its members who delivered them with suitable gestures to the leader of the musicians. The lines were in the form of questions to which the musician replied according to what the poet had inscribed for him. The performance of this dialogue soon became a popular event and thereafter every procession had a ' scene ' acted in this way.

Shrines to Dionysus were built and placed at the foot of a hill where the songs and dialogues were enacted with the audience seated around the hillside— the earliest form of theatre. Members of the procession formed themselves into a chorus which, assembled in the circular dancing space or orchestra, chanted and danced to the music of the Pipe. The Leader led the chanting and his contribution alternated with the singing of the rather noisy male chorus. The festival commenced with rites at the altar and the production of plays became part of the religious rite.

THE GREEK STAGE

The actor introduced by Thespis with the chorus and its leader became the early pattern in which the plays were written. He also invented the large clay mask expressing happiness or sorrow which the actor wore to show the spectators the type of character he portrayed. All action in the play took place in the orchestra and serious dramatic incident was supposed to have taken place off-stage. Aeschylus, 525 B.C., the greatest of Greek tragedians, rewrote songs and recitations and made the innovation of writing them in plays with characters for two actors. He was a man of the theatre and had the director's eye for scenic effect. The Greek stage was built at the foot of a hill and consequently was banked up at the rear with a drop to ground level. The edge of the stage was a line interrupting a view of open countryside with the temple of Dionysus at the side. His plays were timed to start before daybreak and so stage-managed that the dialogue coincided with the natural drama of the sun flooding the countryside and rising in an indigo sky previously lit with stars just before the dawn. He acted in his own plays, like Shakespeare, and it is said wrote ninety plays of which only seven have survived. A prophecy foretold he would die by a blow from heaven and there is a legend that he was killed by an eagle, who, unable to crack the shell of a tortoise, mistook the poet's bald head for a stone and dropped the tortoise on it.

Thirty years later, Sophocles, 495 B.C., introduced three characters in his plays and wrote in verse. He was good humoured, pleasure-loving and his characters were written for actors. He is credited with the introduction of scene-painting though Aeschylus made the greatest improvement in the machinery of the stage.

The skene was at first a slender wooden structure capable of being altered to what each play required. Doubling of parts was essential when performing in a vast arena, as the time it took for the players to enter and leave the stage delayed the performance. In the skene, the actor could change his mask, used not only to identify the character but also to project his voice to the audience, many of whom were seated at a great distance from the stage. The actor with the best voice won the day and the strength of his voice was the quality applauded. He grew in popularity and, like all performers, reacted to his audience. His 'fans' gave him encouragement and no doubt some business was introduced that 'brought down the house.' In the fourth century B.C. a law was passed to restrain enraptured actors and telling them not to make improvements in the texts of classical plays.

The Athenian Theatre

When the façade of the skene became a permanent stone setting, which in Athens was one hundred and fifty-two feet wide, the Greek audience continued to regard it as scenery. Machinery was used for spectacular effects and a stage direction at the end of *Medea* by Euripides, 484 B.C., reads: ' Medea is seen on the roof, standing on a chariot of winged dragons, in which are the children's bodies. She rises on the chariot and is slowly borne away.' Realism was always important to the Greek audience who desired to see with their own eyes the spectacle of a god borne aloft no matter that it was done in broad daylight with a crane and creaking pulleys. Other effects were invented later; trapdoors were included also in the floor of the orchestra, and a prototype of the cyclorama used today—the *hemicyclon* was employed, being a semi-circle of canvas to improve a distant view.

The theatre in Athens held 30,000 people and everyone was expected to attend the religious festival. The front row of seats was reserved for the priests and the Priest of Dionysus occupied a specially carved armchair in the centre. A vast amphitheatre was needed to accommodate this number of spectators and the last row of seats was two hundred and twenty-seven feet from the front of the orchestra. The Greek theatre is sometimes given as an example of the benefit gained by thrusting the actors into the midst of the audience. The enormous size of the theatre at Athens tends to dispute this view. Where it succeeded was not by the proximity of the actor to the spectators but by his power to dominate and entertain them. The actors not only told the story of the play but were able to penetrate the minds of the audience.

The Greek theatre set the seal of theatrical atmosphere and the audience was not by any means the reverent one associated with behaviour in church. An actor or incident could ' stop the show ' and the plays were constantly interrupted with anything handy hurled on the stage. Aeschylus in one of his plays was thought to have revealed a religious mystery and to escape the wrath of the public fled behind the altar. A riot caused in a play by Euripides was only quelled when the author came forward to justify the remark that offended the audience. Several plays were performed at a time and if a performer did not give satisfaction, hisses and groans made him leave the stage. The next play commenced and on one occasion an actor was not ready in time because all the earlier performers were hissed from the stage.

It is remarkable that the great period in Greek play-writing, beginning with Aeschylus and ending with the tragedies of Euripides, was completed in a span of fifty-three years. Equally impressive is the fact that in Elizabethan England all the plays of Shakespeare, Ben Jonson, Marlowe, Beaumont and Fletcher, Massinger, Webster, and Heywood were written in thirty-eight years.

Towards the end of this period, comedy came to the Athenian stage. Aristophanes is the author best re-membered and his situations are so comic that they give amusement today. His plots were cartoons illustrated in verse and satirical of public figures. The players' masks resembled famous personalities; his buffoonery was like the music hall and his wit could anticipate French revue. Athens lost the position of cultural centre at the close of the fifth century. Other city states were building theatres and the old religious faiths were replaced by a material grasping for wealth predominant in the middle class. The internal war of the city states— on the one hand occupied with military ambition and on the other peace-loving, easy-going and philosophical —caused the disintegration of the earlier ideals. The Pelopennesian war between Sparta and Athens from 431 to 404 B.C. reduced the spiritual power of Athens and the theatre survived only as a place of entertainment.

THE ACTOR

As the public taste for comedy grew, so the actor became more important. The comedies that followed were not the caricatures of Aristophanes but were related to life of the middle class. Romance, comedy and pathos were the ingredients and gave a variety of acting parts. The theatres built in other cities corresponded to the new status of the actor. The size of the stage was increased and as the chorus virtually disappeared the area of the orchestra was reduced to the shape of a semi-circle. The machinery of the stage was probably improved then with the introduction of trapdoors and upper stories and balconies in the stage façade. The Roman invasion of Greece further lowered the standing of the theatre which became a place for spectacle and later excessive display. Greek tragedies were translated and performed in the last two centuries B.C., but the Roman lust for incident and visual expression was evident in the translation, which included horrific and gory episodes veiled from Greek audiences.

THE ROMAN THEATRE

The Roman theatre had a raised stage in front of which was the acting space or orchestra. This was semi-circular and not round as in the Greek theatre. (Figures 1 and 2.) The seats were built up around the orchestra and the theatre was a complete building on a level site. The semi-circular auditorium was probably designed to give every spectator a clear view of the stage denied to those in some of the side seats of the Greek theatre. The stage was surrounded on three sides by walls elaborately decorated with columns and statues supporting a wooden roof. Otherwise the theatre was open though coloured linen awnings were used to protect the audience. There was a door in each side wall of the stage and three doors in the back wall

GREEK THEATRE
220° ENCIRCLEMENT

A RAISED PLATFORM
IS BUILT IN FRONT
OF THE VERTICAL
WALL OF THE SKENE,
WHICH CONTAINS
THREE ENTRANCES.

Figure 1

ROMAN THEATRE
180° ENCIRCLEMENT.
A PENINSULAR OR
THREE-SIDED STAGE.

A RAISED PLATFORM
IS ENCLOSED WITH
WALLS. EACH SIDE
WALL CONTAINS AN
ENTRANCE AND THERE
ARE FIVE ENTRANCES
IN THE BACK WALL.

Figure 2

called the *frons scaenae*. The centre door was the largest from which the leading characters made their entrances and in the earlier Graeco-Roman theatres five and even seven doors were provided in the back wall.

Wooden theatres were built at first with the spectators seated on semi-circular tiers of seats not unlike those used nowadays in the circus. The simplified stage had three doors and no curtain and was in view throughout the performance. It was therefore necessary to begin and finish a play with an empty stage. The first stone theatre was built in 55 B.C. for more elaborate displays and afterwards theatres were built throughout the Roman Empire to keep subject races entertained. A drop curtain or *aulaeum* was introduced which was lowered into a recess near the front of the stage to start the performance and raised to terminate it. This method of working the curtain was continued for about two centuries after which it was operated as it is today. With the use of a curtain and other stage machinery, the theatre came to be a place for mime, pantomime and spectacle, and the orchestra was used for mimic sea-fights, gladitorial displays and sometimes as extra seating accommodation for important spectators.

The Roman theatre was entirely a place for entertainment wanted by the crowd. It was not associated with religion, and classical drama, mainly translated from the Greek, was written and regarded as a literary pursuit for the ruling class. In Greece and Rome there were also strolling players who performed on simple portable stages. These were booths with dividing curtains that served as a scenic background and as a dressing room. Plays given with puppets had their place in Roman times and perhaps our Punch and Judy show was developed from the booths of the strolling players.

Actors in Greece were accorded honour but under Roman law were denied civil rights. The Christian Church was firmly opposed to the theatre and clergy were forbidden to enter it but the popular instinct was so strong that the layman could not be entirely prevented from enjoying the spectacle he found there. Opposition to the organised theatre continued and the irrepressible actors were absorbed into the company of entertainers and wandering minstrels.

THE MEDIAEVAL THEATRE

For five hundred years until the eleventh century, there is little to record of dramatic history. In the ninth century, dramatic dialogues appeared in church ritual and over the next two centuries drama was slowly developing. The priests of the Christian Church began to write and act plays derived from church services. Some of the services were already dramatic, being read or sung by different voices in the form of question and answer and by the twelfth century the special dialogues written were included in the new plays performed at religious festivals.

It is thought that liturgical drama of the ninth century began in France and spread to other Continental countries. It was spoken in Latin and later each line was repeated in the native tongue. Probably by the end of the eleventh century it was given entirely in the language of the people.

CHURCH AND PEOPLE

Two lines of dramatic development emerged in the thirteenth century, one from the church which originally opposed it and one from the populace. The living symbols of the church in the Nativity Play of Bethlehem were first presented by Saint Francis of Assisi and through him arose the new order of painting, poetry and of drama. He spoke of colour and pageantry and the observation of natural things which was afterwards noticed by Leonardo da Vinci when he said: ' The eye, which is called the window of the soul, is the chief means whereby the understanding most fully and abundantly appreciates the infinite works of nature and the ear is second in as much as it hears the things which the eye has seen.' Central Italy was also the background at this time of the popular movement and in 1258 a company called the Disciplinati di Gesu Cristo improvised songs and dramatic poems that were religious in character but had no traditions behind them.

TOURNAMENTS

Beyond the church simple entertainment was enjoyed by nobleman and peasant. The tournaments of the eleventh and twelfth centuries gave knights an opportunity to wear armour and colourful emblems of chivalry to show off before their ladies. At first they were mock battles but when blood was drawn tournaments were frowned on by the Catholic Church and the Court; lances were blunted, swords became pointless and armour in both men and horses was padded. In the late thirteenth and fourteenth centuries they were more of a skilful entertainment and the field of the tournament— the wooden enclosure or lists—gave the appearance of a stage with richly costumed actors. The joust with two knights fighting with lances across a barrier was the fashion and became an enviable form of pastime.

At the courts of noblemen there were poets sometimes of lowly origin who through their talent were acknowledged as equal by their lord. They were the troubadours* who wrote romantic poems and songs accompanied by minstrels or musicians of lower rank. The procession to the lists was attended by the troubadours and minstrels who played in the streets and during intervals in the tournament. The troubadours were also required to write a description of the scene in verse from which we have gained detailed knowledge of the event and in the evening they sang and played for dancing indoors which after the prizegiving was a fitting climax to the rejoicings. Prizes were precious stones, falcons and horses and the lady giving the prize also presented a kiss which one participant said he would ' treasure sweetly.'

* From the French 'trouver,' to find or invent, see p. 19

The outdoor entertainment during the day was continued at night and was an early indication that the entire performance could be transferred indoors for presentation in the great hall belonging to a nobleman. This in fact occurred in the reign of James I when a tournament was staged indoors decorated by Ben Jonson and Inigo Jones assisted by Shakespeare and Burbage for which they received 43s. each. The procession in the streets, watched at a safe distance by admiring yeomen, was stage-managed in elaborate detail by the Heralds and the College of Arms. They were responsible for decoration of the lists and seating, proclamation of the tournament, exhibition of heraldic shields and assembling the judges and minstrels.

The knight presenting a challenge was not content with merely fighting at the lists. He dramatised the event by creating an allegorical story as a reason for holding the tournament. And the part of the story seen was the prowess of the knight in gratitude for a favour given by his lady. The armour worn by the knight and costumes of the lady and servants belonged to the characters in the fantasy. Scenery that was used was in the form of symbolic units representing a mountain, a forest and a gate providing entry to a strange realm, the whole forming a tableau to indicate the scene of the battle. At the beginning of the fifteenth century more pageantry was introduced and a hundred years later was so elaborate that it included a pavilion decorated with turrets and flags, a scenic mountain on the top of which sat a beautiful girl with a castle and a fountain to complete the picture. The procession was heralded by two ' wild ' men with trumpets and followed by two ladies riding horses that were handsomely disguised, led by two men. The leading combatant brought up the rear and on one occasion rode in a pavilion representing a ship which with all its appurtenances was a formidable size. Apart from the crew, the vessel was fully equipped ' with all manner of tackle ' and the sides were covered with linen painted to represent water.   On entering the lists there was a great salvo of gunfire.   The men drawing a pavilion were sometimes dressed as animals and portrayed a dragon, lion, ibex and hart, being heraldic emblems.   Many elements of pageantry and scenic display were introduced at this time and became available to the theatre in later years.

MINSTRELS AND TROUVÈRES

Minstrels originally came from Spain.   When the country was occupied by the Moors the Christian population retreated to the mountains of the Pyrenees to continue the struggle against the Muslims.   Gradually they reconquered the peninsula and the minstrels found inspiration in the music and gaiety of the Spanish people. The roving musicians sang to the strumming of the mandolin and entertained with antic and pantomime. They sang at inns, attended feasts, carried news from city to village and their ditties were made up of anecdotes of political events.   Unless they found employment in a troupe under noble protection—and entry was strictly confined to artistic merit—they wandered from place to place and the idea of a minstrel announcing himself with a song at the castle wall to gain admittance is a romantic fiction.   They crossed into Southern France and Italy and eventually were found throughout Europe.   Little did they think that one day their entertainment would sweep the globe and become popular amusement.   The Beatles wearing mediaeval hairstyles, playing guitars and with the quick wit of minstrel antic have rescued a tradition. Their performance appealing to the masses is as welcome now as it was then.

The sagas and folk-lore of the Norsemen came down to France and in Provence were united with the songs of the expressive minstrels of Southern Europe.   A new form of story-telling was created in poetry by the troubadours who, when the fashion reached the courts of northern France, were called *Trouvères*. They flourished during the twelfth and thirteenth centuries at the time when Miracle plays were performed in the church. The trouvères were the poets and cultured leaders of the minstrels at court entertainments. Their stories reflected contemporary manners and ideals and gained widespread recognition through the influence of the Crusades. The nobles maintaining a troupe were given entertainment resembling the music hall, with jugglers, acrobats, performing animals, musicians and singers, all introduced by the trouvère, who recited the popular stories. His fortunes waned in the fourteenth century when ensemble performances were given by the minstrels and eventually the solo entertainer with a troupe became the court fool or jester.

EARLY ENGLISH STAGES

Crowds attending the religious festivals and plays became so great that the church could not accommodate them and the plays were performed on platforms called *mansions* outside the church or on an open space in the town. In one play, no less than sixty-seven mansions were constructed, the actors walking from one to the other.

The mansions were elaborate scenic units built on platforms, their design influenced by the internal architecture of the church. The small stages had pillars supporting an ornate roof or another room and represented the temple, a palace and the houses of Adam, Abraham and Joseph. Heaven and earth were shown on two levels and between them was a cloud mechanism which transported an actor portraying an angel. Hell was the gaping mouth of a monster from which devils sprang attended by smoke and flames. This was in the fourteenth century and a hundred years later a simple winch was used with the aid of a trapdoor under or above the stage. After a trapdoor or panel had been opened, an angel could descend from heaven and flowers grow from the floor of the stage. The principle of the mill wheel was introduced and paradise in the form of a globe turned around like a revolving stage.

It is believed that the first striking clock with a dial was made in Italy in 1335, and continental clocksmiths became very successful in devising intricate mechanisms. Some public clocks included figures of the Nativity that were made to circle round and move their arms when the hour struck. The clockmakers and black-smiths had ample experience to invent and construct machinery in the mediaeval mansions and they were specially engaged. Dragons were made to fly, trees and flowers were mechanical and they knew how to imitate clouds, rain and snow. Decoration of the mansions was lavish and the rich colours of stained glass windows and gilded altar screens were reproduced. Paint, dye, gold and silver leaf were used, and timber, paper and canvas were employed in building them.

When the mansions were put up outside the church or in the town they were placed in a rectangle rather like the stalls in the market place. The plays were per-formed in rotation and the spectators went from one mansion to the next as the plays were changed. This method continued in Europe until the end of the six-teenth century. The English mansions mounted on wagons and called *pageants* were taken round the streets. The pageants stopped at convenient places and the audience watched each scene in turn. It was performed in the pageant itself or the stage was extended by placing an open wagon in front to provide a forestage. The stage of the pageant was divided by curtains behind which the actors dressed and the upper floor included machinery and a trapdoor for spectacular effects. In Belgium, curtains were used to hide the action, for an Englishman visiting a royal procession said: 'The pageants were shewed and suddenly closed with curtains drawn craftily.'

The plays were called *Mysteries* from their symbolic religious origin, and when enacted outside the church were performed by the townsfolk; members of particular guilds playing scenes appropriate to their trade. They were followed by *Miracle* plays describing incidents in the lives of saints. The *Moralities* were the last of the mediaeval plays and the actors portrayed various vices and virtues in their conflict for the soul of man.

Open-air performances were also given around circular earthworks and the plays were acted in the centre while the audience sat on a stepped bank surrounding it. There is a ruin of one of these stages at St. Just in Cornwall. The manuscript of a morality play *The Castle of Perseverance,* performed early in the fifteenth century, indicates mansions or 'skaffolds' around the perimeter and a castle set in the middle of the earthworks.

Research into documents relating to the tournaments, Miracle plays, pageantry of royal and civic processions, and the short plays called 'Interludes' that followed, has unearthed a mass of fresh material indicating the considerable influence of early mediaeval ritual on the Elizabethan theatre. Evidence that much of the staging of plays in later years was derived from these sources was found in the chronicles, church records, tapestries and accounts for labour employed in royal celebrations. Dr. Glynne Wickham, in his *Early English Stages,* has given a comprehensive and detailed account of the period completed after twelve years of research. Stage managers of period plays and pageants will find it a superb work of reference.

THE PLATFORM STAGE

In the tournaments the combat area was invariably at ground level and when speech was introduced to the 'tableaux vivants' of the Middle Ages, the actors needed a platform to project their voices to the audience. There were so-called booth theatres for performances in the market place with a stage mounted on barrels or trestles. The stage had a curtained area at the back open at the top and the players, mostly an odd assortment of minstrels, could be seen above the market stalls, and from windows of adjoining houses. Stage management of royal processions and civic events included a number of spoken tableaux addressed to the eminent personage and his friends along the processional route through the streets. The citizens performing them were members of the trade guilds which suggests that the tableaux were related to the Miracle plays also performed by the guilds outside the church. Wealthy merchants were inclined to charitable deeds and they built stone water cisterns or conduits in London which served the double purpose of helping their fellow citizens and also providing acting spaces for their civic occasions. The flat top of the water conduit became a permanent stage and the first to be used in this way was situated in Cheapside. (Plate A)

MEDIAEVAL SCENERY AND ' EFFECTS '

Typical scenic units like those found in the tournaments were also made for the processions. Richard II came to the throne in 1377 when he was ten years old and for his procession an imitation castle was constructed on or near the water conduit in Cheapside. The castle had four turrets and in each of them was a beautiful girl of about the King's age. When the procession approached, the girls clad in white scattered golden leaves in his path, showered imitation gold florins and filled gold cups with wine from spouts at the two sides of the castle. A mechanical angel situated on the top of the castle was ' devised with such cunning that on the King's arrival it bent down and offered him a crown.' The conduits arranged to supply wine instead of water must have been

PLATE A

Mediaeval Conduit, Sherborne, Dorset

a considerable attraction for they provided red and white wine and each one was sufficient for a thousand people.

Other outdoor stages were around a market cross, in the roof and niches of a gateway or erected in conjunction with a triumphal arch. The octagonal acting area of the market cross was twenty feet in diameter and supported on a vaulted roof twelve feet above the ground surrounded by a low parapet. The gateway and arch had slender acting facilities and a platform was constructed projecting off the ground with one or two platforms above it. They were used with trapdoors and the elaborate machinery devised for spectacular effects. The stage technicians became proficient in all kinds of supernatural devices which delighted the audience then just as much as they have done since. In 1603 the conduits fell out of use, probably won over by the exciting mechanical display of the two- and three-level stages.

THE LORD MAYOR'S SHOW

One example of mediaeval entertainment and pageantry survives today. The annual event of the Lord Mayor's show with its decorated mechanised floats and trade associations descends from the festivities arranged by city livery companies to honour the election of their Mayor. The first Lord Mayor's procession was in 1545, after which it returned each year. The scale in which it was presented, with the help of the leading writers, painters and craftsmen of the day, suggests an important link in theatre history before the time of the public theatres. The association continued after the first Globe theatre was built when Ben Jonson was the author of the procession in 1604 presented by the Haberdashers company. The shows were prepared in the elaborate detail of a modern stage production. Plans were drawn, models constructed and everything necessary for the scenic display thoroughly considered in advance. The livery company organising the show invited tenders from poets responsible for the theme and the painter-craftsmen appointed to decorate and put the wheels in motion. When the contract was obtained, author and director (the craftsman was promoted to this title early in the seventeenth century) sub-contracted with their fellow craftsmen. A variety of callings became engaged to construct, paint and invent the stimulating and impressive spectacle. Actors were employed and Richard Burbage, one of the sons of James Burbage, participated on more than one occasion.

Some idea of their technical ambition appears in the show of 1613, the subject admitting certain vices and virtues in dramatic form and written by Thomas Middleton. There were ornate pageant wagons to Truth, Error and Envy, and the *pièce de résistance* was a scenic mountain depicting London Triumphant, at first observed in a fog or mist attended by four monsters. The mechanical cloud rose to show the mountain bathed in the light of many stars, beams of gold shooting to and fro. In the finale, accomplished at night, flames spurted from the head of Zeal and set fire to the chariot of Error, which it reduced to 'glowing embers.' On a royal occasion the author devised a water-show with the Seven Deadly Sins burnt in effigy on the Thames and resolved into a splendid fireworks display. The Elizabethan stage was well supplied with pageantry and effects essential to 'make-believe' in the theatre that were contrived for these shows.

THE ENTREMET

Among indoor entertainments of the fourteenth and fifteenth centuries presented in the great houses of the nobility and clergy were the old custom of *Mumming*, the

'Entremet' of the French Court, and poems narrating a popular story written early in the fifteenth century. Mumming, as the word suggests, was an entertainment given in dumb show, and it is said was a survival of the ritual in Graeco-Roman performances. It was an amateur recreation by people of humble birth in which the participants disguised themselves in costume not as actors but to hide their identity. Associated with calendar festivals when gifts were presented, it was the only known form of evening amusement where a group of people enjoyed themselves actively taking part and it became the recreation from which later dramatic entertainment was derived.

The Entremet was a spectacular entertainment given in the banqueting hall of the French Court. This was at the time when the nature of minstrel groups was changing and the narrator trouvère declined in favour of ensemble playing by amateurs. The example of the Miracle plays performed by amateurs such as clerks attached to the church aroused interest in the stories recited by the trouvère. When these were dramatised, parts existed for actors playing in ensemble, and they were performed in this way in France by the end of the fourteenth century. A hundred years later there were distinct groups of performers maintained by a nobleman and travelling in groups throughout the year under his patronage. There were troupes of musicians, troupes of actors and solo entertainers performing as jesters. The actors went 'on tour,' travelling at calendar feasts to towns where they knew in advance they would be welcomed. This practice continued in England until the time of Shakespeare, when his friend Burbage was touring the provinces in 1577-8, the year following the building of his first theatre in London.

The French court entertainment was held at calendar festivals and at the time of royal celebrations. As may be gathered the principal functions were to eat, drink and be merry and the repast set before the guests was of such immense proportions that consuming it occupied some time. Intervals were necessary to assist digestion and these convivial interludes were enlivened by the minstrels. The earliest description of an indoor auditorium was in 1389 when the banqueting hall was arranged with a table at one end raised on a dais for the King and his privileged guests. Facing them at the other end was the minstrel gallery and along the two sides of the hall were tables for other guests. In the open centre area were scenic units of the tournaments representing a castle, pavilion and a ship; the highlight of the evening being a combined assault by the occupants of the ship and pavilion on those concealed in the castle. The ensuing melée was so considerable that a number of spectators were almost suffocated and the festivities brought to an early conclusion.

The plan of this auditorium and the kind of entertainment given became the pattern for similar performances called *Disguisings* during the next two centuries. The evening entertainment was developed in England at the time of the street processions and Miracle plays when handsomely decorated pageant wagons were taken indoors and moved around the banqueting hall illuminated with torches. Although the naïve disguisings required little mental effort, they were enhanced by the lighting and other effects of the designer. In 1501 the craftsmen made a pageant wagon in the shape of a lantern that had several windows covered in fine gauze. It contained a hundred lights and twelve ladies seated inside were displayed with great charm.

THE FIRST WRITTEN TEXTS

At the beginning of the fifteenth century, disguising took a new form when John Lydgate, a Benedictine monk and the leading poet in the reign of Henry VI, wrote a number of dramatic poems that were neither plays nor masques. His poems were derived from the chivalrous background of the tournament, the Miracle plays in which actors related a story indicating a moral theme and the allegory and spectacle of the street theatres. At first he used a narrator to introduce a silent mumming. Later actors performed with the narration; other speakers were introduced and scenic units employed. He was the first author to create dramatic entertainment in England that included a written text.

Towards the end of the fifteenth century short dramatic sketches called *Interludes* were performed indoors on social and festive occasions during intervals of a complete evening's entertainment. The subjects of the plays were derived from biblical sources, moral discussions in which various vices and virtues were considered and farcical stories. The plays of the ancient Greek and Latin dramatists were revived, written by teachers and performed in schools and colleges. Interludes became popular for they required a small cast, modest scenery and could therefore be played just as easily indoors as in the market place. This was important to the professional actors whose livelihood was related to the expense involved. Their variety made it possible to interchange plays from the market place to the banqueting hall and the dialogue came to include expressions of contemporary life well understood and appreciated by the audience.

THE ELIZABETHAN THEATRE

From the middle of the sixteenth century the plays were given as a complete evening's entertainment and a stage was first used indoors at this time. It was a raised platform backed by a curtain with properties carried by the actors. The advantage was obvious for it allowed trapdoors in the floor of the stage and machinery for effects and other visual displays, always a great attraction in mediaeval drama. The plays and their stagecraft

aroused amateur and professional interest to other
theatrical opportunities which were afterwards realised
in the masques of Ben Jonson and Inigo Jones to form
the basis of a permanent public theatre.

The first theatre in London called ' The Theater ' was
built in 1576 by the actor James Burbage and when it was
demolished its timbers were used to build Shakespeare's
playhouse, The Globe in 1598. What these theatres
looked like has been the subject of enquiry for many
years and an indication comes from a drawing by a
Dutchman, Johann de Witt, of the Swan Theatre completed about 1596. Although the picture is only a sketch
which may have been drawn from memory, it gives an
idea of the stage and also the building in which it was
installed. (Figure 3.)

Some authorities have said that the Elizabethan theatre
was derived from the stage erected in the courtyard of an
inn. Innyard theatres called *Corrales* existed in Spain as
early as 1520. Houses there were built around a courtyard or *patio* and a platform was put up at one end for the
actors. Spectators watched the performance from the
windows of their houses on three sides of the *patio* and
stood around the stage. The English innyard had two
or three galleries on all four sides with doors through
which the actors could enter. The stage was erected at
one end and the balcony above it could be used as an
upper stage. It is thought that the permanent theatres
were developed on these lines and the stage became the
open-peninsular kind (Figure 17) with the audience surrounding it on three sides and built as an integral part
of the frame or auditorium.

The de Witt sketch, however, seems to indicate two
separate units: the stage with the stage gallery and the
building enclosing it. The drawing shows a circular
auditorium resembling the three-tier Tudor playhouse
and the stage appears to be lightly constructed and set up
in the open central area. Spectators can be seen in the

boxes behind the stage and as the audience was seated in the galleries and standing around the stage, the theatre could perhaps claim to be a form of theatre-in-the-round

THE SWAN THEATRE, BANKSIDE.
Figure 3

(Figure 15) where the audience surrounds the stage on all sides.

The stage was supported on trestles which follows the description at that time of stages built in civic halls supported on barrels or forms. At the back of the stage was the *Tiring House* or stage-gallery on the pattern of the rood screen separating the choir from the nave in mediaeval churches and the screens with a gallery above dividing the reception area from the domestic quarters in banqueting halls. The tiring house contained two doors at stage level with a gallery above used by privileged spectators. There was a sloping roof above the gallery which, at the point where it covered part of the stage, was supported on two decorated columns and pedestals painted to resemble marble. The actors made their entrances through the doors of the tiring house, behind which were their dressing rooms. It is difficult to establish from the original sketch what was above the gallery but there was a contemporary reference to a 'machine room' above the stage and the roof was said to be painted underneath to represent the Heavens. It is thought that the machine room contained a winch by means of which celestial bodies and other exciting objects were lowered to the stage through a trapdoor in the roof. Above the roof and behind it was a loft with a door from which a trumpeter announced the start of the performance.

The round auditorium lends support to the belief that it was related to the 'Game House' known in Tudor England. This was a place of general entertainment that included many kinds of activities such as games, sports and other pastimes, and there is a record of a game-house of this kind existing in Great Yarmouth in 1538–9, forty years before Burbage built his theatre. This evidence, given by Dr. Glynne Wickham in the second volume of his *Early English Stages,* is further substantiated by the name of the Elizabethan theatre always called a playhouse. The word 'play' was derived from the Anglo-Saxon word 'pleg' and a pleg-hus or playhouse is defined as a place for the play, gymnasium, wrestling place or amphitheatre. To carry the suggestion further, it is known that Burbage was a carpenter and therefore would have knowledge of building methods in use and information concerning buildings of a similar kind to his theatre. Furthermore the funds for building his theatre were provided by a wealthy tradesman—a grocer—who no doubt would be just as interested in recovery of his capital as in the use to which it was put. What would be more natural than to assume that he gave his support for a building that had a variety of objects apart from the main one of giving Burbage a permanent London home for his company?

The roof of the auditorium and stage appear to be tiled in the de Witt drawing but other references mention a thatched roof and a Swiss traveller, Thomas Platter of Basle, when he visited England in 1599 described a performance of *Julius Caesar* which was very likely performed in Shakespeare's Globe theatre: ' There in the house with the thatched roof witnessed an excellent performance of the tragedy of the first Emperor Julius Caesar . . . The actors are most expensively and elaborately costumed; for it is the English usage for eminent lords or Knights at their decease to bequeath and leave almost the best of their clothing to their serving men, which it is unseemly for the latter to wear, so that they offer them then for sale for a small sum to the actors.' (*Travels in England*, 1599. Translated by Clare Williams.)

Other companies were quick to observe the success of the Globe Theatre for two years later—in 1600—it was copied in almost every detail by a commercial manager Philip Henslowe, when he built the Fortune Theatre. Henslowe's contract with the builder is preserved as are his records of plays and box office receipts that have provided unique information about the Elizabethan theatre. The important difference between the theatres was that the Globe was round or many-sided and the shape of the Fortune was square although this was abandoned when the playhouse was rebuilt after it had been burned down.

The measurements of the Fortune have survived, the building being eighty feet square and the stage forty-three feet wide and twenty seven and a half feet deep. Other information is largely descriptive; a cover over the stage is mentioned and a ' tiring house ' which may have included an inner and an upper stage.

' Convenient windows ' were in the tiring house though the stage directions of the plays are the only record indicating where the entrances may have been situated. Henslowe was a cautious businessman and he altered a theatre custom prevalent at that time. Theatres were usually rented from their owners by the acting companies who provided ' gatherers ' to collect money at the doors. At the Fortune, he engaged his own and each one was given a box with a slot through which the money was dropped. Our term ' box office ' dates from his careful attention to financial details.

The origin of the Elizabethan theatre may be found in the pageantry of the tournaments, street processions, the Miracle plays and the indoor entertainments of the banqueting and civic halls which becoming popular required a larger building to accommodate the audience. The symbolic scenic devices of the early Middle Ages were used though these were not enough to provide much realism and Shakespeare asks his audience to ' piece out our imperfections with your thoughts.' Appreciation of the modest scenic arrangements was encouraged and in *A Midsummer-Night's Dream* he makes fun of the inadequate staging when Moonshine says:

> ' This lanthorn doth the hornèd moon present;
> Myself the man i' the moon do seem to be.'

Nevertheless, the theatres were equipped with scenic devices that were capable of entertaining with gods descending from the heavens and startling appearances through trapdoors. Hell fire, devils and steam were introduced with thunder and lightning, which was made with squibs covered with gilt or satin and running on wires. A cannon, used realistically above the Globe Theatre, set fire to the thatched roof and burned down the theatre. Since the only parts covered by a roof were the stage and the galleries surrounding it, the theatres were open-air playhouses for performances as a rule in daylight. In mediaeval plays paint was used for illumination; gold leaf, powdered silver and varnish were employed and on one occasion an actor's face was made up with red paint to symbolise light. The Elizabethans were fond of fireworks and these were used for their lighting effects though otherwise any illumination needed as for instance the Ghost in *Hamlet* was left to the talent of the actor and imagination of the audience. The standing room of the ' groundlings ' in the cheapest part of the theatre was around three sides of the stage and by paying more the audience could sit in one of the covered galleries. Noblemen were given separate rooms or ' boxes ' and they sat on stools placed on the stage. From 1583 onwards there were other theatres that were roofed and used by professional companies during the inclement weather of the winter months.

EUROPEAN THEATRES

The theatre in Europe developed along different lines after the invention of printing with movable type in the middle of the fifteenth century. Writings of antiquity were rediscovered in which were collected plans and facts relating to the classical theatre and the study of these led to the transformation of ducal halls into theatres with stages for dramatic performances. The halls were rectangular and into them the architect fitted his interpretation of the earlier theatre. A permanent setting was built which corresponded to the play being comedy, tragedy or satire. Italian theatres continued to develop on classical lines and in 1580 a copy of a Roman theatre was begun in the town of Vicenza: The Teatro Olimpico, designed by the architect Andrea Palladio, which was roofed over and contained in a rectangular building.

The study of plans of Greek buildings and the ancient theatre made by Vitruvius, architect to Augustus Caesar, was published in 1537–47 by Sebastiano Serlio as a *Treatise on Architecture*, and it included the first text book on painting in perspective for scenic design. He described scenery built to represent houses complete with tiled roofs and chimney pots which were profiled or 'cut out round on thin boards and well coloured.' Windows were of glass or paper and could be lit by placing little lamps behind them. The buildings in the foreground were smaller than those at the rear so as not to obstruct the view and the perspective was continued in a scenic back drop on which shadows were painted. About this time Serlio built a theatre in the palace of a nobleman and he published his plan for the first raked stage which has continued in use for four hundred years.

Palladio's design for his theatre was in a sense revolutionary for he reverted to the early form of writer's theatre and ignored the pictorial artists then claiming recognition in perspective painting. The Olimpico had the conventional *frons scaenae* of the Roman theatre with the elaborately decorated back wall and two side walls of the stage. It had three permanent proscenium arches or doorways, and two side entrances. Palladio died and the theatre was completed by his son with scenic additions designed by his pupil Scamozzi in 1584. This was the first attempt to bring perspective scenery to the classical stage and the introduction of illusion in the theatre which later became universal. Small rows of wooden houses modelled in false perspective were set behind each of the five entrances to give the impression of streets leading to an open square supposed to be on the stage platform. Acting space in the streets was confined to the immediate front area and anything beyond that destroyed the illusion. Nevertheless actors could use the scenery and partly circulate in the streets to surprise each other, spy on one another and overhear profound secrets that were typical of the plays given at the time.*

THE PROSCENIUM ARCH

The stage was set for the most important development in the theatre: the single proscenium arch through which artists could show a full scene in perspective. In 1588, Scamozzi was commissioned to build a new theatre at Sabbionetta and he enlarged the centre doorway to include the entrances on either side making one opening with an acting space behind sufficient to represent the market square and the houses surrounding it. The theatre was small, seating only 250, and Scamozzi probably found that the space between the side walls restricted him to a single opening with a view of the stage behind it. Meanwhile the designers stimulated by their perspective painting, realised that by cutting the background of a scene in two pieces, these could be pulled aside to reveal a further scene, perhaps in the form of trees to adorn a woodland glade. The inventive enthusiasts made larger pieces of scenery, some of which were made to move. They were quite elaborate and would be spoilt unless the mechanism of working them was kept out of sight. A frame was added to the front of the scene to hide the top and sides and this soon became a permanent part of the private theatres of the nobility. When the Teatro Farnese was built at Parma in 1618, the entire scenery area of the stage was behind the proscenium arch. The original façade of the Roman theatre survived only as decoration and the theatre was the first in Italy on the plan of the picture frame stage. It is curious that the theatre had no curtain when it opened although this was used in Italy a hundred years before. In Renaissance

* The Olimpico can be seen today and is remarkable in showing the origin of the change from the ancient to the modern theatre.

theatres the curtain was lowered into a trough near the front of the stage which followed the practice of the ancient Roman theatre.

THE COMMEDIA DELL' ARTE

From the early times of mediaeval drama a stage or theatre of the people was in existence. Outdoor performances on boards and trestles were given by actors who improvised comedy and obtained a few coins by way of reward. About 1500 in Italy a company which became famous for its nimble clowning and perfect comedy was the Commedia dell'Arte. The term dell'arte was given as a sign of approval that the actors were professional in every sense. The company of comedians which was very popular with the Italian people had little influence on the Italian theatre. And it was through their travels abroad to France, Spain, Germany and England that the characters they created were responsible for a regeneration of the professional theatre in Europe. They influenced playwrights; Shakespeare and Molière used the characters and plots in their plays. Most of the comedy was improvised though there were written prologues and soliloquies. The stock characters created have had the greatest effect and much of the burlesque tradition of the music hall and revue can be traced to the comic miming of these players. One of the best known characters was Pulcinella, who probably descended from Roman comedy and later became Punch of the puppet show. Other comic characters were two old men, one a miser and the other a doctor of laws, inquiring about and meddling with other people's affairs. He appears in Rossini's *The Barber of Seville* and Mozart's *The Marriage of Figaro*. Pedrolino became the French Pierrot and Harlequin and Columbine were other pantomime characters taken over and played in the English theatre.

Like a river with many streams, the trend from symbolic scenery of the Middle Ages to the stage of the landscape artist continued in other countries. The amateur movement in Europe under the Jesuits flourished from the middle of the sixteenth century and in their teaching colleges students acted in stage productions as part of their graduation. The college theatres in France competed with the secular stage and even outdid it in staging and effects. Spectacular productions were mounted and the performances admired by the court and gentry as well as charmed parents. In Holland, the Jesuits performed on a stage belonging to the Rederijker or Rhetoric Societies which they had used with a proscenium arch and curtains for unveiling of *tableaux vivants*, though it did not become a permanent structure. There is a contemporary painting of an open-air theatre at Amsterdam in 1609 illustrating a stage with tableaux curtains; the ornate proscenium arch proudly surmounted with statues of Neptune signifying the Dutch association with the sea.

Shakespeare and the Elizabethan dramatists arrived at a time when conditions were favourable to their work. During the Reformation the religious plays were suppressed and the crowds, denied a popular form of recreation, turned to Shakespeare and his plays for their entertainment. Under Elizabeth I opposition to Rome and Italian influence was relaxed after the defeat of the Spanish Armada and though the popular stage retained a native pride in English life and achievement, the amateur theatre of court entertainment encouraged the European tradition. The nobility travelling abroad brought news of unique and fascinating spectacles which they were keen to enjoy in this country.

JACOBEAN MASQUES

Inigo Jones paid visits to Italy where he became skilled in landscape painting of the back-drop used in Italy as early as 1518. In his partnership with Ben Jonson the court masques acquired Italian theatricality and he introduced the proscenium arch for *The Masque of Blackness* by Ben Jonson in 1605. Coloured lights used in the Italian theatre were the stock colours of red, blue, white and amber still found today. Red and white wine were colour agents and pigments were dissolved in glass bowls like old apothecaries' jars. They were put in front of torches to shine through windows and doors of scenic houses and basins placed behind the torches were used as reflectors. Dimming was performed by suspending a series of metal collars above rows of candles which on the cue were dropped over them to counterfeit a sunset. The advantage of darkening the auditorium was appreciated in a contemporary reference: ' As you know, in nature, a man standing in shadow sees much better whatever is brightly lit at a distance, than does one who stands in an illuminated position . . . Hence I place the fewest possible lights in the auditorium, while at the same time I endeavour to illuminate the stage brightly; the very few lamps in the auditorium I place behind the spectators in order that these should not interfere with their view of the stage.' (From *The Means of Theatrical Representation*, by Leone de' Somi in 1550; translated by Allardyce Nicoll.) Inigo Jones invented machinery for scene changing and his effects included a crystal ball filled with distilled water set in front of torches; sunlight was represented in the diffused light shimmering around the scene. By the novel use of artificial light he succeeded in contrasting one landscape with the next to reproduce the light and shade found in paintings of old masters.

THE SECOND GLOBE THEATRE

Shakespeare was not endowed with the patronage given by the nobility to Italian dramatists but like them he used all the materials of theatrical invention. In Italy the Renaissance was mainly interpreted through the visual arts and although similar classical influences developed throughout Europe, the poetic influence was stronger in England. The second Globe theatre, built in 1614, had an inner curtained stage behind the ordinary one and this isolated central opening could be regarded as a proscenium arch. It will be seen that although the main trend in Europe was towards visual representation, the Elizabethen theatre with its apron stage in front of a curtained one was ideally suited to poetic drama.*

The design followed the pattern of the first Globe theatre without any of the Italian innovations of Inigo Jones. Ben Jonson was working with Inigo Jones and Shakespeare at the same time so Italian improvements would have been known to Shakespeare though they were not included in his new theatre. There are various reasons for this and one of them may be found in the dramatic construction of his plays. It is quite possible that presenting them with landscape backgrounds and scenery would have been difficult; this in fact is experienced when they are given in a picture frame theatre. Probably an important influence is the origin of the scenic devices used in the Elizabethan theatre which were derived from mediaeval pageantry and street processions of the trade guilds. During the middle ages there was a stronger bond with the Low Countries than with France or Italy and merchants travelling from the Baltic brought news of local customs and events. The design of the Globe theatre was not unlike the stage used for the ' Landjuwelen ' festival in Holland which combined a pavilion with an arcade background. Properties representing trees, fountains, arbours etc. were also carried on and off during the performance and were sufficient visible symbols to describe where the action was supposed to be happening.

* A replica of this type of theatre with an inner curtained stage exists in Norwich. An amateur company, the Norwich Players, was created by Nugent Monck who built an Elizabethan stage for them in the Maddermarket theatre.

The shape of the Globe auditorium and stage was directly related to the plays performed there which demanded a close relationship with the audience essential to poetic drama. A parallel example of theatre building occured in Holland. The Schouwburg in Amsterdam built in 1617 was restored in 1637 by Jacob van Campen who was well acquainted with the Italian landscape stage. Nevertheless his design corresponded to the traditional stage of the Rederijker Societies with a permanent multiple setting and a circular auditorium with tiers of boxes. When the theatre was rebuilt in the Italian style in 1664 a tribute to Shakespeare was given in the inscription:

> ' All the world's a stage,
> And all the men and women merely players.'

SCENIC DISPLAY

Scenery was already used in England in the time of Henry VII for court masques and pageants. During his reign the Office of the Revels was developed and continued under Henry VIII and in the reigns of Elizabeth I and James I. The Master of the Revels was an important personage whose qualifications included skill in improvisation, a knowledge of perspective and architecture and appreciation of ' histories, comedies, tragedies and shows.'

Shakespeare and the Elizabethans were aware of the splendours in court entertainment though their indigent theatre was unable to afford them. In his day, the technique of scene construction was advanced and scenery was built of canvas, stretched on wooden frames and painted. The visual interpretation in court masques was given royal favour and scenic display intended to delight the eye greatly admired. So much so that a clash of conflicting views between poet and artist was recorded in England and on the Continent. The Spanish playwright Lope de Vega wrote dialogue that was satirical of scenery and stage effects, and was the author of the famous phrase: 'Give me four trestles, four boards, two actors and a passion.' Ben Jonson in his partnership with Inigo Jones was slow to appreciate the challenge to his genius by the introduction of landscape scenery. He continued to write the masques but the decorative invention of Inigo Jones and skill in arranging changeable scenery and effects brought a new aspect to dramatic entertainment. It marked the end of the Elizabethan dramatists' stage and the beginning of theatre illusion which Jonson realised when he declared that the scenic elaboration gave enjoyment to the eye rather than the ear. In the theatre words and action are related and down the centuries the argument between poet and artist has continued. It was versed by an Elizabethan playwright:

> ' Gallants, I'll tell you what we do not mean
> To show you here, a glorious painted scene,
> With various doors, to stand instead of wit,
> Or richer clothes with lace, for lines well writ.'

Censorship of plays and players started during the Reformation, existed throughout Shakespeare's lifetime and culminated in sole control by the crown in the reign of James I. Shakespeare and his company became part of the Royal Household and only those companies licensed under Royal Patent were entitled to perform. The Master of the Revels acting for the Lord Chamberlain controlled the theatre and licensed plays for acting as well as publication.

THE RESTORATION THEATRE

Under Puritan rule the theatres were closed and with the restoration of Charles II in 1660 new theatres were built to use the mobile scenery of the Italian theatre. The Theatre Royal, Drury Lane, designed by Sir Christopher Wren, was one of the new London playhouses to influence the construction of theatres in later years. Following the Italian design it was a rectangular building in which the area of the stage and auditorium were almost equally divided. A second stage used by the actors was in front of the scenery or working area and jutted out into the audience where it occupied about one third of the auditorium. The apron stage of Restoration theatres, called the *proscenium*, included two doors either side which in the Georgian theatre became the single doors each side of the proscenium arch. Actors could leave by one door and immediately reappear through the other which may have provided some merriment though did little to advance theatre illusion. The audience accepted the convention that the doors represented adjacent rooms or belonged to separate buildings.* The scenery area of the stage behind the proscenium arch remained a pictorial background and all the acting was done in front of it on the apron stage. The spectators sat on wooden benches in a sloping ' pit ' in front of the stage or in rows or tiers of seats facing the stage. There were boxes in the side walls for use by the nobility, and gallants of the day liked to be accommodated on the stage where no doubt they could closely observe and comment on disturbing elements in the play. Candles were the source of all illumination in the Caroline theatre and gave a distinctive enchantment to the scene.

The Georgian Theatre

Popularity of theatre-going increased in the eighteenth century; larger audiences arrived and managers needed room for them. The acting area was moved further back to provide more seats, additional tiers in the shape of a horse-shoe were built and the stage boxes were continued in the form of *loges* around the auditorium. Spectators now occupied the entire auditorium except

---

* There is evidence in the stage directions of the plays performed there that the Theatre Royal, Drury Lane, had six proscenium doors.

for the forestage and pit used by the orchestra. The view of the stage from the side boxes was limited and early in the nineteenth century balconies were built facing the stage. The dress and upper circle balconies installed in later years without pillars and supported by the cantilever system have survived to the present day. By the middle of the nineteenth century, the actors were confined to the working area of the stage and the opening was surrounded by the proscenium arch painted and embellished to resemble a gilded picture frame.

An important addition to theatre illusion occurred when gas lighting was introduced early in the nineteenth century. The new illumination allowed dimming of the stage and darkening of the auditorium. Many designers took advantage of the medium to produce settings that were enhanced and given atmosphere in the warm and soft lighting.

In 1876, Wagner held the democratic opinion that everyone paying for admission was entitled to a clear view of the stage. His sketch for the design of the Wagner Festspielhaus in Bayreuth, Germany, stipulated that all seats faced directly towards the stage and every spectator had a clear view of the full depth of the stage setting. Only rows of seats slightly curved were used and boxes were eliminated. Much of the pageantry of continental playgoing was gone and the social institution of the opera house whose purpose included exhibition of the audience as well as the play disappeared. The fan-shaped design of the rows of seats is followed in some modern theatres and is evident in cinemas.

CHAPTER 2

'CAN YOU MARK A SCRIPT ?'

THIS was the question I was asked when applying for my first engagement in London as assistant stage manager. The stage manager interviewing me had many years experience and his question led directly to an essential part of the stage manager's duties. I was keen to obtain the engagement and although I could claim only a modest knowledge of marking a script, I replied with a confident ' yes ' and got the job.

Shortly afterwards I found myself at the prompter's table at the side of the stage where the company was assembled in a London theatre. We read the play which I found difficult to follow and could not imagine what sort of audience it was intended to entertain. The actors read their parts quietly, barely indicating humour or emotion and I left the first rehearsal disappointed in the play and the players. As rehearsals proceeded a change took place. With the director's instructions and invention of the actors, the play developed and I found that the author's dialogue and situations provided a comedy which eventually became a great success. The play by Vernon Sylvaine was the first of a series written for a particular team. He became a superb exponent of farce—a difficult medium which passes almost unrecognised in the theatre. His characters that were larger than life and situations so outrageous yet believable, made audiences laugh for several years. Like most comedians he hoped to become established with a serious play and perhaps this was the reason that during the war he moved to Ayot St. Lawrence. Bernard Shaw lived there but Vernon Sylvaine said he really went to be near Shaw, who was a vegetarian, in order to get hold of his meat ration.

In the three weeks of rehearsals I continued prompting and marking the script; the latter task requiring some dexterity in keeping up with the rapid introduction of ' business ' and ' moves '. Occasionally I caught a glimpse of the stage manager and gave him notes of requirements called for in his absence. I found that most of them he anticipated and began to wonder how he knew what would be required though apparently occupied elsewhere. Eventually we came to the day of the dress-rehearsal and I arrived at the theatre to find that overnight, scenery had been set up, furniture, wardrobe, properties and electrical equipment installed and several members of the staff whom I had briefly recognised were in discussion with the stage manager. I discovered that throughout rehearsals the stage manager had organised the work and departments which produced this result. I learnt how the organisation of the stage was divided; how each task was allocated to personnel of different departments. How it was all co-ordinated so that when the time came for assembling the components of the production, the stage manager was confident his plans would contribute to a flawless performance.

THE SCRIPT

My interview occurred shortly before the first rehearsal and my first task was to read the play, for the author's script is the basis of the production and in it the stage manager enters all the directions to the actors and staff employed in performing it. In order to be thoroughly familiar with the play two or more readings are necessary and by going through it carefully, he will note various details. At this point I should mention that I always carry a stiff covered notebook in my pocket. During rehearsals the stage manager is expected to remember a vast number of instructions and it is impossible to recall all of them by memory. Write everything down. No matter what it is—make a note of it. Never mind if you keep the director or star waiting; they will be extremely relieved when later the point crops up, the question is asked and you have the answer. Without this personal notebook the stage manager is lost. Consequently a stiff cover is useful for even in the train you can quickly feel in your pocket that your notebook is safely with you.

Recording. There will be several copies of the play and the stage manager should keep an accurate record of them. During rehearsals the play undergoes considerable revision and I have known as many as three editions to be typed before the acting or production script is developed. The stage manager will find that copies of the play have already been distributed. Apart from those in the producer's office, copies have been given to the director, designer, principal actors and potential backers. One copy is forwarded to the Lord Chamberlain for licensing if the play is a new one and intended for production in the commercial theatre. He retains it and if alterations are not required a Licence is issued. A second copy is normally sent to the Lord Chamberlain, which he returns with his official stamp of approval on each page. This copy with the Licence is given to the manager of the theatre where the play is first performed.*

The stage manager should as soon as possible make a file record of all scripts to include the following information:

(1) Edition and number.
(2) To whom issued and date.

The record will be enlarged during rehearsals and will depend on the changes incorporated. When sufficient material has been included to call for typing of entirely new scripts, a second edition will be in existence which must be recorded as before.

An instance where a change in the script occurs is the

---

* Since this was written, the Lord Chamberlain's power to censor stage plays is abolished under the Theatres Act 1968.

director's discovery that a scene written early in the play advances the action too quickly. The scene may be so entertaining that the balance of the play is improved if the situation occurs elsewhere and the author is asked to transfer it to a position later in the play. The author's task may be complicated when he is writing parts for actors working as a team. A well-known company included two stars who played together for a number of years and one of them was anxious that his part should always be approximately the same length as that of his partner. Arriving at the first rehearsal he counted the pages and if they did not tally, the harassed author was told to make amends. He also suffered with gout and the author had to arrange his plot to include rest periods for the star throughout the play. Needless to say the author aged perceptibly in his efforts to re-write the play and accommodate the star. An experienced author will have a good idea of the playing time of scenes and acts in his play. But sometimes it is found that material written for an act is not long enough to sustain the time between intervals. In this case the director will advise that the act is played as a scene with the intervals re-arranged accordingly. The foregoing are examples of changes which the stage manager must record. When scenes are re-written or deleted, the original material should be preserved as sometimes it is decided to return to a scene (or the dialogue from it) during the try-out tour of the play.

The author's manuscript may be the original work receiving its first production or (as occurs in repertory) the script may be in the form of a published play, including all the directions of the original production. In the case of the first production, the script will be typed and the stage manager should choose the cleanest and clearest copy to keep for his prompt script. The typed play will include the address of the author's agent and the producer's and stage manager's name and address are added to it.   The prompt script is the stage manager's most valuable possession (ranking second only to his wife and family).   He should safeguard it almost with his life and by this I mean stay with it wherever it is and at the end of the performance return it to his dressing room.   This is helpful in other ways, for in his absence his assistant will know where to find it.

It will also be useful to secure a second copy for use later as a duplicate prompt script.   Provided the script is typed on thick paper, it can be used throughout rehearsals for marking and everything else decided by the director.   Eventually it becomes a complete record of the production.   A script typed on thin paper should be avoided.   Pencilled marks sometimes go through the paper and it is necessary to re-bind the script interleaving it with blank pages.   Typed scripts should be in double spacing with the stage directions clearly marked in red or underlined.

A play typed by a professional firm is bound as a complete work in a stiff cover.   Sometimes, however, the acts are typed separately in paper covers and the whole play should be clipped in a stiff-backed folder. In order to assist quick reference to various parts of the play, it is a good idea to stick a gummed tab to the scenes which will provide a convenient index.   The Act and Scene is written on the tab and normally Roman numerals are used to indicate the acts and Arabic numerals the scenes: Act III, Sc. 2.

When a printed play is used, two copies are required; the play being printed on both sides of a page.   A loose-leaf folder or stiff exercise book is obtained with twice the number of pages, and the printed pages are taken apart and pasted on alternate pages in the folder.   A blank page will then face each printed page and the blank page is used for marking during rehearsals.   The size of the pages in the folder should be large enough to allow a good margin around the printed page.   With rapid directions there is not sufficient time to mark the blank page and the margin is used as the print is too small for recording. A few leaves left blank at the beginning and end of the folder will be found useful for notes such as cast lists, scene plots, etc.

Parts. Directors vary in their preference for complete scripts or parts provided for the actors. Some directors like to have complete scripts distributed; others prefer to have the author's original stage directions deleted or parts typed to include dialogue and short cues. The cues should, however, be sufficiently long to make sense and plenty of space between the lines should be allowed for pencil notes:—

Part of the Mayor. Act III.
(*Enter with Ernest the Policeman, Mr. Growser, The Inventor, The Magician, Captain Higgins, Larry and Dennis.*)
I do not wish to say anything of an offensive nature, gentlemen.
(cue) . . . *would be a refreshing change, sir.*
But the appearance of none of you is that of a respectable citizen of Toytown. We have no mirror handy, but I can assure you that were I to meet any member of this party outside the Town Hall I should hesitate before claiming his acquaintance. Hesitate for some time.
(cue) . . . *I should look the other way.*
I beg your pardon, Mr. Magician!

It is usual to type parts on one side of half sheets of quarto paper and they are bound in a stiff cover. Two or more copies of the parts are typed and the top copy should be retained for rehearsals. The other sets may be used for auditions and will be required for the understudies. The leading actors normally have complete scripts but if alterations are made before use, the stage manager should edit the copy so avoiding delay during rehearsals. Parts are numbered and recorded in the usual way.

Plots. Reading the play the stage manager formulates

his production plan. His reading will not only make him familiar with the play; he is also watching for technical difficulties in staging it. For instance a telephone conversation may occur and the actor is heard speaking to someone who is a long way from the scene in which the play is set. Within a page of dialogue the character arrives on the stage and obviously could not have travelled the distance in the time. There may be difficult costume changes or other discrepancies. Consequently the stage manager notes details of this kind and makes preliminary lists or ' plots,' as they are called, as follow :—

(1) Characters in order of appearance. As far as casting is complete, the names of the artists playing the parts.

(2) Acts and Scenes.

(3) Settings. It does not necessarily follow that the author's description of the setting is used. The rough plan of each set should be made after the scene conference with the author, director and designer.

(4) Lighting. Nowadays lighting specialists are usually called in to light the play. But the stage manager is sometimes asked to do the lighting and frequently is expert in this branch of the theatre. He will make provisional notes in his plot of the time of day and year of each scene and the lighting required.

(5) Properties. (a) used by the actors
                  (b) mentioned as being necessary to the plot and used to furnish the setting.

(6) Effects. These may be special lighting effects such as clouds, sea and fire, or sound effects to be produced manually or by electrical reproduction.

(7) Wardrobe. Costumes for each character and whether time has been allowed for quick changes.

The above notes will form the basis of the plots used by the stage departments and in later chapters will be explained in detail. The essential requirements should be discussed with the director and designer at an early stage so that plenty of time is allowed for obtaining them.

Reading. When a play is produced for the first time it is usual to call the artists for a reading of the play. The stage manager will be asked to find a convenient place and one of his colleagues will lend his stage, or a reading may be held in a rehearsal room. Sufficient chairs to accomodate all the cast are arranged in a semi-circle facing a table where there are chairs for the author, director, stage manager and the management. The stage manager commences to read the author's introduction and the cast read the parts they will eventually play. Sometimes it is not possible to secure the whole company for the reading and the stage manager reads for anyone who is absent. Also he reads out the stage directions and anything included in the text which will be used during the performance.

At the reading it will be possible to obtain a rough estimate of the time the play will take to perform. However, if the play is a comedy or farce, the playing time will be much increased by reason of pauses when the audience is made helpless with laughter. In fact, I have known the playing time of a farce to differ by twenty minutes when it was performed to a large or a small audience. *Business* (i.e. dumb show, when there is action without dialogue) can only be timed in performance and consequently the reading will provide an estimate which should be accepted with some caution. As a guide it is generally agreed that a page of quarto typescript (double spacing) will take a minute to perform but here also allowance must be made for pauses in the dialogue. However, at the reading of the play the stage manager will be able to get a fair idea of its length.

The Prompt Script

' Remind those who work the secrets of the thunder barrels to do what is assigned to them by following their instruction slips and let them not forget to stop when God says: " Cease and let tranquility reign".'

This direction appears in the prompt script of a manuscript, *The Mystery of the Passion,* performed in Mons in 1501. In Lee Simonson's book, *The Stage is Set*, the discovery of the manuscript is described: ' Any number of references to the pageantry of mysteries and passion plays had been pried from contemporary records, but no complete description of the setting and direction of an entire performance was known until in 1913 Professor Gustave Cohen, of the University of Strasbourg and the Sorbonne, discovered in the archives of Mons a unique document, the prompt script of a manuscript, *The Mystery of the Passion,* performed there in 1501, completely annotated by the stage manager with detailed directions for the settings used and precise directions for acting the script, which requires four mornings and four afternoons to perform. . . . In anticipating every important bit of action, every necessary costume change, and the preparation of properties and off-stage effects, this prompt script of the year 1501 can still serve as a model for any stage manager today.'

Even in professional companies the stage management is accepted as part of the organisation and rarely obtains further recognition. But it should be remembered that stage management is a craft which has attracted individuals almost since the theatre began. The care and enthusiasm of those working in it is reflected in the performance without receiving the rewards of the actor. But so long as the stage manager does not allow the mechanical side to overshadow the more creative aspect, his work can be wholly rewarding and it is one of the best trainings a would-be director could have. The stage manager absorbs the director's ideas and by his organisation interprets them for the stage staff. His encouragement and humour inspire others who would otherwise find their tasks monotonous and dull.

Marking a script requires concentration, patience and imagination. The object is to furnish an exact record of the history of rehearsals so that in an emergency a newcomer can take over the prompt corner and see a performance through.

The deputy stage manager—who is also the prompter —should provide himself with a table and chair on the prompt side of the stage. It is set at an angle to the stage which allows him a view of the acting area and also a glimpse of the auditorium where the director is conducting the rehearsals. Although the prompt or working side of the stage varies in different theatres, it is normally at the left-hand side of the stage when facing the audience. The D.S.M. should provide himself with a notebook, pencils and an indiarubber. The notebook is used for directions not recorded in the script, such as details of wardrobe: Mr. Jones to wear a buttonhole, or Miss Worthington to have a handbag containing the important letter. A good watch is also required for timing the play later in rehearsals. The script as received from the author includes certain stage directions but these are usually confined to a description of the setting and possibly business in which an actor is directly concerned. The play is staged by the director, who either prepares the movement of the actors beforehand or in some cases works extempore. Whichever method is used, the stage manager will have to record it.

There are no hard or fast rules in marking a script, but the following method is normally used. Imagine you are looking down on the acting area and you have divided the stage into sections following the diagram in Figure 4.

The stage is divided into fifteen sections covering the entire acting area. There is a centre area running down the length of the stage and subdivided into three sections: (a) *Up C* being at the rear of the stage, (b) *Centre* and

(c) *Down C* nearest the audience. On either side there will be areas marked *Left* and *Right Centre* with subdivisions and the area to the limit of the setting is described *Left* and *Right* subdivided as before. It follows

AUDIENCE

PLAN FOR MARKING A SCRIPT
TO SHOW THE MOVES OF THE ACTORS

Figure 4

that the position of an actor standing at any point in the acting area and the direction in which he moves can be described and marked in the script by recording his position as indicated in the diagram, i.e.

(Enters from door *UC* and goes to desk *RC*.)
(Crosses to *DL*.)
(Rises and crosses to chair *LC* at fireplace.)
(Crosses to window R and looks out.)
(Exits by door *UC*.)

The positions are also marked in relation to furniture in the setting which helps to identify them.

When recording the moves, the speed at which everything has to be entered in the script can make it look untidy. This is where a soft indiarubber and several pencils are necessary. The rubber will take out pencilled moves without disturbing the typescript, although sometimes it is better to put a line through a move if the director and artist are not entirely agreed that it should be altered. When the scene is rehearsed for a second time the stage manager will have a record of the former position. The pencils should be HB and sharpened to a fine point.

I have always preferred to mark the moves in the text rather than in the margin. Marginal notes can be forgotten and are not erased, which causes unlimited confusion later on. When a final script is completed after the play is produced, moves can be indicated by numbers and entered on the blank page facing the text. Directions which the stage manager will enter are cues for the lighting, effects and ' cuts ' in the text. The cuts should be lightly pencilled and if definitely confirmed, scored through with a stronger line. Lines deleted, however, should not be so completely erased that the words underneath cannot be read if required. Sometimes words already deleted are restored and then the word ' stet ' is written next to them. It is important for the stage manager to be sure that the director, actor and prompter all know the exact cut and if there is any doubt, the words on either side of the cut should be read out so that all agree with them.

Further directions for the stage manager to record are tempo, emotion and characterisation and as these could run into extensive description, it is usual to adopt some form of shorthand. In fact a stage manager proficient in shorthand will find it extremely useful. Musical signs such as crescendo and diminuendo are helpful in recording tempo. While prompting, it is very important to observe when there are pauses in the dialogue. It can be disturbing if a prompt is given during a pause and this is indicated by the sign ⌒. Underscoring and dashes are also used in addition to the intersection of vertical lines between words to indicate exceptional pauses. A stage movement or cross is abbreviated by the letter X. XDL means cross to the area down left. For complicated moves involving several artists, a brief sketch of their positions on the blank page opposite will help to clarify the direction. In discussion between the director and artist there may be far too much to jot down in the script. The stage manager will soon learn to pick out words or a short phrase which will sum up the direction. Characterisation, emotion and interpretation are recorded in this way.

The cues for lighting, effects and anything concerning the stage management are written on the blank left hand page opposite the text with a mark indicating the point in the script where they occur. When the cues are confirmed, they are marked with coloured pencil; different colours being used for *Curtain* (*Red*), *Lighting* (*Green*) and *Effects* (*Blue*). The cue is described on the left hand page and underlined. With a ruler, a horizontal line in the appropriate colour is drawn across the page and continued on the opposite page under the text ending in an arrow at the point where the cue is required.

Before the dress rehearsal, the stage manager will tidy his script. He will go through it to decide that all the directions and moves are clear and erase everything that has been finally deleted. The calls for the artists, giving them time to get from their dressing rooms to the stage, will be marked on the left hand page with the lighting and other cues and it is a good idea to indicate these cues in block capitals. As they are important, the warning cues i.e. the cue advising the stage manager that the actual cue is approaching, should allow sufficient time before they become operative. In order to remind the stage manager that a cue is arriving in the script, a vertical line in the appropriate colour is drawn from the warning cue down the page and continued on the following page to the exact point where the direction occurs. Pages of a marked script are shown in Figure 5.

It should be remembered that the prompt script is the acting or performance copy of the play. At the dress rehearsal, changes continue to be made when perhaps it is found that the position or size of a piece of furniture makes it difficult to perform a move as rehearsed or lighting and effects cues are altered. The stage manager continues to mark the script in the prompt corner but after the dress rehearsal the script is official and must be a record of the play as performed. Notes given to the stage manager by the artists are not written in the prompt script and the director's instructions to the artists and staff are the only details included.

The stage manager's work in marking a script is exacting. It calls for tact and patience in dealing with others who are working creatively. He should keep a clear picture of the play as the director rehearses it and by doing so can often anticipate his instructions.

The stage manager will learn to know and understand his artists and the stress of rehearsals can be relieved if the artists feel they have a stage manager on whom they can absolutely rely. Give them as much help as possible. Some artists study their parts quickly; others have difficulty in memorising. A considerate and cheerful attitude works wonders particularly if the stage manager has initiative, is an observer of human nature and makes allowance for some of its frailties.

Prompting. I have heard it said that prompters 'are born.' Whether this is true is a matter of conjecture but the fact remains that some people are more adaptable to the delicate task of prompting than others. Women are good prompters; their natural instinct and patience in helping others makes a woman the first choice for this exacting work.

As already mentioned, the deputy stage manager is prompting and marking the script and it is essential for the same person to be engaged in these duties throughout rehearsals and opening performances. The artists become accustomed to seeing the D.S.M. at the prompt table near the side of the stage. They get to know one another and a close relationship is developed. In the first week of rehearsals, the play is in the planning stage;

(*NOTE: The call for BEGINNERS ⑤ Mayor, Secretary
and Doctor is marked three pages before
the end of the previous scene*)
CALL ⑥ CURTAIN UP *All rooms and*
                    Ernest
                    Growser
                    Brass
                    Dennis
                    Larry

Lights to open:-
F.O.H. FULL
Spots on bar FULL
Floats: BLUE ½, PINK FULL, GOLD FULL
FLOODS on window backing BLUE and PINK
500 W FLOOD GOLD on door backing
FIRE SPOT and FIRE ON

WARN LIGHTS ·CUE ②

*Marked pages from the prompt script after moves
have been entered. For the opening of an Act,
the left hand page will include calls for the artistes,
orchestra, bar bells, and lighting cues for house
lights and stage lighting.*

Figure 5

the artists are reading their parts and the D.S.M. can
concentrate on marking the script. When the director
has given his preliminary instructions and the artists have

ACT ONE   Scene 2

The Mayor's study. There is a door up C.
RC is the Mayor's desk and behind it a very
ornate chair with a high back. On the desk are
a blotter and inkwell with a number of quill pens,

⊗ *Also bundles of*
M/S with coloured
tape and mediaeval
seals. Silver tankard
on the desk.

a bell and some books which look important.⊗ A
window is in the R wall through which can be seen
some of the more influential buildings of Toytown
There is a fireplace L with an armchair R of it.
Down L stands the Mayor's safe with a bunch of
large gold keys hanging from the keyhole. There
is a chair R of the door/and a bookcase down R.
another chair below /   *from door C and*
the desk   *goes to desk*

Mayor is reading
large M/S which
he puts down
with a sigh as
the Secretary enters

When the CURTAIN rises the fire/is burning
merrily as it is two days after/Christmas and
inclined to be cold. The MAYOR is standing by
his desk, on which is his hat. He rings the bell.
The SECRETARY enters,/with a quill pen behind
his ear, carrying papers and/a feather brush. *which*
                                        he puts on the desk.

MAYOR	*/Sits at his desk* /I'm not feeling at all well this morning.
SECRETARY	Dear, dear, dear! *X to safe DL opens it*
MAYOR	I'm afraid I've been overworking myself.
SECRETARY	Dear, dear, dear! *at safe: busy tidying M/S*
MAYOR	Don't keep on saying, 'dear, dear, dear!' in that silly way ↓ I tell you a most important thing and all you can say is 'dear, dear, dear'. I'm not at all well; I have a severe pain under my waistcoat and I can see spots. *(Secretary finds stone jar marked GINGER BEER in safe* *and closes the safe) X to L of desk puts jar near the Mayor*
SECRETARY	Fancy that! Spots! /Well I never! ∧ *considers* ⊙ *, Secretary closes*
MAYOR	Spots! You know what spots are? Well, whenever I close *eyes* my eyes I can see them; quite distinctly./ That shows I'm not well. /Don't go to sleep when I am talking to you! ∧ ⊙ *No reply from Secretary*
SECRETARY	I'm not asleep. I was just shutting my eyes to see if I could see spots. And I can; red ones. *Picks up feather brush* *dusts Mayor's chair*
MAYOR	Nonsense. You're pretending. I'm sure you can't see the
Secretary *busy dusting* *R and* *above Mayor*	sort of spots I can see. I'm very unwell; I've been working too hard. And how I'm going to sign all those papers when everything looks spotty I don't know. *Secretary* *dusts top of Mayor's wig then XC*
SECRETARY	*/Stops dusting* /But you don't sign things with your eyes shut. If you see spots when you close your eyes the only thing I can suggest is that you keep them open.

MARKED PAGES FROM A PROMPT SCRIPT

had time to memorise, the serious business of prompting
starts. It does not mean that the D.S.M. will henceforth
be prompting alone, he or she must continue to write in

moves and other directions which at this point in the rehearsals remain fluid.

Prompting should be confident and done with deliberation. The D.S.M. will find different characteristics in the actors who vary considerably in memorising and their ability or desire to take a prompt. He will observe difficult passages in the dialogue and when prompting occurs frequently in a particular place, it is useful to mark the position lightly in the margin of the script. Generally a key word is sufficient for the actor to regain his train of thought and by careful observation the prompter will note the word and give it when required in the inflexion the actor is using. If the prompter does not know the inflexion, he should give the prompt in a monotone. But at all times it is helpful if the prompter can sustain the mood or tempo of the scene by giving the prompt in the inflexion or tempo of the actor. In the event of a complete 'dry-up,' the D.S.M. provides more than a key word and gives a phrase of dialogue conveying enough sense for the actor to recollect his line.

Some memorising is necessary by the prompter. Inflexions contain pauses and by memorising the inflexion of a sentence, the D.S.M. will help himself and the actor. He is not likely to prompt when the actor is pausing and if the prompt is required will automatically give it in the tempo of the actor. Speech is music to the ear and an actor will often recall a word or line by the reading given to it rather than by the line itself.

The D.S.M. should keep a finger on the place in the script where the prompt is required and he is then able to watch the actor's face. The actor will normally turn towards the prompter when he forgets his line and seeing the prompter's face is more reassuring than the top of his head. There are occasions when the actor has his back to the prompter and a glance at his hands is sufficient to see that a prompt is required. Almost unconsciously the actor extends his fingers, a sure sign that he is in difficulty.

In early rehearsals the prompt should be given in a strong clear voice and aimed directly at the actor. Later the voice may be lowered but whispering is of little use. During performances the same method is followed and a good prompter will speedily recognise the pitch of voice necessary to convey it to the actor. It does not matter if the audience hears the prompter. And it is surprising the amount of voice employed before the audience is conscious of anything above a murmur.

Prompting can be unique in disclosing a human failing. I remember an elderly actor who was rather deaf and for professional reasons unwilling that it should be known. The calamity happened and at a large theatre he forgot his line. I gave the prompt and when the actor did not take it, repeated the line with more volume. Nothing happened. I continued to repeat the line and suddenly a voice from the dress-circle took it up. The audience laughed and the situation was resolved when another actor led his despondent colleague over to the prompt corner and the play continued.

Discretion in prompting is part of the stage manager's skill. Small errors when they occur early in rehearsals should not stimulate the prompter into activity. It is more important for the rehearsal to go on with everyone getting the 'feel' of a scene than that it should be interrupted for minor faults. Invaluable help is given when the prompter makes a note of the error and tells the actor after the rehearsal. In fact a celebrated actor once asked me to note his 'lapses' and list them at the end of the day. I did all I could and throughout a long run was encouraged with liquid refreshment from his private supply.

Prompting should be regarded as the support given to the actor in an emergency. It is sometimes advisable to let an actor find his feet (or head) and by doing so, he acquires confidence. But when a prompt is needed, it must be given quickly. The speed of a prompt can frequently avert ' dropping ' a scene and if the prompter regards himself as integral to the team his efforts will be amply rewarded.

CHAPTER 3

REHEARSALS

'Now Lucifer goes into the Earthly Paradise in the form of a
serpent. Note that the personage of Lucifer does not move from
hell until he is told to in what follows; but another person
performs the serpent and goes to Eve, for the reason that Lucifer
will not have time enough to be put into the body of the serpent.'
—*Mons* script.

I HAVE mentioned the division of duties between the
stage manager and his assistants and for the first part of
this chapter I shall discuss the work of the stage manager
before and during rehearsals. Later we shall meet ' The
Company ' which in stage language means the actors
and others concerned in the performance. In the time
of Shakespeare, the company interpreting and acting the
plays also owned the playscripts, costumes and properties.
When the Globe Theatre was built in London, Shakespeare was an actor in the company which formed a
syndicate to provide funds for building it, and so he
participated in ownership of the playhouse. His financial
success was not derived from his plays but from his
interest in the company enabling him to invest in houses
and land in Stratford-on-Avon.

The General Manager

The stage manager is called to the producer's office
and, if the production is a heavy one, will be engaged for
two or three weeks in advance of rehearsals. If the play
is a small one, it will be sufficient for him to attend to
preliminary details for a few days before the first week
of rehearsals. Most of his early discussions will be with
the general or business manager. Frequently the general
manager is a former stage manager and their talks will
be an exchange of ideas. It is not unlike the meeting of

members of other professions who enjoy a chat concerning their mutual interests. They get down to a discussion of the play and between them prepare a rehearsal and production schedule which will include the following details:

(1) Director, Designer and list of actors with their addresses.

(2) Date of first rehearsal.

(3) Number of weeks of rehearsal. (Usually three but sometimes four or longer.)

(4) Place of rehearsal. (The stage manager is asked to find a theatre, or if this is not possible, a rehearsal room for the first week.)

(5) Dates and Towns for the preliminary tour.

(6) Date of Dress Rehearsal.

    (a) Is it possible to have a dress rehearsal with scenery in London?

    (b) If not, the dress rehearsal will be on the Sunday (or Monday with a heavy show) in the first town of the tour.

(7) Scenery. Where it will be built and painted and can the actors see it before the dress rehearsal?

(8) Photographs. The name of the photographer and date of the photograph call.

(9) Publicity Agent.

(10) Assistant stage managers and understudies.

The selection of assistant stage managers is important and the number required will depend on the nature of the production. The deputy stage manager is the first to be chosen. He will be sufficiently experienced to attend to all details of the stage manager's side of the production and will be able to take complete charge in case of sickness or any other cause likely to interrupt the stage management of the play. The other assistants will normally be selected for their particular qualities and their ability to understudy certain parts; this decision being made in consultation with the director. During

PLATE 2

So Wise, So Young (John Knittel), Lyceum Theatre, Edinburgh.   Act I, scene 1

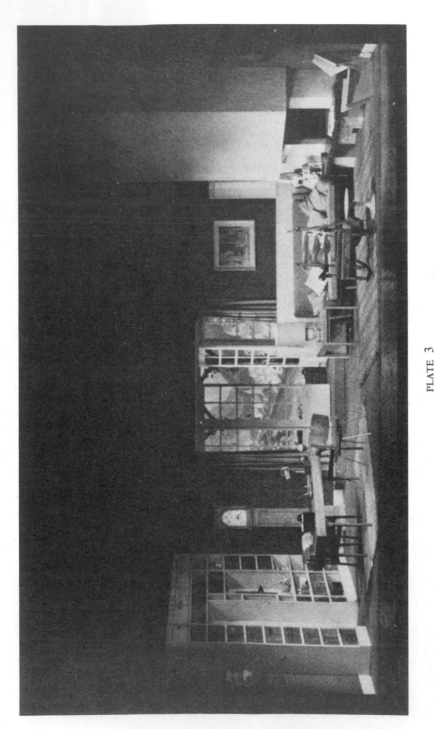

PLATE 3

So Wise, So Young (John Knittel), Lyceum Theatre, Edinburgh.   Act I, scene 2

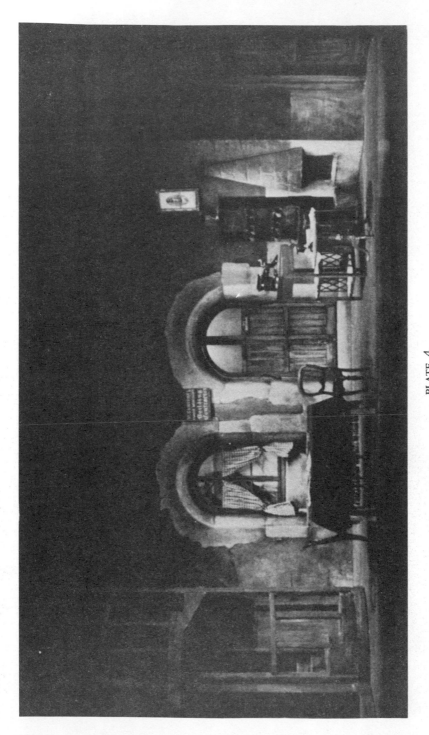

PLATE 4

So Wise, So Young (John Knittel), Lyceum Theatre, Edinburgh.   Act II, scene 1

PLATE 5

So Wise, So Young (John Knittel), Lyceum Theatre, Edinburgh.   Act II, scene 2 performances, the stage manager must be able to detach himself from the play in order to view an entire performance from the audience. The number of his assistants should, therefore, be such as to enable them to run the play competently in his absence. Some stage managers are fortunate in being able to retain one or two assistants who work as a team from show to show. This is beneficial for methods differ and when the stage management has worked together for some time much of the initial preparation is reduced and the running of performances is arranged on a preconceived pattern.

The address list is given to the stage manager who will keep it up to date. The list should contain the address and telephone number of everyone connected with the production and several copies are made for distribution to the producer, director, designer, business manager, company manager, the assistant stage managers and publicity agent. Theatrical addresses and telephone numbers should not, however, be handed out to all and sundry. Particularly the address list given to the stage door of theatres is confidential. By virtue of their calling, actors can be a prey to interested members of the public.

If the play is a musical one, the composer, conductor and orchestra will be discussed and the engagement of a deputy pianist for rehearsals arranged. As orchestral rehearsals approach, the stage manager will make provision for adequate seating and music stands for the orchestra. The business manager advises on any other problems, which vary in their solution with different managements.

THE DIRECTOR

Shortly afterwards there will be discussions with the director and designer. The stage manager may know the director's methods and it is not uncommon to find directors working with the same stage manager on several productions. Their work is so closely bound up that a director favours a stage manager with an intimate knowledge of his work. On the other hand it may be their first meeting and the stage manager must adapt himself to the director's methods. Some have a detailed schedule indicating rehearsals and method of production from start to finish and keep to their programme as nearly as circumstances will allow. Others do relatively little in advance and work without preparation. Their method is still artistically effective, as it relies to a large extent on the co-operation of the artists in creating their roles. They sometimes leave the outline of moves to the rehearsals and create the production when they see it performed by the artists. (These are brief notes on the methods employed and are only intended to supplement information given in many books on the subject of direction.)

If there is a pre-arranged schedule much of the stage manager's work is made easier. On the other hand he must do everything to help the director, and those without a programme need more assistance. There are moments when everyone in rehearsal is so absorbed in the playing or development of a scene that all else is forgotten. The stage manager must use his tact and judgement if it is necessary to interrupt or call a halt. Time is important and he must decide when other work should be done.

The director will discuss casting with the stage manager, who will ask him to arrange time for the selection of understudies. A cast list should be drawn up as soon as possible which will show the *character* with *principal* and *understudy* concerned in playing and covering it. The director will indicate difficult lighting or sound effects and properties which may have to be specially constructed. He will say if he is content with ' substitute ' furniture and properties at rehearsals. By the second week of rehearsals the designer has normally chosen the furnishings and the exact items may be used by the artists, so that they become accustomed to them. In meeting the director the principal link is forged in the stage manager's work and thereafter the various parts of the production are assembled and, by his organisation, lead to the final presentation.

THE DESIGNER

The first essential in discussion with the designer is a ground plan of the setting. The plans are to the scale of half an inch to one foot and copies are made on tracing paper. This facilitates setting of the scenery as scene plans may be laid over a plan of the stage and difficulties in setting observed, i.e. architectural obstructions in the stage for ventilating or lighting. Scale models in cardboard are made from the designs and show how each setting will appear. (Photographs of model settings are shown in Plates 7 and 17.) Figure 6 is a plan of the setting shown in Plate 2. The size is not to half an inch scale as it is reduced to fit the page of the book. The way the doors are hinged is indicated by semi-circles and the steps are given numbers to indicate the ascent of the spiral staircase.

With the ground plans and the models, the stage manager will study the following details:

The practicability of the settings in relation to the scenes to be played in them

    (a) From the point of view of the artists,
    (b)   ,,   ,,   ,,   the stage,
    (c)   ,,   ,,   ,,   the lighting.

He will by this time have a good knowledge of the play and a general idea of the movement and staging of the actors. For instance, a scene may be played involving an eastern potentate on his throne attended by several members of his entourage and favourite slaves. The stage manager will decide whether there is sufficient room and support for the delectable company and, if

A GROUND PLAN OF A SETTING

Figure 6

MOUNTAIN AND SKY CLOTH

WALL ROW

ROSTRUM 6" HIGH

DOUBLE DOORS

STEP

WINDOW

SEAT

SLOPING CEILING OVER
STONE STAGE—CLOTH UNDER

FIREPLACE BACKING

FIREPLACE

DOOR BACKING

DOOR

RETURN

C̶L̶

STEPS UP

10

11

9

8

7

6

5

4

3

2

1

BALUSTRADE

TRUCK 6" HIGH WITH
STAIRCASE BALUSTRADE
AND DOORS.

DOOR

not, indicate that the platform must be enlarged and strengthened accordingly. The designer may consider the proportion and style of his setting is diminished, in which case a conference is required with the director to decide whether to increase the size of the platform or reduce the number of feminine attendants.

The entrance from doors, stairways etc. should be in accordance with those indicated in the script and the stage manager will note the way doors open (i.e. on or off stage) and in the case of windows, if they are sash, casement or french windows, and whether they are *practical* (i.e. to be used by the actors). Questions such as these occur in rehearsals and the stage manager—being an encyclopaedia of information—provides the answer. He will attend to the requirements of staging the scenery and satisfy himself on these lines:—

(1) Can the scenes be set on the stage for which they are intended?

(2) Is there enough side room on the stage to accommodate scenery when not in use?

(3) The ultimate success of a stage design is that all parts of it can be seen from most seats in the theatre. This is not always possible but he will decide that awkward lines of sight are not apparent in the design.

(4) If a quick change of scene is required, the stage manager will indicate whether the setting can be changed in the time allowed.

(5) Lighting will be considered and particular difficulties discussed, such as the area allowed for lighting a brilliant landscape.

The master carpenter and the property master will co-operate in answering questions 1–4 and the chief electrician will make his observations concerning No. 5. Their assistance will be considered in chapters relating to these departments.

In his work of co-ordinating the various parts of the

production, the stage manager will be required to undertake duties for several departments and this can involve overlapping of responsibility. The designer's function, in addition to design of the settings, includes obtaining the furniture and scene dressings and if special or period properties are indicated he will design or obtain them. The stage manager gives copies of his preliminary plots to the designer, who will have more elaborate plots concerning specific articles or methods of overcoming difficulties in the scene design. The designer will often delegate part of his duties to the stage manager, such as obtaining properties normally found in the type of setting under review. This can take up much of the stage manager's time but if he has a good knowledge of the facilities and sources where particular articles may be found, he can greatly assist the designer in his task.

The stage manager is one of the few staff members who is in regular contact with rehearsals. Properties undergo change during this time, when perhaps the director observes that an item is required which has not previously been indicated. In characterisation of a part a suggestion may be made that an actor should use a certain article— perhaps a snuff box or a hunter watch with an elaborate gold chain. The stage manager will obtain it and with a natural flair or sense of the theatre he will know instinctively the kind of article required. Other matters crop up in rehearsals affecting the designer and, apart from the director, the stage manager is often the only person possessing exact knowledge of what is required. He informs the designer, who then makes the necessary adjustment in the design and conveys details of the alteration to the scene builders.

Lighting is an element of vital concern to the designer. The atmosphere of the setting, furnishings and costumes can undergo immense change when illuminated and the colours and strength of the lighting installation will be discussed with the stage manager. I have mentioned that a lighting specialist is sometimes called in to light the play and he is responsible for the preparation of a lighting plan. In a large production this is a formidable project. The specialist who approaches the situation on a scientific basis, and has the intimate knowledge required, devises a plan which indicates the entire lighting installation sufficient for any contingency. In the absence of a specialist, the stage manager is responsible for the procurement of everything necessary to light the play. After making his plan, he consults the chief electrician who indicates the extent of his theatre install-ation, and the stage manager provides a list of the additional equipment required, which the chief electrician obtains for him. In the event of difficult lighting effects it may be argued that the director will know what he wants. However, directors who are also theatre technicians are few and some prefer to leave the mechanical solutions of lighting problems to the specialist or the stage manager.

I recall a play in which actors impersonating two heavenly bodies were installed on either side of the setting and during the play made celestial observations about the characters and situations engaging their attention. The problem to be overcome was to distinguish between the earthly mortals in the play and the divinities studying them. Several suggestions were made when eventually the use of ultra-violet lighting was put forward and this proved to be a successful and—which is more important—entertaining solution. Ultra-violet or black light, as it is sometimes called, is light which only becomes visible to the naked eye when in contact with an object rendered susceptible to U.V. lighting. The object may be painted with a liquid having this property or materials may be used which possess it. The actors performing the deities were clothed in U.V. material and the liquid suitably dissolved with their facial make-up. The ethereal effect, when the stage lights were dimmed, leaving the U.V. illuminations, did justice to anything devised by the Magic Circle. This was an occasion when the stage manager obtained the special lighting equipment, advised on the properties required, and was responsible for rehearsing them before the first performance.

Provision of cue lights and sound reproduction of effects by tape or disc are further aspects of the electrical department which the stage manager discusses at the lighting conference with the designer and chief electrician. When the design is examined, the stage manager takes note of the position of the deputy stage manager in the prompt corner in relation to the setting. The design may not present any difficulty and may include a convenient window or other area down stage from which the prompter has a good view of the play. If the scene is completely enclosed, a small aperture is cut unobtrusively in the canvas of the scene nearest to the prompt corner and covered with gauze. The prompter looks through the opening and gives cues for lighting, etc., in addition to prompting. Cue lights are arranged to operate from the prompt corner to essential parts of the setting. For instance, an actor may be required to make an entrance during a pause in the dialogue and the D.S.M., observing the action, gives the cue. Details of the system are given in chapter 10.

The division of responsibility between the designer and stage manager concerns aesthetic selection by the designer and advice by the stage manager on a practical solution to problems encountered.

PUBLICITY AGENT

The stage manager gives the cast list to the publicity agent and keeps him informed of convenient times during rehearsals when artists may be interviewed about their personal publicity. Photographs are needed and brief biographical notes of the artist's career obtained.

Artists like to mention films or television shows in which they have performed, and with their stage appearances, these form an outline for their publicity. The notes are handed to the stage manager, who passes them to the publicity agent. Later he will want to know the time arranged for the photograph call, when artists will be photographed in their rôles for display outside the theatre and use in the press.

THE COMPANY MANAGER

In large productions, a company manager is engaged to deal with the business side and attends to all expenses incurred, which includes the payment of salaries. The stage manager gives him accounts relating to the stage departments and obtains the necessary funds from him to pay them. The company manager is in effect a deputy for the general manager and much of the stage manager's work with him will be on the lines of those described concerning the general manager.

THE STAR

A special relationship exists between the stage manager and the leading performer. He or she has to accomplish the maximum amount of work in the play. The part and dialogue are the longest, more changes of costume are needed, and everything is done to help this artist so that time and effort are preserved. The star is often the motive or spark kindling the dramatisation of the play. The physical and nervous energy required to enact the leading rôle call for control and stamina in the star and courtesy and attention from those surrounding the artist. The display of good behaviour in the theatre is as welcome there as anywhere else, and much can be gained by respecting certain traditions. The star accepts courtesies by virtue of rank and the stage manager should give the star the security his position affords. He should be alert to the behaviour of his staff and see that traditional courtesies are observed. Mistakes do occur and if the stage manager accepts responsibility, explains the cause and reassures the star, he will find more often than not that the artist will be the first to appreciate his efforts. The personal attention of the stage manager can produce an indefinable bond affecting the well-being and performance of the star. Promptness and attention to small necessities such as comfort and relaxation help the star, who will value the sincere interest of the chief member of the staff.

Much of this would seem to be fairly obvious advice, but artists in the theatre, ballet and music are often dedicated and their life is sacrificed to the special purpose they have chosen. An actor concentrates mainly on his own performance, which is an integral part of the play. The stage manager is concerned with the play as a whole and his success in the job is derived to a large extent from his skilful handling of others. He is often the first to meet an artist leaving the stage after a difficult scene and his attention can do much to convince the artist, who perhaps may be doubtful that the scene was well played. At other times a tactful and cheerful personality will give confidence.

The executive nature of the stage manager's task is illustrated in the chapter on Leadership in *The Art of Living,* by André Maurois, published by The English Universities Press. Another book is the classic *The Oracle*—a manual of the art of discretion—by Baltasar Gracián. The English translation by L. B. Walton is published by J. M. Dent and Sons. It has been described as a guide, especially to those who intend to enter public life, and is wise and humorous observation of men and affairs with the reflection: 'If you can't be good be careful.'

THE COMPANY

Before the cast is assembled the stage manager will find a place in which to rehearse. A stage is the first choice, and in London, with a number of theatres within a small area, a colleague can often arrange the loan of his stage. Stages are in great demand for rehearsals and plenty of notice should be given, with the exact times the stage will be wanted, so that the local staff may be informed. Cleaning and maintenance of the theatre occupy time during the day, and when everyone is comfortably settled in rehearsal the sound of a high-pitched vacuum cleaner innocently switched on spells chaos to artistic endeavour. The master carpenter, property master and chief electrician should be interviewed and they will arrange for the curtain to be taken up, provision of chairs and tables and the necessary lighting. Rehearsal lighting is a production expense and the electrician should be told when rehearsals are finished for the day. The account for electricity consumed is given to the stage manager at the end of the week. He will also receive accounts for the staff called in to clear the stage and ' set-up ' for the evening performance. Smoking is a hazard requiring particular attention. Plenty of ash trays should be provided and the wishes of the local management respected. Some stipulate that smoking is not allowed, having suffered in the past from careless offenders.

A stage may not be available and a rehearsal room is the alternative. The largest possible room should be obtained, for rehearsals undertaken in an area much smaller than the dimensions of the stage setting are a waste of time. Moves and position are restricted and have to be replanned when the actual setting is used. Intimate scenes between two or three people can be rehearsed adequately but for anything requiring the full acting area a stage is a necessity. Thirty feet by fifteen feet is the minimum size but even so actors are unable to project their voices in an enclosed space. Amateurs often rehearse at the homes of friends and once their lines are known the stage manager should do his best to arrange a stage with an auditorium where they can work under the conditions of performance.

Having obtained the loan of a stage, the stage manager will ' mark out ' the settings. For convenience I shall assume that the theatre is empty and the stage manager has the use of a clear stage. The settings must be marked out to the scale of the scene plans so that the actors rehearse within the exact area of the settings and the furniture is placed correctly where it will be used. Marking is done with chalk lines which are later painted over with water paint; colours being used to indicate the different scenes.

Figure 7 is a plan of the setting shown in Plate 6. The original plan is to scale of half an inch to one foot and the measurements taken from it and transferred to the stage will show the actual measurement of the setting.

The line *AB* or width of the scene is called the *setting line* which is intersected at *X* by the *centre line*. *AB* is measured on the ground plan and the length found by using the scale. For instance, if *AB* measures thirteen inches on a plan with a scale of half an inch to one foot, it will represent twenty-six feet on the stage. Having found the distance between *A* and *B*, it is measured on the stage with a tape measure. A *snap line* made by rubbing a piece of string with chalk is used to join *A* to *B*. It is held taut between the two points and by lifting the middle is snapped on the stage when the chalk will show the line required. Half the distance between *A* and *B* is the intersection of the centre line and this position is also marked. (The setting line is described in chapter 5 and the master carpenter will indicate the usual one for his stage with the position of the centre line. Working up the centre line, the measurements of the setting are marked on the stage and ' arcing ' of the corners is described in the next paragraphs.)

MARKING OUT A SETTING

Figure 7

SETTING LINE

To mark the centre line, a piece of string measuring more than half the length of the setting line is held diagonally at point *A* and an arc is described on the stage. A piece of chalk tied to the end of the string is used to draw the arc. The same procedure is followed at point *B* and where the two arcs intersect will be the position of the centre line which is joined to the setting line at X.

The next points to be found are the upstage corners of the setting; points C and D. Again using string with a piece of chalk tied to the end, find the measurement of the diagonal XC as converted from the ground plan. Holding one end of the string at X, describe an arc. Then find the measurement of BC and holding the string at point B describe a second arc. Where the two arcs intersect will be the point C. The same method is used to find point D. Points B and C are now joined by drawing a chalk line between them and a line is drawn between points C and D.

The position of the fireplace YZ is found by measuring the distance from the centre line to point Y on the ground plan and transferring it to the stage. The line DY is then drawn to the measurement of the plan. The right angle AZ is drawn on the stage and having marked point Z, it is joined to Y and the situation of the fireplace is shown. The door $Up\ C$ is indicated by finding points E, F, G and H, and finally the french windows are marked on the line BC. With the aid of chairs, benches, etc., the outline of the setting is enclosed, leaving openings as required for the entrances.

Early rehearsals are sometimes held in a room and continued on a stage when it is more convenient to mark out the settings on an old stage cloth (described in chapter 5). It can be folded and relaid on the stage which saves time in remarking the settings. Important pieces of scenery such as rostrums (platforms), steps, staircase, etc., can be obtained from the scene builders and will be required for rehearsals. In scene stores, doors from other settings can be found which are very helpful. As they have been previously used, the doors and frames surrounding them may be set in position on the plan of the setting. Two wooden telescopic braces are attached to the frame on either side and screwed to the stage or held in place by stage weights. Entrances can be timed accurately and the actors become accustomed to them.

Calls. The stage manager will be required to notify the company of the time and place of the first rehearsal. The director may wish to see all the artists or may give the stage manager details of his rehearsal schedule. The word ' *call* ' is used to indicate a notification of rehearsal or other attendance in the theatre. In stage language, it is also used to describe the appearance of artists at the end of the play in response to applause and is used in the prompt script as a reminder that artists are to be warned that their entrance in the play is near. A call is sent out by the stage manager to the artists required and it is his duty to inform the company throughout rehearsals when they are requested to attend. The call may be given by telephone or by a postcard and should be given immediately the time is known. As rehearsals proceed and the whole company is present, verbal calls are given or pinned to the notice board at the stage door. The artist is really expected to find out at the end of the day's rehearsal when he will be wanted again, but the methodical stage manager will take care that the artist does not leave the theatre uninformed. The precaution saves delay which, apart from the confusion, can be expensive when rehearsal salaries are being paid.

Rehearsal Attendance Book. It is the duty of the stage management to keep the attendance register up-to-date. An exercise book is ruled for each week of rehearsal with columns for artists' names, characters in the play and days of the week. At the foot of each daily column, the place and time is entered with a note of the scenes rehearsed. Attendance of artists is recorded by a tick entered opposite their names. With large companies including chorus members, it is customary for their names to be entered in a list at the stage door. The rehearsal book is also a useful guide in calling. When verbal calls are given out, the stage manager marks the book with those actually present on the stage at the time. The register is helpful in other ways as a diary of the work performed during rehearsals.

The deputy and assistant stage managers are responsible for the conduct of rehearsals. They arrange the furniture and show the actors where the properties may be found. For the first days of rehearsal, when moves are planned and the actors are reading their parts, substitute furniture and properties are used. Three or four bentwood chairs placed in line give the approximate length of a sofa and other articles can usually be obtained from the property master. ' Hand properties ' which are the smaller articles used by the actors should be assembled. Although they are not required while parts are still being read, it is helpful to the actor to have them directly he knows his lines and is able to use them. Walking sticks, swords with their belts and anything relating to large or cumbersome items of wardrobe should be provided as soon as possible so that the artist becomes thoroughly accustomed to them. In pantomime, for instance, when animals are impersonated, the ' skin ' should be obtained at the earliest moment and worn continuously. Other properties such as documents, keys, tea trays etc. are also substituted during early rehearsals.

' Effects ' will be needed and are usually indicated or operated by the assistant stage manager from the prompt corner. A number of effects to be operated by the effects man must be rehearsed at an early stage and will require concentrated rehearsal to the point that he memorises his cues just as much as the actor. When complete scenes are rehearsed, they are timed. As this is important information for the director, timing should be accurate and a strict record kept. Details of time sheets for use during the performances are described in chapter 10.

Towards the end of the first week of rehearsal, when

the director's method is becoming established, the stage manager should organise a close liaison with his deputy. The D.S.M. is the eyes and ears of the stage management, responsible for giving the stage manager the notes concerning their department which have been encountered during the day. On these instructions the stage manager either acts personally or arranges for the A.S.M. to carry out the necessary task which may be obtaining a special property, arranging a new effect or attending to scenic alteration. (The A.S.M. is popular with the company when she makes their tea.) Although the stage manager is away for much of the time, he is able to keep in touch with the pattern of rehearsals through his assistants.

As scenes begin to be roughly set, the stage manager should watch a rehearsal in order to note changes in the scenery or lighting which may have developed. A door may be required to stay open in a certain position or a window not previously used is now opened by the actor and the first details of lighting can be noted. Later, when the whole play is given a ' run through,' the stage manager will watch it from start to finish. At this point in rehearsals, he will be able to consider the work of his department and observe the general pattern of the play. The lighting will be a first consideration and he will take note of additions to the requirements originally discussed. His powers of observation are taxed to the full and he is alert to everything likely to promote a successful performance.

CHAPTER 4

THE STAGE STAFF

' Note that Joseph must have pincers in his belt and Nicodemus a hammer . . . Remember to get ready four new ladders to be used in lowering Jesus, for the Carpenter and others can easily help without speaking'.—*Mons* script.

THE practical work of the stage is performed by four departments who work under the supervision of the stage manager. Each department has a departmental head and a clear knowledge of the division of responsibility is essential. Although the staff found in a professional theatre is considerable, this need not be viewed with alarm by the amateur stage manager. It may, however, be helpful to know the correct function of the departments when the amateur society is allocating duties to its members.

THE MASTER CARPENTER

He is generally considered to be the senior member of the staff and apart from the electrical installation, the entire fabric and mechanical side of the stage is under his control. He is a carpenter who has often learnt his craft with one of the scene builders, with which he combines a knowledge of building. The system of counterweights and lines used for lifting the scenery, the safety curtain, fireproofing, the house tabs (curtain) and the scenery brought in for each production are his concern. He is versatile in the use of various materials and works with metal, wood, cloth and rope.

During rehearsals the stage manager will consult him regarding the plans for setting the scenery and will show him the running order of the play. The length of the intervals will be discussed and the time allowed between scenes for quick changes of scenery. His advice is valuable when the theoretical planning of the scenery is considered from a practical point of view. Often the master carpenter can indicate a practical difficulty in the design and offer a solution, relying on his experience in working the stage to do so.

He will require the fullest information concerning the scenery and is supplied by the stage manager with a complete set of plans. Depending on the amount of scenery to be lifted or ' flown ' he will prepare and test all the pulleys and ropes to be used. When the scenery arrives in the theatre he discusses its disposal with the stage manager. With a heavy production, including a number of scenes, the area off-stage has to be carefully judged and ' packs ' (or sets of scenery) are arranged around the walls in a position where they can be most conveniently used. He decides on the proper ropes or counterweight lines to ' fly ' those parts of the scenes which are lifted and he builds the set pieces, which sometimes are erected on ' trucks ' or moving platforms and placed in position later. Before the dress rehearsal he will be given a definite time to rehearse his staff in setting and changing the scenery.

In London theatres the master carpenter is assisted by one or two day-men who are experienced stage-hands. One of these men is usually appointed in charge of the flies and the other is a charge-hand controlling a group of stage-hands for the performance. During the day, the master carpenter and his day-men are occupied in maintenance of the theatre equipment and also concern themselves in keeping the scenery in good condition. The amateur carpenter will not need all these qualifications but a sound knowledge of carpentry and a flair for nautical ropework would be assets welcomed by any amateur society.

THE PROPERTY MASTER

In many ways the property master has duties akin to the master carpenter though he is more intimately concerned with the production than with the permanent stage. He is capable of turning his hand to a variety of jobs and is frequently a craftsman in a particular field. Papier mâché work is one of the well-known specialities in this department. In the provinces there used to be a property master who was the fourth generation of his family working in the same theatre who were expert in papier mâché—the craft being handed on from father to son. Nowadays the opportunity for this work is limited for it was the spectacles and pantomimes of Victorian days that were largely responsible for the use of papier mâché objects.

Nevertheless, the genius of a property master can transform a dull object to a pot of gold. In a production such as *Treasure Island,* sea chests, barrels, the map of the island in green oiled silk, crates of treasure and piles of ingots will test his skill. He is also concerned in the provision of stage meals and is responsible for effects that are manually reproduced. In changes of scene, he and his assistants handle small items such as rostrums and mantelpieces and he organises the placing and disposal of furniture. All furniture set in the acting area is carefully marked as any divergance from the planned position can be a risk to the actor. The property department requires efficient rehearsal which is done when the scene changes are organised with the master carpenter.

The property master can be invaluable to the stage manager by giving advice concerning the hire and purchase of articles and frequently has a remarkable knowledge of sources of supply ranging the length and breadth of the city. As soon as possible the stage manager should give him the *property plot* (a detailed one is shown in chapter 7) and the various requirements for the action of the play and scene changes are considered. Alterations in the plot often occur and it is essential to see that it is kept up-to-date by constant revision. His duties include keeping the furniture in good condition, polishing metal ware, washing china and arranging the setting of properties for the performance.

THE CHIEF ELECTRICIAN

The chief electrician has in the past decade adapted himself to a variety of new equipment installed in the theatre. From the time when the electric control board was placed in an inaccessible position on the side of the stage to the current trend of installing it behind the dress circle and at the back or side of the stalls with a view of the stage and operated by electronic method, great changes in theatre lighting equipment have occurred. Apart from the electrical installation, he is responsible for the heating and ventilating systems and more recently, electrical devices which have been introduced for the movement of scenery. He is, therefore, an engineer with knowledge of the installation and maintenance of several kinds of machinery.

The other stage departments receive advance instructions concerning their duties but the chief electrician and his department rely on the lighting rehearsals for the information necessary to light the play. The stage manager gives him every assistance beforehand by informing him of the running order of the play and providing him with details of special effects. In addition there will be a plan of the lighting showing the number of lanterns and other equipment to be used. The colours of the mediums for insertion in the lanterns will be indicated with a selection of alternatives. From this material the chief electrician can form an idea of the requirements and will consult his stock list of equipment in the theatre to minimise the expense of hiring it. He will be in touch with the lighting contractors and will be prepared for delivery at the theatre of the lighting equipment ordered by whoever is lighting the play. Each theatre presents different problems and the chief electrician will obtain any additional equipment he considers is necessary.

Colours of mediums for the battens and footlights are cut and inserted before the scenery is erected and all the permanent installation is overhauled. When additional bars or barrels for the lanterns have to be installed, the chief electrician superintends the work in advance.

Apart from the production his duties in daily maintenance are heavy. He is responsible for the entire theatre electrical equipment and may be required to attend to the washing machine in the wardrobe, a fuse in the advertising sign, or a short-circuit in an ancient cable entering the theatre from the main supply. He records the current used for the production and provides a weekly note of this item of expenditure for the management. The number of his assistants varies with the size of the production and the operation of the lighting board.

THE WARDROBE MISTRESS

The wardrobe mistress gives personal attention to the artists and is responsible for the care and renewal of all costumes. Although modern clothes require periodic attention, costumes in a period play require constant supervision. Stage costumes that are specially designed and made by a firm of costumiers are expensive and the wardrobe mistress who can make costumes from the designer's sketches is invaluable in saving the management expense.

Her room should be sufficiently large to enable clothes to be stored, cleaned and repaired. She is in charge of the dressers for the artists and through them receives information concerning the artists' costumes. The stage manager also notes the appearance of the company when viewing the play and reports any defects in their costumes to the wardrobe mistress. She can be very helpful in maintaining a happy atmosphere in the company and by her personal and sympathetic attention artists are assisted in their performance.

The stage manager provides her with a ' dress plot ' and a dressing room list and indicates where quick changes of costume are needed. A quick change room is arranged on the stage and the wardrobe mistress instructs the dresser in the assistance the artist requires. She gives a note of her expenses each week to the stage manager, which includes payment of the dressers and the call-boy.

SHOWMEN

They are the members of the stage, property and electrical departments who are employed during the actual performances. Payment is ' by the show ' on the basis of eight performances per week.

PAYMENT

In London an agreement exists between the Society of West End Theatre Managers and the National Association of Theatrical and Kine Employees concerning payment of stage staff. In provincial theatres the rates of payment vary but are normally in accordance with the London agreement. When amateur shows are performed in a professional theatre, the agreed rates of payment apply. Overtime is a heavy item of expenditure and the stage manager should keep this in mind. From his record of rehearsals he will be able to check the corresponding time entered by the staff in their time sheets.

ACCOUNTS

The departmental head receives time sheets each week from every man employed. These show the number of performances attended and any overtime. After checking them, he enters the total in his account book, with his own salary and items of out-of-pocket expenses. The account books are given to the company or stage manager, who verifies them and obtains the amount of money required from the management. Although the week is taken from Monday morning to the final curtain on Saturday night, account books are made up on Thursday so that payment can be given on Friday at a *treasury call*. The artists and stage-management also receive their salaries on Friday usually before the evening performance.

Two separate accounts are required during the week that a play is produced. Production expenses are itemised to the rise of the curtain on the first performance in one account, and running expenses from that time to the end of the week are shown in the second account.

The heads of the stage and electrical departments are permanently engaged and even when the theatre is closed they remain to keep it in order. Other staff, such as the stage door keeper, fireman and housekeeper, are also on the permanent staff. The work of the theatre is carried out in the morning and, apart from matinees, leaves the afternoon free before the evening performance. During rehearsals it is a considerate action to remember that the staff are not called upon to work outside their normal hours, and that the routine work of the theatre is continued. The heads of departments are frequently able to help the stage manager in lending items from their permanent stock and may know where other items can be found. Expense is saved and a gratuity, offered in the right (or liquid) spirit, often works wonders in this direction.

CHAPTER 5

THE STAGE

'All those who no longer speak this day go off by the secrets underneath the earth', (i.e. the trapdoors)—*Mons* script.

ALMOST the whole of the stage in our theatre is behind the proscenium arch except for a small area containing the footlights, which is known as the *forestage*. Sometimes this is extended to form an apron on which the actors perform near to the audience. It corresponds roughly to the apron stage of the Elizabethan theatre, though the practice of acting in close contact with the audience began in France in 1637. When the first performance of *Le Cid* was sold out, the management placed chairs for late-comers on the stage apron and afterwards patrons were encouraged to occupy the sides of the stage. This was resisted by Molière, who chose to keep the play within a frame where as he said: 'it could withdraw the better to project itself.' Theatre-in-the-round is another innovation where the performers are surrounded by the audience on all sides. This kind of stage is more suitable for drama emphasising the spoken word and is not helpful in staging plays written for the picture-frame theatre. Much of the illusion is lost by mingling of the players with the audience and whatever may be said against the traditional theatre it remains one in which attention is focussed on the acting and the production has a distinct form. Simplified stages that do not illustrate the action have never survived and some kind of scenic picture is inseparable from a vigorous performance. Plays were originally derived from religious sources and their presentation was firmly based in magic and ritual. The theatre of 'make-believe' is therefore a powerful stimulus in

SECTION OF A STAGE

Figure 8

reviving the imagination that is subdued in a modern world concerned with material things.

THE STAGE AREA

The plan of a stage such as will be found in many theatres in London is shown in Figure 9. The surface is made of strong wooden planks, sometimes of teak, which are over a framework of timber or steel. The boards are laid so that they run from the front to the back of the stage. Bridges and traps mentioned later run across the stage and it is easier to cut the boards between the joists supporting them when the traps are installed. On entering the stage of one of the older theatres we are immediately conscious that it is not level but is inclined from the footlights to the back wall. This is called the *rake*. The slope of the stage may be constant or it may be level at the back and then commence a gradual descent towards the audience. The rake is normally half an inch to one foot. In other words if the rake is continual the floor of the stage drops half an inch for each foot from the back wall and a stage forty-eight feet deep would be two feet lower at the footlights than where it meets the back wall. The rake was intended to give the audience a better view and scene painters in the past used it to obtain an illusion of perspective. Theatres nowadays are built with flat stages; the rake being used to raise the level of the seats in the auditorium.

The stage spaces to the right and the left of the acting area are called the *wings*, the name being derived from the profiled and painted screen which in old theatres was pushed on-stage in a groove. The wing, representing the side of a setting, was held at the top and the bottom in grooves and the space where they were used was known as the wings. A series of small boxes, called *dips*, are let into the stage floor in the wings. These enclose the lighting points to which the cables of the

ST. MARTIN'S THEATRE — STAGE PLAN

Figure 9

movable lighting equipment are attached. The forestage is usually covered with linoleum and the footlights are inserted in a sloping trough placed along the
front edge of the stage.

STAGE CLOTH

The acting area is sometimes covered with linoleum,
though a surface of planks is found in most theatres.
In order to cover it, a *stage cloth* of canvas or strong
linen is stretched over the acting area. The edge down-
stage is wedged in the *carpet cut* (described in the para-
graph on *cuts*) and the other sides are tacked to the stage.
The stage cloth is painted in harmony with the scene to
represent a carpet, floor boards, paving stones or other
surface.

BRIDGES AND TRAPS

In larger theatres the stage includes a series of *bridges*
and *traps*. The bridges are platforms cut into sections
of the stage which are operated manually or mechanically
to rise or fall in a particular area. They occupy a fairly
large space running across the stage and three or four
may be installed in a well-equipped theatre. The traps
are inserted in the stage below the area of the bridges
and nearer to the footlights. They are smaller platforms
used to a large extent in pantomime. Traps are of two
kinds: the grave trap and the star trap. The grave trap
is found in the centre of the stage and is about six feet
in length and two or three feet wide. It sinks below
the stage to a depth of about nine feet. Star traps are
about two feet square and are installed to the left and
right of the grave trap. They are named from the star
made of triangular pieces of wood hinged to strips of
leather which when the trap is not in use lie flat and
undetected in the floor of the stage. The platform is
underneath the star and supports it. When a spectacular
effect is produced the trap is lowered below the stage

and counterweighted. A performer stands on the platform and at the moment required the counterweights
are released and the platform flies upwards to eject the
artist through the star several feet above the stage.

A trap (or cut) is sometimes used to drop cloths and
flats to the cellar below the stage. It is cut to accommodate the length of the longest cloth, being about
eighteen inches wide, and the cloth is wound up on a
roller or dropped in a series of folds. An old method and
one worth remembering is the *sloat box* used to lower a
cloth when a trap is not available. The box is the length
of the cloth and contains a roller on which the cloth is
wound or the cloth is dropped into the box in folds.

Bridges and traps are rarely used today but sometimes a
bridge can be used to good effect in place of a built platform
to raise the level of the stage. Trapdoors played an
important part in mediaeval mystery plays. They were
used for entrances and exits and instead of walking across
the stage to a remote exit the player made a speedy
disappearance through the trapdoor. After a quick change
of costume he reappeared as if by magic elsewhere.
(Plate B.)

Cuts

When a stage cloth or large carpet is laid on the acting
area, the down-stage edge is secured in the *carpet cut*.
This is a narrow trough running across the stage parallel
to the footlights and is usually found where the forestage continues beyond the acting area. It has a hinged
lid and the up-stage edge allows enough room for
insertion of the stage cloth which is firmly held when
the lid is closed to meet the floor of the stage. Cuts are
sometimes included at the back of the stage and are
used for lowering cloths below the stage.

The Proscenium Arch

The opening dividing the stage from the auditorium
is built architecturally to correspond with the proportions

of the theatre. For this reason it is very much higher than the space required for viewing the performance, and a permanent fixture known as the *pelmet* is attached to the proscenium arch to reduce the height. On either side of the proscenium opening are steel channels used to guide the *safety curtain* and behind them are steel wires for guiding the *house tabs* or curtain as it is generally known to the public. This curtain has a series of rings sewn to the edge of the material which slide up and down the guide wires when the curtain is raised or lowered. In provincial theatres, there is sometimes a third curtain made of canvas attached to wooden bars or *battens*. The curtain is painted with advertising matter and usually has a blank space for slides to be projected from the auditorium during the interval.

THE SAFETY CURTAIN

The fireproof curtain, or *the iron* as it is called by the stage staff, is a compulsory installation in all theatres displaying scenery and where performances are given for payment. It consists of a strong steel framework with panels of asbestos and steel which at short notice can close the stage area from the auditorium. The safety curtain is suspended on steel wires and operated electrically or by hand with the counterweight system described later. It is held aloft by a brake and controlled from a position near the prompt corner. The stage manager should be aware of a fire safety precaution that in setting scenery or furniture it must not interfere with the free descent of the safety curtain. (Figure 54.)

THE CURTAIN OR HOUSE TABS

The *act drop* or curtain divides the stage from the auditorium before and at the end of the play and between scenes and acts. There are three types and formerly there was a fourth on the pattern of the advertising curtain but used as the act drop. The first type consists of a heavy pleated curtain (lined with other material to make it withstand light and sound) attached to a strong batten. An iron chain is inserted in the bottom hem to give it weight and preserve its alignment. There is normally a centre opening and therefore the curtain is made in two parts which overlap. The purpose of the division is to enable artists to make a quick appearance at the end of the play. This type is the one known as the *house tabs*, the word *tab* being an abbreviation of *tableaux*. They were formerly known as tableaux curtains for the sudden appearance of the artists was an effective and dramatic situation. The word *house* was included because they are part of the furnishing of the auditorium and seen by the audience. The curtain is raised and lowered by ropes and the sides are attached to the rings which run up and down the guide wires.

The second type is a pleated curtain which is parted in the middle when required to open or close. Each curtain is drawn to the side of the stage in a festoon and the method is used when there is insufficient headroom for the curtain to be lifted out of sight. There are two hauling wires attached to the centre edge of the curtains which pass through rings sewn diagonally across them. They are controlled by a single wire around a winding drum or winch situated at the side of the stage. The winch includes a ratchet brake mechanism which is released before the curtains return to the stage by their own weight.

The third type is a pair of curtains on runners which are drawn to the sides in the manner of window curtains. They are slower in working but are recommended to the amateur as they are simple to operate and there is less wear through creasing. The hauling wires are wound round the drum in opposite directions so that the curtains open or close according to which way the drum is turned. (Plate C.)

The act drop is a relatively new name for the curtain

PLATE B

Section of the stage floor showing a bridge

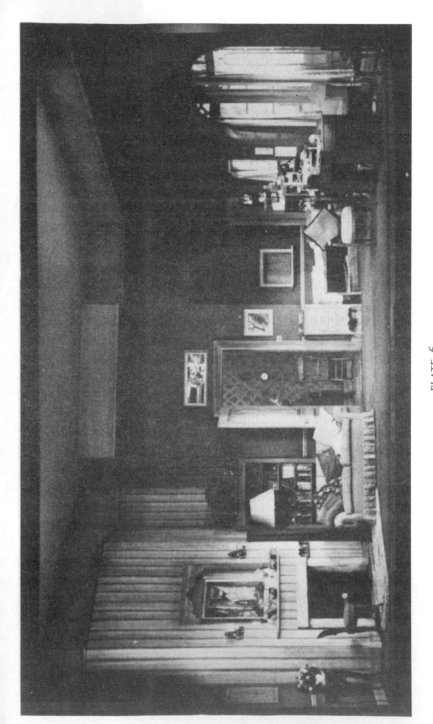

PLATE 6

The Shot in Question (Michael Gilbert), Duchess Theatre, London

PLATE 7

The Shot in Question, Model

PLATE C

Floor winch

as in the Roman, renaissance and restoration theatres it was used only at the start of the play and to finish it. When the actors left the stage at the end of an act the audience knew they could expect an interval, although this did not mean a tedious wait for the performance to continue. Scene changing was done in full view of the audience and became something that every spectator was there to watch. Henry Irving was the first to hide the mechanical part of the play when he lowered the curtain between scenes for his production of *The Corsican Brothers* in 1881.

THE GRIDIRON

Towards the middle of the seventeenth century the Italian scene designers were attempting various methods of arranging quick changes of scene. Their success is doubtful, for in one of the text books of Nicola Sabbattini, he advises that the attention of the audience should be distracted by pretending to start a brawl at the back of the auditorium or, as this might be dangerous, an unexpected blast of trumpets or fanfare of drums could be heard while the scenery was being changed. Nevertheless, it is probable that they were experimenting in lifting or *flying* scenery in addition to moving it on the stage.

Scenery is lifted by means of the *gridiron* or *grid* as it is commonly known. There are a number of joists supported by heavy beams which are built up as high as possible above the stage and the grid consists of wooden rafters or steel girders running across the stage and supported by the joists. The girders have a gap of a few inches for ropes to pass through attached to the scenery suspended below the grid. The ropes are threaded through pulley blocks fixed above the joists to take their weight, and three single blocks and one triple block are used for the ropes on which each cloth is flown.

THE FLIES

The *fly floor* or *fly gallery* is a narrow platform built along a side wall of the stage at a height of about thirty feet so that it does not interfere with scenery moved on the stage. All ropes for lifting the scenery are secured or *tied off* to the *fly rail*, which consists of heavy beams running along the fly gallery. Wooden or metal *cleats*

FLY RAIL CLEAT
Figure 10

similar to those used in ships for attaching ropes are fastened to the inner edge of the fly rail. Sometimes a second gallery is built on the opposite side of the stage and is used for adjusting scenery in difficult operations. The counterweight system described later is often installed on one side with the fly gallery for the hemp ropes on the other side of the stage.

The ropes referred to as a *set of lines* are arranged at intervals of a few inches from each other and are provided over the stage area wherever it may be required to fly a cloth or piece of scenery. Three ropes or set of lines are used for each cloth and starting at the fly rail are threaded or *reeved* through a triple block on the grid and continued through three single blocks to fall in position across the stage where it is intended to fly a cloth. The ropes are described as *long, centre* and *short* lines; the long line being the furthest away from and the short line nearest to the fly rail. The ends are fastened to a wooden batten attached to the edge of the

Figure 11

cloth. To set a cloth, the flyman pulls on all three ropes and on the stage the master carpenter instructs him to adjust the long, centre or short lines so that the cloth is level. When this is so, the flyman ties off all three ropes together to the fly rail and the cloth is said to be *on its dead*. (The word *dead* is used to describe the exact height by which any piece of scenery is raised or lowered to its correct position and is also used when scenery and lighting or other equipment is no longer required.) (Figure 11.)

Two cleats one above the other are attached to the fly rail to serve each set of lines. The lower cleat is used for securing the cloth or other piece of scenery permanently in the correct position, i.e. on its dead. The other cleat is employed for making fast the slack rope when the cloth is raised. *Trimming* of a cloth, i.e. adjusting it to the right height, takes time and in a quick scene change when the cloth is dropped to the stage all the flyman has to do is to untie the ropes from the top cleat and let them slide through his fingers. When all the slack rope is out the cloth, held by the ropes attached to the lower cleat, will be in the exact position.

The knots used in tying ropes to scenery are the *bowline*, the *rolling hitch* being a variation of the clove hitch and the *slip knot*. They are chosen for complete security and speed in untying. The bowline is used for a direct lift and when scenery is pulled sideways the rolling hitch is tied, as it cannot move along the batten. The slip knot is used for temporary attachment into a ring, though it will not hold a batten. (Figure 12.) A small sandbag is tied to a line or set of lines to prevent them from slipping through the pulley blocks when they are hauled up to the grid. The weight of the sandbag also helps to bring the lines down again to the floor of the stage. Large sandbags are used for counterweighting a heavy piece of scenery. They are tied to the set of lines immediately below the triple or *head block* on the grid above the fly rail and when the ropes are hauled the weight of the sandbags counterweights the scenery.

Bridles or *grummets* are used in flying a large cloth in order to distribute the weight along a wide batten. The ends of two rope bridles are attached to the top batten of the cloth and the loops so provided are fastened to two lines from the grid. The batten is then supported at four points, though flown on two instead of the three lines normally used.

Hanging irons are used with heavy scenic units which

THE SLIP KNOT

THE BOWLINE
Figure 12

SANDWICH BATTEN

CLOTH

THE ROLLING (CLOVE) HITCH

need additional security or when battens are not available to which lines may be secured.   They are flat and
hook-shaped pieces of metal with a ring at the top

HANGING IRONS
Figure 13

FLYING IRON
Figure 14

through which the flying rope is tied. (Figure 13.) They
are screwed vertically at strong points—the ends and
the centre—to the bottom of a piece of scenery and
additionally bolted when used with very heavy loads.
(See French Flats, chapter 5.)

A *flying iron* (Figure 14) is a rectangular piece of metal

with a hinged ring (to provide a flat surface for touring) and is used for bolting to the stiles of scenery or the sides of a boat truck.

Sometimes a cloth has to be moved and when other lines are not available it is *brailed*. A brail line is stretched across the stage from one fly gallery to the other and is attached to a set of lines which are moved up or down-stage or from side to side and retained as required. When an item of scenery or a light fitting has to be hung in a particular place where there are no lines, a *spot line* is introduced. It is a line suspended from a pulley block attached to the grid in the exact position where the line is needed. The line is reeved through the block and continued through another single block to the fly rail.

Hemp ropes are used and these, in addition to other machinery for flying, require constant supervision. The Head Flyman is an important member of the staff for it is his responsibility to attend to the security of everything flown above the stage.

Steel wire cable $\frac{3}{32}$ in. thick is used in flying when a hemp line cannot be concealed. It is virtually invisible and being flexible is not likely to break under strain through kinking of the wire. *Piano wire*, sometimes called *Trick wire*, was formerly used for this purpose.

THE COUNTERWEIGHT SYSTEM

To haul up a heavy piece of scenery by rope often requires the combined strength of several men, and in modern theatres the counterweight system is installed. It consists of steel wires attached to a steel barrel used for securing the scenery and which is balanced by heavy weights hung on the other end of the wires. The weight can be adjusted to about that of the scenery, and by balancing it the scenery is lifted or lowered with a minimum of effort. The steel wires are reeved through blocks in the same way as the ropes but instead of being

tied off at the fly rail, they are fastened to the counterweight cradle containing the weights which moves up
and down in grooves near to the side wall of the stage.

For ease in operation, a rope is attached to one end of
the counterweight, passed through a block at stage
level and taken up to a block above the grid, from
which it is attached to the other end of the counterweight. By pulling on the rope, the counterweight is
controlled and the scenery raised or lowered to the
stage. The system may be operated from the fly floor
or at stage level and the brake on the hauling rope is
installed wherever it is used. The weights take up a
good deal of space and a loading gallery is built above
the fly floor or at stage level to accommodate them.

When a heavy piece of scenery has to be taken off the
counterweight barrel, weights equivalent to the weight
of the scenery are taken out of the counterweight cradle
for the barrel to remain balanced by its own weight.
The scenery is then released from the barrel which is
flown away, and the method is known as *overhauling*.

Although the counterweight system appears to be a
modern invention, it was known more than three
hundred years ago. The Italians discovered it and
when performances were given to the French court,
they were astonished to see 'Heaven changed to Hell
half a dozen times in the course of a single evening.'

THE SETTING LINE

This is the basis from which the designer works when
designing his scenery for the stage on which it is to be
presented. It is an imaginary line and in Figure 9 starts
at the up-stage edge of the *tormentor,* though its position
varies in different theatres. It runs across the stage and
the scene designer decides where to start his scene by
drawing the setting line on the ground plan. The
master carpenter marks the stage according to the plan
and builds the scenery from this position.

Revolving Stages

The revolving stage was invented by the Japanese and was used in their popular theatre by 1760. Two revolves were introduced later, one operating inside the other, and spectacular effects were made possible when stage lifts were also included in the outer revolve. From 1898 the revolving stage was taken up in Germany where it was adapted and copied in most of their theatres.

The advantage of a revolving stage (which consists of a circular platform operated by an electric motor or manually by means of a winch and steel cable) is that a number of scenes can be set on it to revolve in turn towards the audience. It presents difficulties, particularly if the play is toured. Only a certain number of provincial and London theatres have revolving stages and the alternative is to hire one. This is expensive, involving labour and time in building it, and therefore a play is rarely designed with a revolving stage when it has to be toured. A further difficulty is that the stage must be flat and consequently the area surrounding the revolving part of the stage must be built up. As the diameter of the section that revolves is smaller than the width of the proscenium opening, a false proscenium (described in chapter 6) has to be mounted to mask the scenes, which in turn restricts the acting area. On the whole, it is generally agreed that simpler methods of changing scenery are to be preferred.

Tumbling

A method for lifting a cloth in theatres or halls without sufficient head room is the use of a *tumbler* or roller attached to the foot of the cloth. In this way, the cloth is rolled up rather like the old-fashioned blind, but it is rolled from below. The tumbler projects on either side of the cloth where the hauling ropes are wound. The ropes are taken up and reeved through two pulley

blocks attached to a ceiling beam and the free ends
returned to the side of the stage. When the ropes are
pulled, the tumbler revolves and the cloth winds itself
around it. The weight of the tumbler helps to keep the
cloth taut. The tumbler is made of two lengths of half-
round batten with the cloth sandwiched between them.
Pieces of curtain pole may be used but an experienced
carpenter should construct the long tumbler as the roller
must be made accurately otherwise the cloth is caught in
folds and creased. *Tripping* is another useful method when
a cloth has to be taken out of sight and the space overhead
is insufficient to allow for normal flying. The cloth is
taken up as far as possible and a second set of lines is attached to the lower batten of the canvas. The lines are
passed behind the cloth and hauled up followed by the
batten and canvas which folds over itself so that the cloth
becomes approximately half its height.

LINE OF SIGHT

The stage manager should know the fundamental
positions in the auditorium from which scenery is viewed
to ascertain how much of it can and can not be seen by
the audience. The proscenium arch is the frame through
which the performance is seen and it conceals some parts
of the stage. However, when an empty stage is viewed
from the front seats in the theatre, we can see the back
wall, much of the wings at either side, and by looking
upwards our line of sight is taken to the grid and sometimes beyond it. The designer has to achieve correct
masking of his scene which means everything is hidden
except what is intended to be seen by the audience.
The stage manager will be asked to help the director
and designer in this respect and there are four main
points in the auditorium for viewing the setting which
he should know. They are: (1) The centre seat in the
front row of the stalls for looking at anything suspended
above the setting; (2 and 3) the seats at the end of the

front row for observing that the sides of the setting are properly masked; and (4) the upper circle or gallery in order to see that as much as possible of the setting is visible from this viewpoint. If there are boxes on either side of the stage, the lines of sight from these should also be considered, and sometimes end seats behind the front row give a view of the side of the setting that needs masking.

CARPET RUNNERS

Silence in the wings and around the acting area is essential to the well-being of the actors and fulfilment of their performances. To achieve this, lengths of coconut matting are placed wherever there is likely to be traffic of footsteps around the setting and the entrance to the stage from the dressing rooms. The runners are bound at each end with strips of lead so helping them to lie flat and keep their position. They are not secured permanently as they have to be lifted for scene changes. The stage manager should be continually on the alert for noise near the stage, and to quote an example, although the usual precautions were followed, someone once informed me that I had the heaviest feet in the theatre.

THE OPEN STAGE

The traditional theatre at the turn of the century had many secrets, and the mystery by which its effects were achieved contributed to the enjoyment of the performance. With the advent of the cinema, audiences were entertained to dramatic situations on a grand scale and staging of these in the theatre became out-of-date. Competition brought to the provincial theatre by the motion picture closed many theatres, and in its turn the cinema suffered a similar fate with the arrival of television. After the last war, drama groups attracted to the live theatre discovered cinemas, recreation halls and chapels which were often unsuitable for staging of plays in the conventional manner. To provide an alternative arrangement, the *arena stage* or theatre-in-the-round was employed which in the early part of the century was used in Germany by remodelling the acting area in the shape of a circus ring with the audience seated around it. (Figure 15.) The audience completely surrounds the

ARENA STAGE
360° ENCIRCLEMENT

ENTRANCES   WILL VARY   ACCORDING
TO ARRANGEMENT OF SEATING

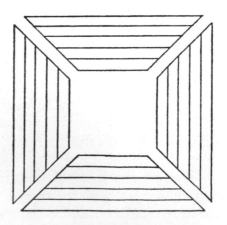

Figure 15

acting area and there is no separation between stage and audience which are contained within the same space. Entrances are made through the audience, sometimes by ramps placed conveniently, or from under the stage. Another form is the *transverse stage*, where seating is arranged on two opposite sides of the acting area and the audience face each other across the stage. (Figure 16.)

ENTRANCES

TRANSVERSE STAGE

Figure 16

Much has been said in support of this kind of performance, the principal reason being that it involves the audience more intimately and therefore favours the live nature of the performance. Television and film, for instance, provide a two-dimensional view which in the arena stage becomes a three-dimensional one. Nevertheless, it should be observed that from his seat the individual member of the audience continues to have a two-dimensional view often interrupted by the face of his opposite number on the other side of the arena.

Production difficulties are masking of the actors by each other and the need for skill in the choice of furniture and properties to give the best possible view of the performance from all sides. Lighting requires adaptation from methods used in the proscenium theatre and is described in chapter 8. Voices, facial expressions and gestures are mainly directional and therefore their effect will be modified when seen from different parts of the arena. On the other hand, the simplicity of staging with no more than essential furniture can be of value in student performances. A larger audience is accommodated, close to the performance, and provides a stimulus to individual effort and development of the actor.

A large room or hall used for transverse stage performances can be adapted to a variety of plays and the amateur has an advantage over a professional company through the simplified form of production. The seating may be arranged at opposite sides of the room or diagonally across opposite corners. The audience can be seated on three sides of the acting area or the seats may be rebuilt in smaller sections with gangways giving access to the acting area which by its shape can serve a particular play. The seats permit a flexible arrangement and several forms of presentation are possible which give variety when a number of plays are given in repertoire.

Encirclement of the open stage by the audience is 360° in the arena stage, or the audience may be seated in a semi-circle with 220° or 180° encirclement as in the Greek and Roman theatres. (Figures 1 and 2.) This form may be varied and the Festival Theatre, Chichester, comprises an open or *peninsular stage* arrangement in which the audience is seated on three sides of the stage. (Figure 17.) The seasonal nature of the theatre precludes the use of expensive scenery or stage machinery and a permanent setting consisting of a platform with a series of steps is situated at the back of the stage which, with additions, is made the basis of various settings. The increased seating capacity of the auditorium is valuable in a theatre whose economy depends on a limited season.

The theatre is experimental and the impression is

gained not so much of what kind of performance will be given but rather how a particular play will adapt itself to the rigidity of the stage and its open spaces. Plays written for the conventional theatre are not seen at their best under these conditions though the success of productions at the Chichester theatre testifies to the skilful and inventive direction of the plays performed there.

ENTRANCES

A VARIATION OF THE PENINSULAR STAGE.

Figure 17

The Globe theatre where Shakespeare's plays were first performed had a stage that jutted out into the audience who surrounded it on three sides. He called it ' this wooden O ' though probably it was made up of straight segments rather like the sides of a threepenny bit. It will be seen that the peninsular stage included in some recent theatres was used by Shakespeare and continues to be a solution for staging plays in which drama and the spoken word need a close relationship with the audience.

In the proscenium stage, Shakespearian verse makes a great demand on the actor's skill. Much of the enjoyment of the text, written for an audience able to follow it intimately, is lost when the actor has to speak slowly with exaggerated gesture to spectators in the furthest part of the auditorium. When the plays are given with realistic scenery other problems arise. For instance, in the opening scenes of *Twelfth Night* the scene is changed five times in less than ten minutes and the designer has to create a simple arrangement for the play to continue without interruption.

The Globe theatre is supposed to have held 3,000 people in which actor and spectator were closely associated and the great advantage in the production of Shakespearian and other period plays is the accommodation of the audience near to the stage. In a theatre seating 2,000, the furthest spectators seated around the stage are only thirteen rows from the front. More than twice this number would be needed to hold a similar audience in a proscenium theatre.*

Another form of open stage is found in the design of a theatre on a compact site too small for conventional use. The *end-stage* is one where the audience faces the acting area which is placed at one end of the auditorium. It is a proscenium type stage with a maximum opening and qualifies as an open stage because acting area and audience are contained within the same space. (Figure 18.) There is little or no encirclement by the audience and the action is seen against the walls of the stage. Entrances may be made and action seen through openings in the back wall.

The Mermaid Theatre and the Hampstead Theatre Club in London and the Phoenix Theatre, Leicester, are of this type and built with a slender budget on sites in which shape and size were restricted. When it is realised that building of a traditional provincial theatre would cost about £300,000, it is commendable that acting spaces, where drama is seen and enjoyed, are provided in these theatres at a fraction of the cost. The Phoenix Theatre, Leicester, was built in six months for under £30,000 and the Hampstead Theatre Club in three months at a total cost of £17,000.

* From *A Life in the Theatre* by Tyrone Guthrie

The changed attitude of the theatre-going public in the last twenty years has encouraged forms of presentation which in the days of realism and theatrical illusion would not have been accepted. The visible presence of mechanical aids to the production such as the lighting equipment and construction of scenery is now tolerated in the open-stage technique. New theatres may therefore include certain aspects of this design though the

END STAGE
ENCIRCLEMENT NIL.

ENTRANCES

Figure 18

end-stage with little audience encirclement will need modification.

The adaptability of the open stage is often stressed but lies principally in reseating the audience and altering the acting area. In the proscenium type theatre it can well be achieved with certain alterations in design. The ebb and flow relationship between audience and performance may then be obtained in production methods using different stage levels and the transition of scenes from the acting area to the auditorium.

An interesting example occurred in the production of *Lock up your Daughters* at the Mermaid Theatre and its transfer to Her Majesty's Theatre for a successful run.

The eighteenth-century play with music was first produced on the open stage of the Mermaid Theatre. The close relationship between audience and performance there contrived to emphasise the intimate scenes, some of which were played down-stage of the acting area. The production was mounted around a small revolving stage flanked on either side by platforms, approached by steps, on which a formal indication of the scene was built, such as a window and a bed with period canopy. The orchestra was situated behind the setting and was visible through the stylised trellis separating the scenes played on the revolving stage.

When the play was transferred to Her Majesty's Theatre, which has a traditional proscenium, the curtain was permanently taken up and the pelmet raised to provide the maximum opening. To reproduce the effect of the open stage, the orchestra pit was enclosed and the acting area of the stage extended by an apron into the auditorium. The acting area was covered with a temporary surface to accommodate the revolving stage and the setting was then installed as at the Mermaid Theatre. The orchestra remained at the back of the stage, all the lighting equipment was visible and scenes begun and terminated by a change in the lighting. The intimate nature of the production continued with the rapport between audience and performer largely maintained although in a traditional theatre with a much greater seating capacity than at the Mermaid.

THE ADAPTABLE STAGE

New forms of theatre are in demand not only from producers, designers and actors desiring to move away from the so called ' peep show ' limitation of some traditional theatres but also from repertory companies presenting a variety of productions which require alteration in the relationship between performer and audience. Opera and classical tragedy are best seen under conditions of detached spectacle provided by the division of audience and performance in the conventional proscenium stage. Drama, emphasising the spoken word and definition of character, is improved by the close relationship with the audience found in the apron or open stage.

QUESTORS THEATRE

Figure 19

To include adaptability in a theatre from a proscenium type to one of 180° encirclement, such as the peninsular stage, demands a substantial alteration in the seating and the method—unless resolved in the original design—will remain a technical and economic problem. A remarkable achievement for an amateur company has been made by The Questors, Ealing, London, who have built their own theatre, which includes four types of acting areas under one roof. They have a proscenium stage, a proscenium with forestage, a peninsular or three-sided stage and an island stage or theatre-in-the-round. (Figure 19.)

The design appears to be derived from the peninsular open stage which is contained in the stalls or pit area and is surrounded by fixed horse-shoe tiers of seats on a steep rake. For use as a proscenium stage, seating is placed in the stalls area, the front two rows being removed when an apron stage is required. In the island stage arrangement, the proscenium surround is removed and the stalls seating placed in tiers on the area of the permanent stage. This seems to be the least satisfactory form as the combination of permanent and improvised seating lacks symmetry which is essential for the balance of seating surrounding the island stage.

Difficulties in providing an adaptable stage in a large theatre by mechanical methods have been overcome in a small one, seating under five hundred, with the help of willing labour in an amateur organisation. The theatre is shown to be capable of housing four types of stage and the company deserves the highest praise for its enthusiasm and enterprise.

The design of the new Barbican Theatre for the Royal Shakespeare Company in the City of London indicates an ingenious compromise between the proscenium and open stage and also offers a novel treatment of using scenery. The company requires an adaptable stage for the contemporary staging of Shakespeare and a repertoire of modern plays for which they have designed an open ' space stage.' By this is meant an acting area poised in space at the focal point of vision of the audience. (Plate D.)

Complicated scenery and stage machinery are not intended; the minimum amount of scenery is to be employed and the acting area is presented as a stage picture to be used empty. To achieve this, the stage is surrounded at the back by movable gridded screens which will perform the two functions of defining the shape of the acting area and of masking the sight lines into the back-stage areas. The gridded surfaces of the screens, besides their decorative purpose, have a practical use; scenery is to be created by attaching doors, windows and other scenic items to the screens. When they are set behind the acting area a large free area is provided and by setting them in a forward position the acting area can be enclosed.

The stage machinery comprises a grid over the acting area down to the front edge of the stage and there will be two large bridges or lifts behind the acting area situated at an angle of 45° to the stage axis. These sections of the stage can, therefore, be raised or lowered to serve productions and scenery will be dropped below the stage for storage. It is intended to raise and lower the stage mechanically by 'hinging' the front edge to provide a rake and to drop the stage a few inches for use with trucks. The acting area is to be built on a sectionally de-mountable framework so that any section of the stage floor can be removed and machinery for a production installed as required.

Wide sloping ramps which seem to emerge from the audience provide access to the down-stage area. Additional entrances from the sides are between two-fold returns adjoining the ramps and the up-stage panelled screens. A shaped fire curtain as wide as the auditorium and as high as the ceiling is designed to fall along the front edge of the acting area to seal it completely from the auditorium.

For proscenium staging of plays, the returns near the stage ramps are removed to provide unobstructed wing space on either side of the acting area. The ramps are raised to a position level with the acting area and wall panels normally positioned in the wings are moved along the edges of the ramps to form a proscenium opening of thirty-five feet. A framed border will mask the top of the opening.

The auditorium has a capacity of 1,275 seats and the whole audience is seated within sixty-five feet of the stage with a full view of the acting area. Three balconies containing only a few rows of seats and a lighting gallery overlap one another and are continued right round the side walls to create the ' non-proscenium " one room " relationship between stage and auditorium ' described by the company. For the proscenium stage all the seating in the side galleries will be screened off thereby reducing the capacity to 900 seats. Of special interest to the stage management is the box provided for them

GEORGIAN THEATRE
Figure 20

behind the main auditorium. Here all the equipment found in the prompt corner is duplicated so that a production can be controlled from the auditorium with a clear view of the acting area as well as from the stage.

The theatre estimated to cost £2,210,000 is bound to arouse controversial interest and the design which is probably unique emphasises the staging of plays in Shakespearian verse which is the principal concern of this company.

Many traditional theatres have succeeded in being adaptable because their size made it possible to stage a great range of productions from drama to lavish musical plays. True adaptability, however, lies in the ability of a theatre to afford a flexible relationship between the audience and performer. We have only to look at the plan of an eighteenth century playhouse to realise how this was achieved in the design of the stage, proscenium arch and the auditorium. (Figure 20.)

The Georgian theatre had a proscenium arch and a forestage occupying the entire area of the traditional orchestra pit. It was also common practice to enter the forestage by doors on either side of the proscenium arch. The auditorium seating was in the shape of a horse-shoe and offered 200° encirclement of the forestage acting area. The actor-audience relationship could, therefore, be adapted from the isolated spectacle of the traditional theatre to the intimate contact of the full apron stage or the half forestage using the proscenium doors.

The influence of the Georgian theatre may become a trend in the design of new theatres and in fact is already doing so. The Playhouse, Nottingham, has an adjustable forestage and a proscenium one in a circular auditorium. The shape of the auditorium reduces the impression of a physical division between stage and audience, although sight lines from the perimeter seats and the loges on the side walls suggest that they are intended for greater appreciation of the open stage. The Yvonne Arnaud Theatre at Guildford also has a circular auditorium, and the apron stage is provided by a rather cumbersome arrangement of filling in the orchestra pit with rostrums which later may be improved by the installation of a lift.

Essential to the enjoyment of the traditional theatre are the magic detachment and ' suspension of belief ' associated with the proscenium stage. The flexible nature of the eighteenth century theatre—with adaptability from detached spectacle on the one hand to intimate audience relationship on the other—may offer a solution to the design of future theatres intending to preserve the traditional atmosphere.

Designed for adaptable staging in the form of proscenium, open peninsular and arena stages, the newly constructed Northcott Devon Theatre, Exeter, built on

NORTHCOTT DEVON THEATRE EXETER
Figure 21

a site given by the University, has accommodation for
about 450. (Figure 21.) The proscenium opening i.e.
the distance between the side walls is fifty-four feet and
the seating in the fan-shaped auditorium rises directly
from the stage which is not a platform but a flat space
on the same level as the first row of seats. When used
as a proscenium stage the proscenium opening is
reduced by enclosing the side areas with curtains or

masking flats. The width between the end seats in the front row is twenty-eight feet and therefore the average stage setting of twenty-six feet may be used with the area of the orchestra pit employed as a peninsular stage.

Additional seating stored under the stage is carried up by the lift in the orchestra pit and placed on the stage area for theatre-in-round productions when the total seating capacity is increased to about 600. The stage seats comprise two-thirds of the area surrounding the arena stage and with the curved seating in the auditorium enclose the circular acting space on all sides. However a similar situation arises as in the Questors Theatre where the permanent accommodation is much greater than the temporary seating on the stage and the actor may be influenced in his performance by the large number of spectators seated in the auditorium. These are seated several rows away from the stage and consequently the intimate relationship between actor and audience claimed for the arena stage is not provided.

The design, however, offers a good view of the acting area in three different forms of staging and does not entail any alteration of the seating in the auditorium.

FIRE PRECAUTIONS

The responsibility rests with the firemen employed in the theatre and the stage manager should be aware of the appliances used in the case of fire. The Licensing Authority insists on certain apparatus and although amateur performances may perhaps not be under its control, the amateur stage manager is well advised to make provision in the way of a few buckets of sand and water placed at strategic points. In the professional theatre the combustible property of scenery and stage effects erected in an enclosed area is watched with caution. When it is necessary to use a flame of any kind such as a candle or a torch, permission must first be obtained from the Fire Brigade controlling the theatre who normally make a rigid inspection of the proposed effect before it is allowed.

The construction of a theatre includes the installation of an automatic smoke vent in the roof of the stage called the *Lantern* which has sloping windows arranged to fall outwards in case of fire. (Figure 8.) They are controlled by a rope running down the wall to stage level. When the rope is released the windows open, so causing a draught to take away smoke and flames. The apparatus includes a *sprinkler* system, fire hoses, axes, blankets and fire buckets with water and sand. Sand is used for an electrical fire. The sprinkler system is a series of pipes attached to the roof of the stage, under the fly floors and ceilings. Water in the pipes is immediately released should the temperature rise above a certain point and the system is also operated by a handle situated near the control of the safety curtain in the prompt corner. In some of the older theatres, the handles for the safety curtain and the sprinkler system are very alike and it is always advisable to look carefully before operating them. No unauthorised person should be allowed to touch the handle, yet I can recall the young assistant stage manager who innocently attached the lead of a dog awaiting its entrance to the sprinkler handle. Fortunately the dog was a distinguished performer and no harm was done.

CHAPTER 6

SCENERY

' It is imperative that the theatre makes us see every specific
place called for by the action of the play—here a temple, there a
palace, a public square, the streets in back of it, in short everything necessary to show the eye what the ear must listen to.'
—Voltaire.

SCENERY is an important part of the stage manager's
responsibility and when the design is made, he must
satisfy himself that it is practical for the stage where it
is intended to be used and that the scenery is built to the
required standard. Changes of scene need careful
organisation, and although the master carpenter instructs
his staff in the handling of the scenery, the stage manager
approves the method and usually prepares the plan with
the master carpenter when difficult changes of scene are
encountered. Consequently the stage manager and his
assistants must have a thorough knowledge of the construction of scenery and the methods employed in using it.

FLATS

The principal units of scenery are flats. These are
wooden frames over which canvas is tightly stretched
and they may have a special use for surrounding doors,
windows, fireplaces, etc. They vary in length and width
and are normally from 12 ft. to 18 ft. in height and up
to 8 ft. in width. The height of the proscenium border
sometimes allows greater length up to 24 ft., but difficulty in handling prevents greater width. Hinged flats
are used for a wide area of scene to allow for travelling
and storage. The components of the wooden frames
are the upright sides called *stiles*, and the horizontal
sections known as *rails*. They are strengthened by
battens and *shoes* or *toggles*. Figure 22 shows their

CONSTRUCTION OF FLATS AND METHOD OF LASHING THEM TOGETHER

A Stile	D Shoe or Toggle	G Rail
B Rail	E Cleat	H Batten
C Rail	F Sash Line	

Figure 22

construction and method of fastening them together. The frames are made of 3-inch by 1-inch deal or pine and the joints are morticed and tenoned. In the United States the joint is secured with a corrugated metal fastener driven in edgewise across the seam and flush with the wood. It is strengthened with a *keystone* or a *corner block* secured above the join and corrugated fastener. The keystone is a piece of $\frac{3}{16}$-in. three-ply shaped like a rectangle and the corner block is a small triangular-shaped piece of three-ply. They are set in $\frac{1}{4}$ in. from the edge of the frames to prevent damage during scene shifting.

LACING OF FLATS

Figure 23

Flats are held together with light rope known as *sash line*. The rope is attached to the stile of one flat, being tied to a *grummet* or *lashline eye* which is a metal eye-piece screwed to the stile. It is taken over the cleat on the adjacent flat and down the stile to cleats or screws on both flats where the rope is pulled taut and tied with a *slip knot* so that the joint may be broken quickly. Flats that have had long use are inclined to warp and when this occurs they are *laced*. Screws are attached to the inner edges of the stiles and as the line is taken down the flat, it is laced around the screws before it is tied to the cleats below. (Figures 22, 23 and 24.)

TYPES OF CLEATS
Figure 24

Other methods of fastening flats together and to heavier items such as rostrums or other built pieces are with a *pin hinge* and a *carriage bolt*. The pin hinge is an ordinary hinge one half of which is screwed to the edge of each flat. The pin is replaced by a short piece of heavy wire bent over at the top to prevent it falling through the hinge. When the flats are brought together the wire is inserted through the two halves of the hinge and removed to break the joint in a quick scene change. (Figure 25). Scenery under strain or required to bear a heavy load is fastened with a $\frac{3}{8}$-in. carriage bolt inserted through a hole bored in the frames that are joined over each other and screwed down with a washer and a wing

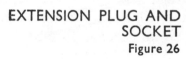

WIRE PIN FOR
PIN HINGE
Figure 25

EXTENSION PLUG AND
SOCKET
Figure 26

nut. The *extension plug and socket* (Figure 26) is used to fasten an extra piece to the top of a flat which may not be masking properly. The height of the flat is increased and the method is called ' topping up.'

FRENCH FLATS

In Plate 14 the entire back of the scene is what is known as a *french flat*. It was necessary to fly the back wall for the purpose of a quick change of scene. The flats were laid face down on the stage and long wooden battens called *stiffeners* secured firmly across the frames, with hanging irons attached to the rails at the bottom of the flats. Steel wires or rope slings were fastened to the hanging irons, run underneath the battens and attached to a bar flown from the grid. The door was removed and the entire back wall or french flat was lifted to the flies. (See also paragraphs on ceilings and trucks.)

BOOK FLATS

The flats on the right-hand side in Plate 14 are *book flats*. These are flats which are hinged to provide ease of handling in a scene change. Book flats are used as backings for doors and when standing at an angle to one another are more or less self-supporting. When found in exterior scenes, they are called *wings*—this word also covering the area at the sides of the stage. A *threefold*

BRACING A FLAT
Figure 27

The Cruise of the Toytown Belle (S. G. Hulme Beaman),
Models, Granville Theatre, London

PLATE 8 (*above*)   Act I, scene 1   Outside the "Dog and Whistle"
PLATE 9 (*below*)   Act I, scene 2   The Mayor's Study

The Cruise of the Toytown Belle (S. G. Hulme Beaman),
Models, Granville Theatre, London

PLATE 10 (*above*) Act II, scene 1 The *Toytown Belle* in
Harbour

PLATE 11 (*below*) Act II, scene 2 The *Toytown Belle* at sea

The Cruise of the Toytown Belle (S. G. Hulme Beaman),
Models, Granville Theatre, London

PLATE 12 (*above*)　Act II, scene 3　The Raft
PLATE 13 (*below*)　Act III　The Island

PLATE D

Model of the proposed Barbican Theatre for the Royal Shakespeare Company in the City of London flat is also hinged but an additional small section of 2-in. batten called a *jigger* or a *tumbler* (U.S.A.) is hinged between the second and third flats. The jigger raises the edge of the third flat so that both outer flats may be folded inwards over the centre one.

EXTENSION BRACE
Figure 28

BRACING

Flats are supported by *braces*, which are expanding sections of wood attached at one end to a screw eye in the back of the flat and the opposite end to the stage by means of a *stage screw* or *weight*. (Figures 27–30.) Iron

braces are also used though they are not telescopic.
Another type of support is the *french brace* which is
hinged permanently to the flat, opened out when required
and secured to the stage. It is a right-angled wooden
support and is very useful when strengthening flats
around a door to prevent movement.

BRACE WEIGHT   STAGE SCREW
Figure 29   Figure 30

CEILINGS

In a simple room or *chamber set*, the scene is enclosed
by flats and a ceiling. The ceiling is made of canvas
stretched over a wooden frame in a similar way to the
construction of a flat. It is suspended by two sets of
lines attached to the front and back edges of the ceiling.
If it has to be flown, the setting is struck and the ceiling
lowered to the stage. One set of lines attached to spring
hooks is released and the other set of lines hauled up.
Thus the ceiling assumes a vertical position for lifting
away from the stage. Sometimes a large ceiling is

hinged and is suspended on three sets of lines. In this case, the lines on the front and rear edges are held with spring hooks and removed for flying. The centre set of lines is secured near the hinges and when hauled the ceiling folds like a book. The ceiling of the setting in Plate 14 was arranged to close in a similar way. It was hinged to the french flat and the front of the ceiling dropped to remove the spring hooks. It folded down against the french flat and the ceiling and flat were flown away. Ceilings are made to overlap the scene and if it is intended to open the setting for larger stages, the ceiling must have sufficient overhang to enclose the scene when it is enlarged.

Doors and Windows

The chamber set has an entrance door and will have one or more windows with a view of the scene beyond. The door is constructed of a wooden frame enclosed by panels of three-ply. This method is used to reduce weight and provide ease of handling. The door is hinged to the *architrave* which is the frame or moulding around it. To indicate the thickness of the wall seen through the doorway, boards known as *reveals* are screwed to the frame. The flat containing the door has an opening of the appropriate size and the door with its frame and reveal is inserted in the opening and tied to it. In order to allow convenient access, the lower rail of the flat is replaced by an iron bar known as a *sill-iron*, the upper side of which is rounded and sometimes secured to the stage to prevent anyone tripping over it.

Windows are of lighter construction than those found in houses and are not glazed. If the effect of glass is wanted, a good imitation can be made by the use of gauze which the scene painter enhances with a few deft strokes of his brush. Translucent windows are made of tracing linen and stained glass indicated by painting it. For leaded windows, black tape is used. Windows are secured to the flats in the same way as doors and the thickness of the wall is shown by the reveal screwed to the window frame.

Much of the character of doors and windows is furnished by clever scene painting. When realism or solidity is needed, the mouldings are constructed. Likewise picture rails and cornices are built, though by combining construction with painted mouldings a successful effect can equally be achieved. In this event, the mouldings on the back flats are painted and where they project from the sides of the scene they are built.

ROSTRUMS AND STEPS

If the setting represents the hall of a country house or perhaps the interior of a mediaeval tavern, it will possess steps and a platform inviting approach to another part of the building. The *rostrum* or platform has to carry weight and is built to be collapsible so that it may be stored or travelled. The legs are made of 3-in by 1-in. wood hinged at the corners, and when the top of the rostrum is fitted over them the structure is held in position. The top is made of ½-in. to ¾-in. ply or ¾-in. blockboard and is secured by cross battens which finish about 1 in. from the edge and so retain alignment with the legs. It is covered with felt and a layer of canvas to prevent noise from footsteps and the legs are disguised by a *ground row* or other piece of scenery.

Stage steps are usually constructed with *risers* of 6 in. (i.e. the difference between the height of each step) and *treads* of 9 in. to 1 ft. The treads are padded and the whole of the steps canvassed. Occasionally an important staircase is made with steps rising by 4 in. and treads of 18 in. and included in a scene depicting a mansion. Lack of space sometimes requires the construction of a steep staircase and the steps may have risers of 8 in. with treads of 9 in. In this event a handrail must be provided. When the steps have up to four treads, they are made

Theatre Books

Act Now . . . and Improvise! by D. Hill
- 0 85343 596 0: £5.00 - **1996**

The Actor's Art and Craft by R. Laurie
0 85343 595 2: £8.50 - **1995**

Adaptable Stage Costume for Women by E. Russell
- 0 85343 558 8: £5.40

Auditioning: A Practical Guide by R. Laurie
- 0 85343 585 5: £3.60

Beginnings in Drama by M. Browne
- 0 7155 0232 8: £1.50

Choreographing the Stage Musical by Sunderland & Pickering
Cased - 0 85343 588 X: £15.75
Paper - 0 85343 586 3: £11.50

Costume Language: A Dictionary of Dress Terms by S. Davis
Cased - 0 85956 066 X: £17.50 - **1995**
Paper - 0 85956 069 4: £12.50 - **1995**

Creative Drama Book by J. Kase-Polisini
- 0 87602 028 7: £20.00

Manners and Movement in Costume Plays by I. Chisman
— 0 7155 0126 7: £3.00

Mask of Reality: An Approach to Theatre Design by I. Corey
— 0 87602 007 4: £25.00

The Musical Director by W. Hoare
— 0 85343 593 6: £7.50

Musicals: The Guide to Amateur Production by P. Spencer
— 0 85343 592 8: £10.50

Odyssey of Masquers by O. and I. Corey
— 0 878281 09 7: £35.00

On English Costume by M. Kelly
— 0 7155 0290 5: £1.50

The Play Produced by J. Fernald
— 0 7155 0151 8: £4.00

Playing Period Plays by L. Oxenford
One Volume — 0 85343 549 9: £9.50
Parts I-IV in separate volumes: £2.50

Producer and the Actor by F. Newman
— 0 85343 074 8: £1.50

Stage Fights: A Simple Handbook of Techniques by G. Gordon
- 0 85343 581 2: £4.00

Stage Management and Theatrecraft by H. Baker
- 0 85343 556 1: £11.50

Stories to Dramatize by W. Ward
- 0 87602 011 2: £16.00

Textbook of Stagecraft by S. Richmond
- 0 7155 0388 X: £2.40

Theatre, Children and Youth by Davis and Evans
Cased - 0 87602 016 3: £28.00
Paper - 0 87602 017 1: £22.50

All prices exclude postage

Cressrelles Publishing Company Limited
10 Station Road Industrial Estate, Colwall,
Worcestershire WR13 6RN
Telephone/Fax: (01684) 540154

g j

- 0 85343 557 X: £4.00

Drama Improvised (Second Edition) by K. Pickering
- 0 85343 612 6: £5.00 - **1997**

Dramatic Literature for Children by R. Bedard
- 0 87602 045 7: £21.00

Face Is A Canvas by I. Corey
- 0 87602 031 7: £37.00

Further Steps in Stagecraft by S. Richmond
- 0 7155 0250 6: £2.40

Give Them Roots . . . and Wings by D. Schwartz and D. Aldrich
- 0 87602 022 8: £15.00

How to Mine by C. Ross-Mackenzie
- 0 7155 0104 6: £1.50

Improvisation: Project and Practice by R. Newton
- 0 85343 525 1: £1.50

Junior Textbook of Stagecraft by F. Marsden
- 0 7155 0175 5: £2.40

with their own legs. Above that number they are hooked on to a rostrum with right-angle flat pieces of iron which drop into slots cut in the top of the rostrum. To give access to a rostrum, *off-stage steps* are provided with a handrail and hooked on to the rostrum.

CLOTH

A *cloth* is a large area of canvas made up of widths joined horizontally and used to mask the scene. A *backcloth* is used behind the setting and a *frontcloth* for a scene played down-stage. The canvas is fastened at the top to a long wooden batten which is attached to ropes suspended from the grid. To give weight and allow it to hang firmly, another batten is secured to the bottom of the cloth.

Sandwich battens are used for this purpose when the edge of the cloth is sandwiched between two battens screwed together. Four battens are required for a cloth and they are made half-round by planing off two of the edges of each batten. The rounded side of one batten is placed on the stage and the edge of the cloth is tacked to the other side. The second batten is then placed over the cloth with the rounded side uppermost and the two battens are screwed together with the cloth sandwiched between them. The battens are made round to prevent damage to the painted cloth when it is rolled up. The battens at the bottom of the cloth need to be secured 2 in. from the edge. Their weight helps to keep the cloth taut and they hang clear of the stage with the space underneath filled with the 2-in. strip of canvas touching the stage.

The ropes used for flying pass through T-shaped slits made in the canvas and are tied around the top batten. (Figure 12.) An improved method of tying the ropes is by means of a *top batten clip*. (Figure 31.) Holes need not be cut in the cloth and the clip slides over the end of the cloth which can also be folded around the batten—to shorten it—when space is restricted.

TOP BATTEN CLIP

Figure 31

CUT CLOTHS

They hang behind one another to form a frame for the backcloth, and are cut along the edge to indicate foliage or architectural details of a building. When the design is intricate, such as the delicate tracery of leaves, it is strengthened by glueing fish netting to the back of the cloth.

BORDERS

In place of cut cloths, *borders* of canvas are used to mask the top of the scene in which case lengths of unframed canvas known as *legs* complete the scene at the sides. Borders may be quite plain (*sky borders*) or cut in the shape of leaves (*foliage borders*). A black velvet border is employed for masking the down-stage edge of a ceiling.

A *frame border* made of canvas and battened all round may represent a detail of architecture such as the beam of a Tudor house. It is stiffened with a thickness at the lower edge called a *soffit*.

TAILS

Sometimes it is found that borders and the top of flats or wings do not mask the stage entirely when seen from the side seats or boxes. *Tails* are borders secured to the fly rail where they hang up- and down-stage on each side of the scene. In Plate 11 sky borders and tails were used to mask the ship scene and Plate 13 shows a tropical island backcloth framed by cut cloths of foliage.

BACKING CLOTHS

They are for masking windows and are small cloths which can be used effectively when suspended from a curved rail in place of the usual batten. The cloth hangs in a curved position and thereby achieves an optical effect of greater distance. To prevent movement the bottom of the cloth is fastened to stage screws and the sides are also secured.

CURTAINS

The simple curtain setting is the one enclosed on three sides with draped material. Although the main asset is economy, the curtain setting, in order to be truly effective, must be capable of several alternative arrangements. It should be noted that there is a great difference between curtain settings and those made of canvas and wood—a contrast making it difficult to combine them theatrically. Nevertheless, effective use can be made of the two when the curtain setting is used to indicate a special feature and canvas scenery is employed for another. For instance, curtains may suggest the walls of a room and built pieces of scenery may be used to indicate doors, windows and different levels in the form of rostrums and steps.

Further scope for curtain settings is in the form of styled realism when screen settings are employed. The screens of canvas and wood, including architectural features, are folded in two or three parts to stand against a background of curtained material.

The initial cost of curtains may be heavy, but when made of good durable material they are a valuable asset in staging amateur and professional plays. In choosing the material, texture should be the first consideration. The cheaper materials are loosely woven and are not light proof, yet this is an essential requirement for stage curtains. The material should look and hang well, it must be opaque and respond to changes in lighting. Matt surfaces are best as the lighting is reflected by shiny materials. Those most often used are velour, wool serge, hessian, casement cloth and bolton sheeting. Of these, velour is the best and most expensive. It has beauty, is heavy and a good range of colours is combined with richness in texture. It does not crease and is light proof. Velvet, lined with bolton sheeting, should be used if considerable lighting effects are intended. Wool serge has the advantage of being the only material that is non-inflammable. It is cheaper though more loosely woven and lacking the richness of velour. Hessian is a coarse loosely woven material similiar to sackcloth. It is economical but has defects in that it creases; is not light proof and therefore must be lined with casement cloth. It is used often and under stage lighting the colour is enhanced giving the impression of a much richer material. Casement cloth has a good surface but it is too light for use by itself. It is generally employed for backing other fabrics. Bolton sheeting is a heavier material and may be used alone for simple decoration. There is a variety of colours but it is not light proof and should be used preferably to back other material.

Curtains should be made with strong webbing at the top and rings sewn on or hooks specially designed for stage use. A curtain that is entangled because of a broken hook can bring disaster to a good performance. A deep hem should be sewn at the bottom and weighted with lengths of chain threaded through it, which are set up 3 in. in the hem to save wear on the bottom of the curtain. The chain helps in hanging the curtain and stops it blowing in a draught. Proscenium curtains and others opened and closed during the performance, that are not flown, should be suspended from a silent and reliable curtain track. The track is constructed of tubular steel and the curtain hooks are attached to hard-wood bobbins running along it. The curtain is operated with an endless cord held by a weighted pulley near the stage or by a steel cable attached to a winding drum bolted to the stage. (Plates C and E.) Curtains not required to move are suspended from battens or steel bars. A curved tubular steel runner may be obtained for curtains surrounding the stage that have to be opened quickly. There is another type of track which consists of two parallel runners joined at the end by circular runners and providing an endless track on which curtains may be reversed. This is convenient when there is time to adjust the folds of the curtains which otherwise are inclined to settle in untidy positions.

Fireproofing of curtains is an important point to consider. The texture and colours of some materials are affected by the chemical solution used in fireproofing and it is wise to ask a professional firm to undertake this task, who will usually accept responsibility for the result.

GAUZE

Gauze, or *scrim* as it is sometimes called, is fine netting hung in front of a cloth, suggesting an exterior scene, to give the impression of mist. It is also used in transformation effects. By lighting the front of the gauze it becomes almost opaque, the fine mesh giving it this special quality. A painted gauze remains undetected until the front lighting is reduced. Then it becomes transparent and the transformation of scene occurs. Lighting a gauze and its use in special effects are described in chapter 8. Very wide gauze can be obtained, but normally it is joined in horizontal widths. A gauze may be used as a frontcloth and in this event is framed on all sides with slender battens to pull it taut. It is attached to lines from the grid and after the special effect is lifted out of sight in the usual way. The mysterious property of gauze was appreciated even in 1501 when an instruction in the *Mons* script read as follows: 'There must be much light in limbo and great brilliance and melody and the Divinity, like a soul, covered with a tent of gauze must appear, with two angels.'

SET PIECES

Columns, tree-trunks, rocks and any part of the scene which is a complete item are described under this heading. Construction follows the example of rostrums in that a frame of wood is made to which the required outline is added. In the case of rocks and tree-trunks, chicken wire is shaped to the form needed and attached to the frame, then covered with canvas and painted. Columns are made of wooden cores and completed with three-ply or light plastic material curved to give the required solidity.

GROUND ROWS

They represent rocks, walls, bushes, etc., and are made like flats but the edge is extended by three-ply covered with cloth cut to the shape of the design. The method of cutting is called *profiling* and the irregular edge of a ground row is known as a profiled one. Flats made to represent trees also have a three-ply addition profiled to the required shape. (Plate F.)

TRUCKS

These are low platforms on wheels used to mount scenes or sections of them so that the entire scene can be moved to another part of the stage. The platform is strongly built and is about 6 in. high, with a number of wheels or ball-bearing castors enabling them to move in any direction. The platform has sides that conceal the castors and almost touch the ground. When not in use, it is wheeled to the wings and placed in a scene dock or other convenient position. Scenery may be constructed partly on trucks and the rest built in the normal way. Plate 14 shows a scene where a truck was used for a quick scene change. The window and window seat with the flat surrounding it and the window backing were all built on a truck. The back of the scene and the ceiling were arranged for flying and the other flats struck in the usual way. Another method of using trucks is employed in the *scissor stage*. Here trucks are set up- and down-stage in the wings and arranged to move round on a pivot into position facing the audience. A third truck is kept at the back of the stage and can be moved down when the trucks at the sides are not in use.

Wagon stage, *platform stage* and *rolling stage* are other names for a series of trucks moved freely about the stage or run in a track. The *sliding stage* is an arrangement whereby a complete setting is built on a truck and rolled into position to alternate with other trucks in a pre-conceived order. A truck may be split into sections and the halves moved to either side of the stage. Another truck kept at the back of the stage is then moved down into view. In an elaborate arrangement as many as five trucks circulate in turn before the audience.

CYCLORAMAS

In place of a backcloth to represent the sky, a *cyclorama* is installed to give an impressive effect of distance. It is a large backcloth suspended on a curved track attached to the grid. The plan of the stage in Figure 9 indicates its position. The cyclorama moves on runners following the direction of the track and forms a background curving around the stage. Although this is effective, it presents difficulties when scenery is moved in a confined space and consequently a cyclorama is more often used with a permanent setting. It may be of great height, but 30 ft. is normal, and its height successfully masks the top of the setting, thereby dispensing with borders. Providing the grid has sufficient height, the entire cyclorama may be flown. It is then attached to steel bars in the form of three sides of a rectangle with the bars curved at the sides and lifted by means of counter-weighted wires. The success of a cyclorama depends on an even expanse of cloth and it is pulled tight and secured to stage screws around the lower edge.

A built cyclorama is installed in theatres fortunate enough to possess the space required and, being constructed of plaster, is not liable to movement. It is curved at the sides, and the top takes the shape of a dome. The matt surface of the plaster gives many opportunities for atmospheric lighting effects and it has a stage trap (called a *lighting pit*) running the length of its base where lights are concealed for illuminating the lower area.

TORMENTORS

These are wings either fixed or removable that are used for concealing the sides of a setting immediately behind the proscenium arch and sometimes they include small pieces extending up- and down-stage to form a complete structure. Entrances are found at each side, often enclosed with curtains, and above them there is a small opening which the electrician uses for his *perch** lights. They are shown in Plan, in Figure 9. When in

* See soft edge spotlight (chapter 8)

the form of flats, they are known as *returns* and are attached to the setting by line and cleat. (Figure 6.)

FALSE PROSCENIUM

This is employed to frame a scene when the theatre proscenium arch is too large for the purpose and to give importance to the aspect of the setting. It follows the shape of the proscenium opening and is a semi-permanent structure made of a wooden frame and three-ply covered with a neutral coloured material such as velvet. In order to offer a solid appearance it has a reveal along the inner edge surrounding the scene, and entrances are constructed at the sides which the designer sometimes uses as an integral part of the stage setting. A point to remember concerns the lighting. The top of the false proscenium reduces the area from which the lights are directed and consequently additional lights may have to be installed behind it.

LINE PLOT

The head flyman will need a *line plot*, which is a plan of the position in the grid where the lines will be used to fly the scenery. With scale plans of the settings, the distance is measured from the setting line of the scenery to be flown. A line corresponding to the centre line of the scene plans is drawn on a piece of paper and the positions obtained from the scale plans are marked on it. Figure 32 shows a typical line plot with the method of indicating separate or *spot lines* for special pieces of scenery. It is used for the scenes in Plates 8–13.

FLY PLOT

The head flyman will also require a *fly plot* telling him when and in what order the scenery in the flies is to be used. He receives this information from written cues as shown in Figure 33 and acts accordingly when the stage manager signals to him with a cue light from the prompt corner.

ISLAND CLOTH ACT 3

SKY CLOTH ACT 2 SC. 2&3
TOWN CLOTH ACT. 2. SC. I.

ISLAND CUT CLOTH ACT 3

SPOT LINE
FOR TREE
IN ISLAND
SCENE
ACT 3.

GAUZE ACT 2 SC.3.

SKY BORDER ACT 2 SC.1&2
VELVET BORDER ACT 1 SC.2

ISLAND CUT CLOTH ACT 3
SEA CUT CLOTH ACT 2 SC.3

VILLAGE INN CLOTH ACT I. SC. I.

SKY BORDER ACT 2 SC.1 & 2
VELVET BORDER ACT I. SC. 2.

ISLAND CUT CLOTH ACT 3.

SEA CUT CLOTH ACT 2. SC. 3.
MAIL COACH CLOTH (SCENE DROP)

SETTING LINE

FRAME BORDER

LINE PLOT
Figure 32

FIREPROOFING

The regulations of local authorities concerning the prevention of fire are strict, and although the amateur stage
manager may not be subject to the regulations of the
professional theatre, he should know something about
the precautions taken. Scenery supplied by reputable
scene builders is constructed of fireproof materials.

FLY PLOT

SET TO OPEN	Scene drop. Act I, Sc. 1. Village Inn scene. Inset and Act I, Sc. 2. Study. Full set.
AT CUE	House tabs up slow.
AT CUE	Scene drop up fast.
AT CUE	House tabs down fast. During scene change take up Village Inn cloth.
AT CUE	House tabs up fast.
AT CUE	House tabs down fast. FIRST INTERVAL. During interval take up velvet borders and lower sky borders, Town cloth, Sky cloth and Island cloth.
SET TO OPEN	Act II, Sc. 1. Ship scene.
AT CUE	House tabs up fast.
AT CUE	House tabs down fast. During scene change take up Town cloth.
AT CUE	House tabs up fast.
AT CUE	House tabs down fast. During scene change take up sky borders and lower sea cut-cloths and gauze.
AT CUE	House tabs up fast.
AT CUE	Take up sky cloth slow.
AT CUE	Take up gauze fast.
AT CUE	House tabs down fast. SECOND INTERVAL, etc.

Figure 33

This does not include the timber used except in the case of three-ply which is impregnated with a fire-resisting solution during its manufacture. The canvas of flats and all textiles used for curtains or draperies require fireproofing which is done by a cleaning or dyeing firm or sometimes in the theatre. The method is to dip the material in a fireproof solution and allow it to dry without rinsing. The effect is not permanent and has to be renewed periodically. To test it, a part of the seam at the back of the material is held in a flame. If it smoulders for a moment and goes out almost immediately, it is safe; otherwise it must receive a second treatment. Imitation flowers are made of fireproof material. The fireproof solutions recommended by the London Fire Brigade are as follows:

Heavy-weight materials:

Boric Acid	15 oz.
Sodium Phosphate	10 oz.
Warm water	1 gallon

Light-weight materials:

Borax	10 oz.
Boracic Acid	8 oz.
Warm water	1 gallon

SETTING UP

When the scenery arrives in the theatre, the master carpenter and his staff arrange it in *packs* around the walls of the stage. A chalk line is drawn for the centre line of the stage and another to indicate the setting line. The cloths and other items intended for flying are then placed on the acting area. The cloths are unrolled, and after they have been centred by the chalk line, are sent up to the grid. Sometimes they are required to hang out of centre, in which case the appropriate adjustment is made.

If the scene has a ceiling, it is battened, attached to lines and floated a convenient distance above the scene, to be dropped in position later. Following this, all the work required in battening the flats and building the set pieces is completed. The stage cloth is laid and the scene built on it according to the scene plan. Before the scene is completely built, some of the larger items of furniture are carried to the centre of the stage, from where they are set as required.

Lines of sight will be considered and the stage manager attends to these and the masking of the scene by viewing it from the auditorium. The property staff set the furniture and fix the *door furniture* which is the term used for door handles, finger plates, etc. The exact position of chairs, tables and so forth is marked on the stage by sticking small pieces of sellotape behind the furniture. After setting the scene, it is marked with paint on the stage cloth, and when it is struck, the master carpenter shows his staff where to make the packs around the stage. Each scene is dealt with in the same way and difficulties that may be found in a scene change are considered.

QUICK CHANGE OF SCENE

An example of a change of scene from a small setting to a larger one, performed in approximately one minute, is given in Plates 14 and 15. The bed-sitting room was set within the panelled room and struck during the scene change. In order to provide space for the bed-sitting room, the panelled room was altered as follows:

(1) The ceiling which was hinged to the flats at the back of the scene was raised and held by lines from the grid so that later it would fall into position by its own weight.

(2) The flat with the door down-stage right was struck and the rest of the scene on that side opened a short distance off stage to afford entry during the scene change.

(3) The desk was taken apart and the two sections with the drawers were packed on top of one another in the recess up-stage right, the top of the desk with the telephone, wastepaper basket etc. being kept near them off-stage.

(4) The large leather armchair was placed next to the desk sections.

(5) The small table and chair were placed in the curtained opening Up-Right.

(6) The carpet was rolled up to the fireplace, the desk chair being kept at the back of the scene.

This alteration provided a clear area and the bed-sitting room was set within it.

The scene change was performed as follows:

(1) The sloping ceiling of the bed-sitting room, which was hinged to the back flat, was raised and held by lines from the grid attached to the front edge of the ceiling. Simultaneously the electricians detached all lighting cables connected to the scene.

(2) The flats on either side, cleated to the back wall, were untied.

(3) The window flat with window seat and backing were set on a truck and wheeled off-stage right to the wings.

(4) The bed, small table with lamp, desk and round table were carried off-stage right, followed by the armchair, coffee table and the standard lamp. The flower ornaments were also removed. Finally the carpets were rolled up and carried off followed by the two sections of book shelves and the fitted electric fire.

(5) The ceiling was dropped to fall against the back wall, the door was untied and pulled away from the flat when the entire back of the scene with the ceiling was taken up to the flies.

(6) The door and backing were carried off-stage right to the wings followed by the book flat behind the shelves and electric fire.

(7) The carpet in the panelled room was unrolled and the furniture set in position.

(8) The right-hand wall was returned to its marks; one side of the door flat cleated to it and the other side tied to the tormentor.

(9) The ceiling was dropped and the signal given by the stage manager to take up the curtain. Similar quick change of scenes were performed for the settings shown in Plates 2 and 3 (Act I Scene 1 and Scene 2) and Plates 4 and 5 (Act II Scene 1 and Scene 2).

The success of a scene change depends on the planning

beforehand, organisation of the staff and the co-operation of the departments concerned. The three heads of departments plan the scene change with the stage manager and thereafter arrange the details as they affect the staff under their control. The master carpenter and his staff on the stage and in the flies are concerned with the scenery, while furniture and properties are the responsibility of the property master and his staff. The chief electrician and his assistants attend to the lighting equipment. The planning concerns the order in which the change of scene is done and the duties each individual has to perform. The change should be rehearsed at a staff rehearsal when it will be possible to observe and correct any difficulties encountered.

The stage manager watches the scene change from the centre of the proscenium opening where he stands with his back to the curtain. Changes are sometimes performed in complete darkness with the curtain up, and the stage manager carries a torch with a small piece of blue filter covering the lens. With this shielded in his hand, he can help the staff to find the scenery and furniture marks on the stage.

CHAPTER 7

PROPERTIES

'To Ogier Counin for three days employed by him at the inn of
M. le Maistre to make the apple tree of oranges and fig leaves
at 8 sols per day: 24 sols.'—*Mons* script.

WHEN the curtain rises on a scene which gives pleasure
in its detail and careful choice of furnishings and properties, it may not be realised that each item is chosen
for a specific purpose by the designer and confirmed by
the director. The stage management keep accurate
records of the description and situation of every item
in the *furniture* and *property plots*. Stage properties are
divided under two headings:

(a) *Scene dressings* that are part of the setting and include
furniture, carpets, pictures, flowers, ornaments etc.
(b) *Hand properties* which are carried by the artists such
as watches, cigarette cases, spectacles, umbrellas
and sticks, documents, weapons etc.

Properties also include *effects* or noises made off-stage to
produce the sounds of wind, rain, thunder etc. that are
operated manually, or visual effects comprising falling
snow, water, breaking of glass and trick cupboards.

'Property of the Management' was painted or sewn on
all movable articles when David Garrick was at Drury
Lane Theatre. Since then the word 'property' has been
used to describe objects of this kind.

FURNITURE

Furniture is either purchased or hired. In London
there is of course plenty of choice and as the designer
often leaves some of the selection to the stage manager,

148

he should have a good knowledge of it and of the different periods to which furniture belongs.

There are many books on the subject and two museums in London provide great assistance by showing rooms furnished in the style of different periods. They are the Victoria and Albert Museum at South Kensington and the Geffrye Museum, Kingsland Road, E.2. The rooms at the Victoria and Albert Museum are elaborate and are installed exactly as they were found in houses since destroyed. A booklet *A History of English Furniture*, published by H.M. Stationery Office, is obtainable at the museum and gives details of the development of furniture from the Middle Ages to the Renaissance, Restoration and Georgian periods. At the Geffrye Museum, the rooms are arranged in chronological order from 1600 to the present day. There are also many examples of domestic objects from which the stage manager can obtain ideas for unusual and intriguing properties.

It is perhaps interesting to note that the latter half of the eighteenth century produced three of the finest craftsmen in the design of Georgian furniture. Sheraton, Chippendale and Hepplewhite were contemporary and during this period the highest standard of skilled handiwork and design was achieved. All of these craftsmen produced books with their styles, such as Sheraton's *Drawing Book*, Chippendale's *Director* and Hepplewhite's *The Cabinet Maker and Upholsterer's Guide*. They show a fascinating and detailed study of the furniture and other ornamental designs and are invaluable as reference books of the period. A selection from the works is published in three volumes by Alec Tiranti Ltd. *English Furniture at a Glance*, by Barbara Jones, is published by The Architectural Press. It contains over two hundred drawings of furniture from all periods and is an excellent guide where quick reference is needed.

Apart from knowing what is wanted for a particular

setting, the size and shape of the furniture must be considered. The stage manager takes the plan of the setting with him and, when choosing the furniture, measures it so that it will fit the space intended. The director may need an item of a special size and the stage manager spends time in seeking out the piece required and obtains alternatives if the exact size is unobtainable.

BOOKS

In a scene supposed to represent a library a quantity of books is required to fill the bookcases. Real books need not be used and in any event they become a heavy item if the play is toured. A second-hand bookseller is often glad to unload books that are no longer popular and the bindings are useful as book-backs for stage settings. The spines are cut out and pasted to plywood strips covered in black velvet to fit the shelves of the bookcase. It is preferable to use book-backs in this way for a bookcase on the side of a scene as those in full view of the audience tend to receive more of the stage lighting and the illusion is lost when the black velvet backing is illuminated. Rubber latex is used successfully in place of book-backs. It is moulded to the shape of a book and is supplied in sections including an assortment of sizes which are painted and afterwards cut to fit any shelf. The rough texture of latex is also useful when period books are needed and can be painted to represent old volumes. The latex sections are mounted on plywood painted dark grey to fit the space between the shelves. Latex book-backs were used for the bookcases on the side of the scene in Plates 3 and 5 and real books were used for the setting in Plate 15.

CARPETS

It is difficult for an audience to concentrate on an actor's performance if it is interrupted by the sound of his shoes clattering on the bare stage and therefore it is essential to provide a carpet or stage cloth. Sometimes, particularly when scenes are changed quickly, it is impossible to cover the whole of the acting area, but it is always preferable to do so in order to deaden the sound. When rugs are used they should be marked on the stage cloth with paint or adhesive tape at the corners so that they are always returned to the original position.

Curtains

Curtains should be made and hung as they would be at home. They are lined with a suitable material, which is essential when they are closed over windows through which a strong exterior light is seen. Difficulty may be experienced in fixing the curtain track or the pelmet board. The window frame can be slender, leaving insufficient room, and in this event a separate rail is inserted behind the flat and secured with pieces of three-ply to the stiles and rail. The material should be seen in the setting if possible before it is made up. Colour is altered under stage lighting and sometimes the design is not bold enough to register in the theatre. The A.S.M. should make sure that curtains are working properly before the performance and to set them correctly, i.e. open or closed for each scene. Under the fire regulations, curtains are included as inflammable material and must be fire-proofed.

Door and Window Furniture

These are small objects, sometimes overlooked, which nevertheless complete the authenticity of the setting. It should not be sufficient to provide a handle or a knob to open a door. Fingerplates or keyholes are found on most doors and in the theatre give a pleasant touch of decoration. Windows should always have their usual fastenings and sash windows are given metal window lifts whether or not they are practical.

FIREPLACE

There are, of course, many types of fires to be found in period and modern plays, and the implements and fuel to keep the fire alight should be included. Fire-irons, fender and scuttle with a coal fire and for a wood fire, some logs should be placed for further use.

FLOWERS

Artificial flowers, if cared for, can be used several times. They must be fireproofed and the precaution should be noted when artificial flowers are purchased from shops unaccustomed to providing for a theatre. Real flowers should be avoided as petals or leaves may drop off and can be dangerous to the artists who may slip on them. Hence the superstition that it is unlucky to use real flowers on the stage.

MIRRORS AND PICTURES

Care should be taken in hanging mirrors that lights are not reflected and whenever possible they should be placed on the sides of the setting. If it is essential to have a mirror where lights are likely to be reflected, the glass should be painted over with a solution of size which gives a dull appearance. Sometimes a sheet of frosted cromoid, used in lighting, is employed instead of glass and can be decorated by scratching away the frosted side to the pattern required. This was used for the mirror above the fireplace in Plate 16. The glass is removed from pictures to reduce weight and prevent reflection. Pictures are screwed to the rail of a flat or a special rail inserted for the position required. Small pieces of metal called *picture plates* are attached to the sides of the picture or mirror and screwed to the rail through holes in the centre of the projecting part of the plates.

Money

Stage money in the form of notes is sometimes a problem, as the Bank of England is firmly against the use of anything which may look remotely like real paper money. However, the shops dealing in stage properties keep a selection of notes which are not likely to be confused with the real thing on close inspection but are sufficiently authentic to the audience. On one occasion, bundles of notes were required and left in view for some time during the playing of a scene. In this case real notes were used on the top and bottom of each bundle and plain pieces of paper of the same size were cut and made up to form the necessary thickness. Needless to say, they were promptly retrieved by the stage management on the fall of the curtain.

Ornaments

In Victorian settings, there is generally a clutter of china and other ornaments on the shelves of a cupboard or a mantelpiece. In order to assist the scene change, they are held or *wired* to the furniture which also saves time in setting them. They are fixed by fine wire wound round the article and tacked to the shelf. The entire piece of furniture with its contents can then be moved in the scene change and each item will remain in position. The hire of good china is sometimes expensive and a substitute can be provided by purchasing inexpensive white china which is painted to the design required and is often more effective than the original article.

Period Properties

In the choice of properties which may be identified by the audience, special care is required. Those used in period plays need research so that an exact replica is obtained. . Members of the audience are quick to observe what they think may be erroneous and letters are received about the mistakes which give the writers much pleasure.

For example, in *Dr. Angelus* by James Bridie, the period of the play is 1919 and a copy of *Punch* was used. I made enquiries at the publishers and found that the colour of the cover had been altered about that time. I was able to obtain a copy and in a theatre on tour we received a letter concerning it. The writer complained that we were using the wrong copy of *Punch* and was only satisfied when he was invited to examine the one used in the performance. It is gratifying to find that members of the public take this interest in the production and encouraging to the stage manager in his research. Properties relating to the professions need to be authentic and advice from a member of the profession concerned is essential to obtain absolute accuracy. Frequently the author has done research and can give help but usually it is left to the stage manager to make detailed enquiries.

The surgery in *Dr. Angelus* was furnished with period properties and one of them—a medical cabinet—received publicity. The cabinet was not used during the play and had been obtained from a dealer in second-hand surgical articles. During the London run, the property master was dusting it and, opening one of the drawers, found that it contained drugs which had been there for some time. Small bottles and packages with drugs were discovered in other drawers and as one of these had a ' Dangerous Drug ' label, the police were asked to examine them. They were confiscated and the Home Office took possession of the items on their list. It was later revealed that the cabinet had been purchased from a doctor whose home was destroyed in the war. The cabinet had been on tour with the production in several provincial cities and the discovery was not made until a few weeks after the play opened in London. (See Plate G.)

STAGE MEALS

These need not be a headache for the property department if the following points are considered. The food should appear to be real and must be palatable so that it can be eaten with little effort. Smaller quantities are provided as the time allowed for consumption of a stage meal is usually much less than normal. The real thing can be imitated i.e. half an apricot on top of some white blancmange with a coloured slice of banana at the side is a good substitute for bacon and egg. Meat can be represented by a slice of banana soaked in cochineal or a slice of bread dipped in gravy. Sandwiches should be small and as thin as possible. They are moistened in water for dry bread can stick in the throat. Tea and coffee should be freshly made for each performance and the property master told the exact time it is required so that it is hot when consumed. Alcoholic drinks are imitated with water or lemonade in which burnt sugar is dissolved to apply colouring. Champagne for the stage can be obtained from wine merchants who will provide genuine champagne bottles filled with ginger ale, and the cork pops out with sufficient excitement to make the audience envious. Imitation food for dressing can be found in shops catering for small properties and quite a good display of apples, oranges and grapes can be supplied with papier-mâché replicas. It should be remembered that stage food to be consumed should be covered when not in use and only made ready just before it is required. An instance where stage food is needed for ' business ' is the omelette eaten by the comedian. It is made of thin rubber and coloured suitably. The actor can prod it, pull, throw it and much else besides though it firmly resists all his attempts to eat it.

STATIONERY

Letters, envelopes, etc., are made to look as realistic as possible. A printer once told me he was asked to print the address of the locality in the play as the letter-heading whenever stationery was required in plays presented by a well-known producer. This may be exceptional but it indicates the care with which properties are prepared. The written part of a letter should be genuine and as a fresh envelope is required for each performance and the letter occasionally re-written, it is part of the duty of the stage management to arrange it. Telegram and cablegram forms can be obtained from any post office and the officials will often help by providing the tape which is sometimes pasted to the form. For period plays needing old-fashioned documents, stiff cartridge paper may be used, which can be coloured by painting with varnish. When a desk is shown, it should be remembered that the contents are rarely tidy. Envelopes, bills, odd letters, etc., can be employed to indicate the daily use of the desk.

How often when we go to the theatre, we feel that the room is really in use and lived-in by the characters in the play. When the setting is completely furnished, the designer or stage manager takes note of anything which may help in providing this atmosphere. It can be done in several ways. For instance, letters and envelopes are sometimes held behind a picture or mirror; tobacco or some domestic objects can be added to a mantelshelf to make it look untidy. On a sofa, cushions can be arranged with some illustrated papers lying about. Telephone directories and books may be left opened as if they were recently used, and unless it is required for the action of the play, ash trays need not be emptied. A coat can be left hanging over a chair or perhaps a game of chess may have been interrupted. (See Plate 1.)

When matches are used the matchbox is set with a couple of matches sticking out from the box and the artist does not have to fumble for them during the performance. Ash trays should have some damp sand so that cigarettes are extinguished quickly.

WEAPONS

A firearm certificate issued to an individual is obtained from the local police. This is essential before a revolver or gun is hired from an armourer dealing in weapons for the theatre. The stage manager accepts responsibility for the firearms which must be locked up in a secure place. Blank cartridges are obtained from the armourer and it is advisable for the stage manager to load the revolver personally and instruct the artist in its use. The wads from blank cartridges are dangerous and therefore care should be taken that the weapon is not fired in the direction of anyone near the muzzle of the gun. Revolvers and guns can be erratic in performance and the stage manager is well advised to hold a spare loaded one in the wings to be used if the one on the stage fails to go off. When swords, rapiers or foils are used, they are made as harmless as possible by blunting the edge and rounding off the end. This is done by grinding away the edge until a completely flat surface is achieved. Even so, careful rehearsal is needed before a fight is staged. The period of the play must be observed and most armourers will know the exact type of gun or sword required.

Imitation weapons were recommended to actors in mediaeval plays. The soft baton afterwards identified with the policeman's truncheon in pantomime and the sword which probably had a collapsible blade that seemed to enter the victim realistically are mentioned in the prompt scripts of these plays.

EFFECTS

The important thing to remember in producing sound effects is to visualise the exact nature of the sound required. The mental image will be stimulated by how much can be remembered of the sound when it was previously heard. Therefore, it is all-important to

cultivate a good ear; and those most successful in producing stage effects often develop what amounts to a
second sense which is helpful in critical appreciation of
the exact sound required. A sound may have several
components all of which, reproduced in varying degrees,
combine to give the desired effect. For instance, the
sound of a door closing may be regarded as quite a
simple operation. All that is needed is a stout piece of
wood which at the required moment is banged on the
floor of the stage. But if the sound of a door closing is
analysed, much more will be observed. The actual
sound is firstly a hollow one made by the reverberation
of the door closing on a room. Again, the door itself
has a lock and sometimes a bolt, chain and a letter-box.
So it will be seen that what appears to be a simple
operation is really interesting when all the components
necessary to reproduce the sound are realised. And
this goes for most of the sound effects used in the theatre.
The illusion of the performance is helped considerably
when thought is given to the nature of the effect, when
sufficient time is devoted to its rehearsal and it is produced in a sensitive and imaginative way. Effects can
be optical, electrical, mechanical and manual, and
depending on the method employed will be the responsibility of the stage management, electrical or property
departments.

ANIMALS

Recordings on tape or disc can be obtained of most
sounds of this kind, and there are various devices sold
in musical instrument shops which imitate bird calls.
I have found at different times that the stage staff includes
an expert who is always glad to display his particular
gift.

During rehearsals of *The Grass is Greener* by Hugh
and Margaret Williams, I had a strange experience with
a bird call. The sound of a cuckoo was needed and

although several recordings were tried, other sounds upset the effect. Eventually I remembered there was a leading authority who during much of his lifetime had made a large collection of bird calls and I telephoned him at his home.

Explaining what was wanted I gave my name and told him we were rehearsing at the Fortune Theatre opposite the Theatre Royal, Drury Lane. Perhaps he was a little deaf as I had to repeat my name and the theatre before he agreed to see me. That evening I found my way to his home which was a suburban detached house with a tall laurel hedge enclosing a small garden leading to the front door. A street lamp filtered a pool of light to the pavement but the house and garden were in darkness. I rang the bell and when there was no response rang again. The house was silent and although there seemed to be a light reflected in the glass roof of a greenhouse the side door leading to the garden was locked. I knocked several times, went back to the gate to verify the number and decided to ask a neighbour if this was the right address.

The people in the next house confirmed it and told me that as far as they knew the house was occupied. I walked back and noticed a large black car at the pavement which was not there when I arrived. There was no one in sight; I entered the gate and was about to go up the path when two shadowy figures came from behind the laurel hedge. I blinked in the light of a torch snapped on into my face. ' One moment, sir. We are police officers and we have been told that someone is trying to make a forced entry into this house'. They asked my name and took up positions on either side of me. ' I am calling about a cuckoo ' I said. ' A cuckoo?' ' Yes ' I replied, ' I have come to hear a recording of a cuckoo.' ' Ah, a recording' one man said to the other, 'In that case you had better come with us, sir.' And regarding me with indulgence reserved for the cuckoo they shepherded me to the front door.

This time it was opened and an elderly gentleman speaking with a foreign accent asked us to come in. I introduced myself and with the officers keeping me in close surveillance was ushered into a room where we all sat round a table. Our host explained that he had escaped to this country during the war and he and his wife were still afraid they would be found and questioned. After my call earlier in the day, they had telephoned the Theatre Royal, Drury Lane who had no knowledge of a stage manager of my name and certainly they were not looking for a cuckoo. Their suspicions aroused, my host and his wife decided to await my arrival and telephone the police.

We settled into a comfortable discussion about the merits of the male and female cuckoo and were given precise information of the difference in sound between the hen and cock birds. The evening ended on a cheerful note and with a glass of wine, the officers and I were entertained to a selection of bird calls that might have been heard in *Tales from the Vienna Woods*.

BELLS

Telephone and door bells or buzzers are attached to wooden boxes containing batteries and include a length of wire and bell push for operating them from a distance. A telephone bell should always be placed as near as possible to the instrument and very often a good place for it is in a compartment in the footlights where the bulb and medium have been removed. Before the advent of electric bells, house bells were those operated by a steel wire attached to a handle or by pulling a cord. The bell was a small one suspended on a coiled spring and rang for some time in a manner difficult to reproduce in any other way. These bells used in period plays can still be obtained at some of the old established iron-mongers or hired from shops dealing in stage properties. Church bells are recorded and the gramophone shops

PLATE E

Wheeled runner overlap track

PLATE 14

The Bargain (Michael Gilbert). St. Martin's Theatre. London.   Act III. scene 1

PLATE 15

The Bargain (Michael Gilbert), St. Martin's Theatre, London. Act III, scene 2

PLATE F

Scenery building showing a profiled flat

can supply a list of many kinds. When ship bells are needed, it is best to use the actual bell which is suspended in a convenient position. It has a piece of rope or sash line attached to the tongue which is used for swinging the tongue inside the bell. A ships' chandler will provide information showing the bells struck for the various watches heard in a ship at sea.

CLOCKS

These are recorded and can also be reproduced manually by striking tubular chimes as supplied to orchestras. A metronome in a box is used to give the sound of a clock ticking and can be adjusted to the required beat. When a clock face is visible to the audience it is usual to ' paint out ' the face. This is done by painting small lines in gold or black radiating from the centre to the circumference of the face. The lines prevent reading the time and at a distance appear to be decoration. For a clock required to alter its time during the action of the play, the spindle holding the hands is extended and pushed through a hole in the canvas behind the clock. A clock face is then fixed or painted on the back of the canvas and the hands may be worked as required.

CRASHES

A bucket or a strong box is filled with broken glass or crockery and is emptied into another box when the crash is needed. Breaking of a window pane is imitated by dropping some small metal plates on to a paving stone or other hard surface. For the sound of breaking wood, a box of stage weights is dropped on to sticks or wood from boxes used by greengrocers. Another method is to record the crumpling of a matchbox in front of a microphone which is amplified to the required volume. The visual effect of a window pane breaking is obtained by arranging for a jagged piece of glass to fly into place when an object is thrown through the window. It is usually possible to attract the attention of the audience elsewhere and the piece of glass is quickly dropped into the window frame which has strips of wood inserted at the back to hold the glass. To give the appearance of a shot fired through a window pane, wire shaped like a spider's web with a hole in the centre is attached to elastic which is released on to the window frame when the shot is fired.

DOORS

The best method of producing the sound of a door closing is to brace a door in its frame in the wings. It should have a letter-box and one or two bolts which with the sound of the lock closing gives the authentic noise. A door knocker should also be attached which is useful if someone needs to announce his arrival in this way. Alternatively, a stout box can be made about 3 ft. by 2 ft. with a lid. A lock is fitted with a letter-box and door knocker. When the lid is opened and closed, the hollow interior of the box gives a good imitation of a door being closed.

ENGINES

Recordings can be obtained of cars, aeroplanes, trains and factory machinery. Cars nowadays make little noise and it is sometimes best to omit the sound and let the actor announce the car's arrival. A substitute for the sound of an old-fashioned car is an electric sewing machine in a box. By varying the speed a realistic sound of a veteran car or a motor cycle can be produced. To represent the sound of a train, a heavy garden roller is pulled as quickly as possible across the back of the stage with chains, whistles and other mechanical ingenuity to assist it. Two boards covered in sand paper and rubbed together will give a good imitation of a puffing engine.

GUNFIRE

A .45 revolver fired into a dustbin or fire bucket may be used or a good imitation of revolver fire can be made by striking the seat of a bentwood chair with canes. Two men employed in this way can produce a realistic effect of rapid gunfire. For the distant sound of artillery, a thunder sheet is employed and larger explosions are reproduced by maroons described in chapter 8.*

HORSES

Two half coconut shells are knocked rhythmically on a hard surface. Some practice is needed to imitate a horse galloping or trotting on different kinds of ground.

RAIN

The noise of rain is produced by the *rain box*. This is a lightly made box about 4 ft. in length and 6 in. in diameter. It contains partitions which have small holes. Dried peas or lead shot fall through the holes when the box is tilted and a patter of rain or a downpour is heard. Although the sound of rain falling continuously can be disturbing, it may be needed for quite long periods in the play. In this case dried peas, lead shot or rice are used in a bass drum with one of the drumheads removed. The drum is suspended at an angle so that the peas are in one place when it is not in use and a good idea is to keep a piece of stout material handy to cover the peas and stop them from falling out of the drum. To start the effect the drum is revolved with a spinning motion rather like a coin before it comes to rest and the peas moving round inside sound like rain falling continuously. The lead shot or rice will give a different volume and for alteration in pitch the drum can rest on a blanket to muffle the head. The peas will have to be stirred by hand, but in doing so the operator can vary the flow of rain to alternate with quiet lines in the dialogue.

* See also 'Weapons' p. 157.

Visual effects are imitated by suspending a box with rice above the scene. The box is perforated with small holes and when gently shaken with ropes attached to the sides of the box, the rice falls to the stage. To help the effect, a spotlight is focussed across the area through which the rice falls. Water may be used by suspending perforated lengths of piping from which a rubber hose is run to the water supply. A canvas trough must be placed immediately below the pipes to catch the water as it falls. It is rather messy and care must be taken that the water is not spilled on the scenery or anywhere near electrical equipment. An optical effect is described in chapter 8.

RESIN BOXES

Musical and ballet companies need resin boxes. They are wooden trays put at the side of the stage and contain powdered resin. The dancers rub the soles of their shoes in the resin to obtain a firm grip on the surface of the stage.

SEA

The effect is made by taking a garden sieve and replacing the mesh with tightly stretched canvas. The canvas is varnished to give it a hard surface. Small lead shot is swirled round the canvas by circular movement and the sound of waves reproduced. For sea lapping gently on shingle, a long box like the rain box is used. Instead of internal partitions, it has a series of steel spikes, i.e. long nails driven in from the sides. Lead shot is inserted and when the box is tilted slowly from side to side, the shot tinkles past the steel spikes. An optical effect is described in chapter 8.

SHIPS

While scenes aboard ocean liners are best left to the technical assistance of a large theatre, it may happen that a small boat or raft is required to show itself in motion. The boat is mounted on wheels that are eccentric and can also have perambulator springs to give increased movement. It is pulled by ropes across the stage and the mechanical parts of the boat are concealed behind a ground row or cut cloth of waves, rocks or the side of the jetty. (The raft in Plate 12 was worked in this way.) The creaking sound of rigging in a sailing ship can be done by rubbing a piece of leather coated in resin around a bamboo pole. When someone falls into the sea, the splash thrown up over the side of the ship is produced by throwing rice grains into the air from a tray.

SIRENS AND HOOTERS

These are hired from a ships' chandler and attached to a cylinder of compressed air. Being the actual siren, the sound is very effective. Recordings are also available.

SNOW

A box like the one used for rain is flown above the scene. Small pieces of paper torn up to the size of snow-flakes are put in the box, which has a base of small-mesh chicken wire. When the box is shaken the pieces of paper flutter slowly to the stage. It is useful to have a detachable cover to prevent the snow falling when not required. An optical effect is described in chapter 8.

THUNDER

The most realistic effect is produced by a combination of two thunder sheets hung near one another. They consist of a sheet of metal and a sheet of three-ply with handles at the lower edges to hold them. The softer rumbles are started on the three-ply sheet and the steel sheet is used to produce the claps and louder rolls as the storm increases. Drums are also used and for an exceptional storm a series of cannon balls is sent down a long wooden trough to fall into an iron tank. This is usually put in the flies, where its position gives an excellent rendering of a storm overhead.

Samuel Pepys wrote in his Diary about the sound of thunder used to strike a bargain. He was a good-natured materialist; troubled by his impecunious relations and his wife's improvidence, he was as eager to learn how to save money as to have a good time: ' Mr. Batelier told me how, being with some others at Bordeaux, making a bargain with another man at a taverne for some clarets, they did hire a fellow to thunder (which he had the art of doing upon a deale board) and to rain and hail, that is, make the noise of, so as did give them the pretence of undervaluing their merchants' wines, by saying this thunder would spoil and turn them. Which was so reasonable to the merchant, that he did abate two pistolls per ton for the wine in belief of that.'

WATER

When real water is needed from a tap, a small tank is suspended at a height behind the flat. It is connected by a rubber or plastic hose to the tap and all connections must be done by a member of the staff with a knowledge of plumbing. Great care is needed when using water as anything leaking on to the painted canvas will stain it.

WIND

Three methods may be used and they are: (a) recorded sound; (b) a machine by which a small electric motor rotates canes drawing air through wire mesh enclosing a box; and (c) the wind machine worked by hand. This is probably the best and consists of a revolving cylinder with smooth wooden blades attached to the surface. When it is turned the blades are in contact with a sheet of canvas or silk and the sound of the blades against the canvas can be made to reproduce several kinds of wind by rotating the cylinder at different speeds. For visual wind, blowing a small flag in a breeze, an electric fan is used and an occasional puff of wind to disturb a curtain can be simulated by waving a large piece of three-ply to produce the movement needed.

TRICK LINES AND CABINETS

Magical effects such as self-opening doors, walking umbrellas and locked cupboards that open without effort sometimes tax the imagination of the stage management. They are not difficult to reproduce and the veteran property master can frequently give the solution. The key to a cupboard supposed to be locked is filed so that it turns but does not engage the lock. The cupboard door is provided with a ball catch which clicks when the cupboard is opened. The actor inserting the key opens or closes the door at the moment he turns the key and the sound of the ball catch suggests the mechanism of the lock. Later in the play someone inserts a knife or a knitting needle near the lock and after a moment of deft manipulation the door opens, being held only with the ball catch.

There are two old tricks which may be recalled, as they are useful to know. In the Victorian theatre a transformation scene was performed with flats that were hinged horizontally or vertically. The upper half of a flat was made with a flap—*the falling flap*—hinged across the middle so that on the cue it would fall over the lower half of the flat. The hinged section was painted on both sides. When upright it matched the painting on the lower half of the flat. The reverse side of the flap was painted to correspond with the upper half of the flat—previously hidden—and when released an entirely altered flat was presented in view. *Vamps* were first used in a melodrama by Planché entitled *The*

Vampire. They were spring double doors lined with rubber and painted to match the surrounding flat. At a given moment the actor would take a flying leap and disappear as if by magic through the wall, the spring traps closing behind him.

Self-opening doors are operated by a *trick line* attached at stage level to the door and drawn through a hole in the flat to a point off-stage. The walking umbrella is performed by an ingenious form of track attached to the top of the setting and was invented by Messrs. Maitland Moss and Fred Walden of the Malvern Festival Company for James Bridie's *Mr. Bolfry.* In this play the umbrella is made to walk from the fireplace to the door and is suspended from the track XY. (Figure 34.) The track consists of a length of 3-in. by 1-in. batten fixed on the top of the flats on which a carriage travels controlling the movement of the umbrella. It is suspended from fine nylon lines which should be the same colour as the scene behind them so that the lines become invisible from a distance.

The umbrella is held by two nylon lines attached to screw-eyes (C) and (D) at the lower front edge of the carriage. The lines are tied to each side of a piece of stout wire (painted black) about four inches long, fastened to the handle of the umbrella so that it touches the floor at a very slight angle. Attached to the front of the carriage are two other screw-eyes. The one marked (E) underneath the front edge is used to guide the ' lifting ' nylon line to the foot of the umbrella and the other (F) is placed to secure the ' travelling ' line used to pull the carriage along the track. The lifting line is attached to the ferrule at the lower end of the umbrella which should be made heavier with a small lead weight so that it returns to the floor when it is made to walk. In this way the umbrella is held securely by three nylon lines.

At the rear end of the carriage another screw-eye (G)

LINES PULLED A-1
ALTERNATELY B-2

TRICK LINE

FIREPLACE

FERRULE WEIGHTED.

8″

SPINDLES

CARRIAGE,
SIDE VIEW.

1½″
INSIDE

COTTON
REEL

EYE FOR
PULL LINE

SCREW EYE FOR
UMBRELLA HANDLE—
AND ON OPPOSITE
SIDE.

EYE FOR LINE
TO BASE OF
UMBRELLA.

END VIEW

WIRE WITH LOOPS
FOR SUSPENSION LINES

WEIGHT AND LOOP FOR LINE "A"

AS USED IN
SETTING OF
"MR BOLFRY"

Figure 34

takes a line running over the rear of the flats to which a
small weight is attached. This helps to keep the carriage
steady and counterbalances the weight of the umbrella
and carriage as they move forward. The lifting and

travelling lines (A) and (B) are passed through screw-eyes at the far end of the batten in line with the back of the door flat to guide them down to stage level where they are worked by the operator. The carriage is a simple box without ends and includes two cotton reels on spindles which act as ' rollers ' to run on the batten.

The method of working is to set the umbrella at the upper side of the fireplace with the carriage on the track immediately overhead. On the cue the A.S.M. (remaining out of sight) turns the door handle and the door is opened by a trick line just enough for the umbrella to pass through it and be seen in transit by the operator off the stage. The lines (A) and (B) are manipulated alternately by first pulling (A) which lifts the foot of the umbrella and then pulling (B) to advance it towards the door. The umbrella is made to walk in a realistic manner and can even be persuaded to make some breathtaking hops. As the umbrella passes the edge of the door it is caught by the A.S.M. wearing a black glove and pulled out of sight. The door is closed with the lines trapped against the flat above the door and the A.S.M. holds the umbrella and door handle until the curtain descends. The ceiling is cut to provide a walking area for the umbrella and a framed border running across the setting is attached to it. The border hides the track mechanism and should be sufficiently deep to mask the top of the scene at the rear of the setting.

The walking umbrella in *Mr. Bolfry* gave the author his final curtain for the play. During a scene played in a room of a manse in Scotland, the Devil in the person of Dr. Bolfry is conjured at a midnight séance by the young people in the house. He arrives dressed exactly like the Minister, wearing a raincoat and carrying an umbrella. In a subsequent scene, he preaches a blasphemous sermon after which he is chased out of the manse without time to retrieve his umbrella left near the fireplace. The following morning, the

Minister and his wife wonder if their experience was all a dream when suddenly the umbrella springs to life and walks by itself out of the room. The Minister is too astonished to move but his wife who accepts a walking umbrella as she does biblical ' fiery wheels and beasts with three heads and horns ' consoles her husband with a cup of tea and the curtain descends.

Trick lines are used in several ways and I can recall a tropical thunderstorm when they were given full play. The scene was the interior of a bungalow and the effect required was that of an approaching storm which culminated in a tropical downpour attended by a small cyclone. The distant thunder was done with thunder sheets and drums, to be realised finally with cannon balls and an iron tank. Wind machines, rain and lightning effects were brought into action and the climax involved the use of several trick lines for the tornado to blow itself through the scene. The lines were used to shake tropical plants under heavy rain, to blow open the lattice blinds, to swing an oil lamp hanging overhead, to upset a chair and to blow newspapers from a table when the full force of the storm entered the room. It needed organisation, as apart from careful preparation of the trick lines, electric cues were required for members of the staff waiting at strategic points on the stage and in the flies to perform their allotted tasks. Much rehearsal was given to the effect in order to get the progressive timing of the storm and the staff—holding on valiantly until their cues—created an example of patient endurance. At the end I overheard sundry oaths muttered through the thunder claps and was glad the rehearsal came to a successful conclusion. At times like these it may be fitting to relate that in 1500 the following was recorded in the manuscript of a passion play: ' To Master Jehan du Fayt and his assistants numbering 17 persons for having helped in Hell for nine days during the said Mystery at 6 sols a day to each, 45 livres 18 sols.'

PROPERTY AND EFFECTS PLOTS

During rehearsals the stage manager's original plots are revised and he keeps the property master closely informed about any alterations. Before the dress rehearsal, when the scenes are built and dressed, a final plot is completed which will include dressings for each scene, hand properties and effects. Several copies are made and given to the assistant stage manager, property master and his assistants. The situation of furniture and properties used for dressing the scene is noted and the character using a particular hand property named. Personal properties are given to the artists and for these he is responsible. Nevertheless, if anything should go astray it is always the final responsibility of the stage management. For this reason it is safer to keep a duplicate of an important item, thereby saving the day if it is lost. Some properties seem to attract trouble and an artist carrying a sword and scabbard can be helped by seeing it is safely attached to his person before he goes on the stage. At a command performance the leading player was required to dash on waving his sword. By some mischance he forgot it was still in its scabbard which at this critical moment flew into the audience. During the interval he was presented to H.M. the Queen, who graciously remarked that she hoped he had not intended to hit her Prime Minister.

A table is arranged at the side of the stage for other hand properties. These are set in order of use and never varied so that an artist who is perhaps late for his entrance will know exactly where to find the manuscript or other property he requires. An example of a typical property plot is shown in Figure 35. Although the property master will eventually know the situation of the furniture, for complicated settings it is advisable to give him a small plan of the scene with the plot.

PROPERTY AND EFFECTS PLOT

ACT I, Sc. 1.   Outside the 'Dog and Whistle
Rustic seat, C.
Rustic table, L.

Hand properties (personal)
Penny for LARRY (Miss Blackler).
Cutlass, pistols for PIRATE (Mr. Merry).
Police whistle, truncheon, notebook, large pencil for ERNEST (Mr. Roberts).

Hand properties
Chart for PIRATE (Mr. Merry) off L.   Glass of ginger beer for BRASS (Mr. Seaman) and coil of rope for ERNEST (Mr. Roberts).

Effects
AT CUE: 'But if much money we should get, it is good.   Yes?'
Ernest's whistle and glass crash off C.

ACT I, Sc. 2.   The Mayor's Study
Desk UP R.C.—on it: inkwell, quill pens, blotter, books, handbell, silver tankard, Mayor's hat.
Armchair behind desk.
Upholstered armchair at fireplace.
Upright chair R of Door.
Safe down L.   In it: manuscripts with large red and blue seals, jar with ginger beer.
              In keyhole: bunch of large gold keys.
Bookcase down R.   In it: books.
Fireplace L with taper inside fender and flash box off-stage.
Trick line on door C.

Hand properties (personal)
Umbrella, watch and chain, sixpence for MR. GROWSER (Mr. Frost).
Watch and chain, stethoscope for DOCTOR (Mr. Johnson).
Metal-rimmed spectacles for SECRETARY (Mr. Clark).
Red and white spotted handkerchief for BRASS (Mr. Seaman).
Sixpence for MAGICIAN (Mr. Wander), ERNEST (Mr. Roberts) and INVENTOR (Mr. de Vise).

Hand properties
Bag with thermometer for DOCTOR (Mr. Johnson).
Quill pen, feather brush, manuscripts for SECRETARY (Mr. Clark).
Tripod and bowl, wand for MAGICIAN (Mr. Wander).

Effects
AT CUE: 'The whole town is filled with coloured smoke.'
          Thunder, flash box at fireplace, trick line on door C.

Figure 35

Panatrope and Tape Recording

These are the two systems used in the theatre for reproduction of recorded sound. The *Panatrope* is a gramophone solidly constructed for commercial use and can be operated by anyone accustomed to a domestic record-player. It usually has twin turntables, pick-ups and volume controls and depending on the size of the amplifier eight or more loudspeakers can be connected to each turntable. The twin turntables give continuous reproduction from one recording to another and are used in cross-fading between different sounds. When two amplifiers are installed they become independent units and in the event of a breakdown the recording is continued by switching from one to the other. Electrical reproducers develop all kinds of faults and although duplicate pick-up heads are supplied, other faults may arise perhaps in the amplifier or wiring. It is necessary to be prepared for anything that may interrupt an effect essential to the performance, particularly when both turntables are used, and the normal method is to provide a spare single turntable unit and speaker as a stand-by in case of need.

A record may include several effects and a graduated scale is supplied to find the exact point on the disc to start the cue. The scale has numbers or letters to indicate the approximate position and a fine micrometer adjustment to locate any groove on the record. The pick-up arm moves along the scale and is held there at the point required until lowered on the disc by a small lever. Although playing a music recording is not difficult, the reproduction of sound effects has to be learned for it requires skill and a flair for timing. Rehearsal is needed to find the right moment to lower the needle and pick-up which is done with one hand, leaving the other free to turn up the volume control to the mark previously arranged. Some practice is required, though panatropes supplied today are good mechanical instruments with well-designed controls.

The panatrope is usually operated by the A.S.M. and cues are given by a cue light from the prompt corner; by a word cue from one of the actors; or through a clear view of the stage. It is placed as near as possible to the prompt corner depending on the amount of equipment installed there with the space available. The records are labelled to include (1) their number in consecutive order, (2) the description of the cue, i.e. ' clock chimes ' and (3) the scene in which the record is played. The labels are pasted over the record label in the centre of the disc and in the case of commercial recordings there is normally enough room left over to read the original title. Wire containers can be purchased in music shops for storage of records. They are placed in the container in order of use and should be stored in their sleeves to keep them clean and free from dust.

The cue light connected with the prompt corner and a shaded light for the operator are fixed above the panatrope. The A.S.M. will need a cue sheet which should indicate:

(1) The Act and scene in the play.

(2) The number of the cue.

(3) The number of the record.

(4) Description of the record, i.e. title of music or effect.

(5) The band (or section) of the record used, i.e. Band 1, 2 or 3 when there are several different effects recorded on the disc.

(6) The right or left hand turntable.

(7) The pick-up setting, i.e. the mark on the scale and micrometer adjustment.

(8) The volume required.

(9) The loudspeaker: stage or front-of-house.

Additional cues are included when a record is duplicated and when the volume is altered.

The panatrope needs a little time to warm up and it is switched on and tested by the electrician or the A.S.M. before the audience arrives in the theatre. A record is played and each loudspeaker tried in turn. The panatrope is left switched *on* for the performance but the loudspeakers are switched *off* until they are needed. After a cue is performed, the loudspeaker must be switched off again, for the equipment can pick up other electrical sounds and during a quiet part in the play this is very disturbing. It is also a good idea to see that the volume controls are at the ' off ' position before touching the pick-up arm, as otherwise the sound of setting the pick-up may be transmitted to the loudspeakers if one of them inadvertently has been left switched on. Wear of the records is something to be watched and ' direct ' recordings made for special effects need replacement more frequently than commercial discs. Direct recordings are made with acetate discs and the original recorded disc is the one used for the play. Commercial recordings are made on vinylite and pressed from a matrix or master recording. The commercial discs should be dusted lightly from time to time with a special cloth obtainable at record shops. The cloth must not be used with direct recordings as the chemical solvent is harmful to the acetate disc. These records can only be cleaned by holding them under a cold water tap and letting them dry in clean surroundings. Dust spoils a good effect and the illusion is quickly dispelled with a needle heard scratching, so care of the records is important. The panatrope also should be dusted occasionally and a small brush can be obtained to remove particles from the pick-up needle. Stages are not the cleanest places and the panatrope should be closed after use or covered with a cloth.

In amateur performances with a small number of sound cues a good record-player and a loudspeaker giving sufficient volume can provide the effects. In this event there will not be a graduated scale to mark the pick-up arm and a *chinagraph* pencil obtained from a leading stationer or a shop selling artists' materials is used to mark the record. The record is played at the cue and the chinagraph pencil held just behind the needle and pick-up arm. As the disc revolves the pencil is made to touch the record lightly and will leave a white mark around the disc at the groove of the cue. This is a fairly accurate method and is useful without a graduated scale.

A major development in the effects department is the *magnetic tape recorder* which has almost replaced the panatrope although only used in the theatre in recent years. It is not a new invention and was patented in 1898 when the recording was made on a steel wire. At that time it aroused great interest but did not find immediate commercial application. Tape recording achieved recognition about twenty years ago by the gramophone companies when the tape was played back, amplified and the sound passed to the record cutter for production of the matrix from which discs are processed. It has many advantages that include the silent quality of the tape, the longer recording time and the ease by which immediate play-back is available. Editing is done by cutting out parts of the tape or adding to it which is not possible with records. The tape can also be ' wiped ' or erased and therefore used again almost indefinitely; an economy over discs which deteriorate during a period of time.

The idea of a magnetic tape consists in storing electrical impulses with magnetised particles of iron oxide coated on a plastic tape. The music, speech or effect recorded is transferred to the tape by means of a ' head ' which is a coil of wire wound around a core of magnetic iron. The head has a gap through which the tape moves and the current passed through the gap magnetises the powdered iron oxide on the tape. To reproduce the recording the tape is passed through the head of a tape unit like the one used for recording but the head is unable to record or erase the tape. The tape travelling through the gap alters the magnetism of the core and generates a current in the coil which is converted through an amplifier to the loudspeaker. The recording is only transmitted accurately if the speed of the tape during the recording and reproduction are synchronised. Standard commercial equipment is now in use to ensure that tapes can be exchanged and used with a variety of machines.

The value to the theatre consists in the quality of the tape recording and simplified controls. Apart from switching on the equipment all that is necessary is to press a button and operate the volume control. The possibility of error in handling a pick-up is avoided and the recording remains constant throughout its use. During rehearsals the sound effects are made on direct recordings and later transferred to the tape when the production is in its stride. Records are more convenient because it is not so easy to return to a part of a cue recorded on tape. The tape needs rewinding, the cue has to be found and this takes time. The records are used throughout rehearsals and even during a pre-London tour until the director is content with the result. The cues transferred to the tape are edited to the time required and the tape is made to stop automatically by splicing a strip of metal foil into it which makes direct electrical contact as it passes through the head. It is so arranged that the tape stops at the beginning of the next cue which is started immediately by pressing the button. When music is needed for a scene change, more than the exact time is recorded in case the scene change happens to take longer than anticipated.

Loudspeakers for panatrope and tape recordings are placed anywhere on the stage and it is useful to remember that sight plays an important part in realising the effect.

With limited resources one loudspeaker placed behind the centre of the setting can be used for several effects though they are expected to be heard from different sides of the stage. The fact that the actor looks in the direction from which the sound is supposed to be coming establishes it although the loudspeaker may be some distance away. In other words sound is deceptive and because we expect a sound from a certain part of the scene we believe it is heard there. Sounds travelling from one side of the stage to the other require more than one loudspeaker as for instance the sound of a car passing a house. The sound as it approaches comes from one loudspeaker and by manipulating the volume controls it is heard departing through another speaker in the opposite direction. It should be remembered that effects rehearsed in an empty theatre are louder than when the theatre is full and the volume decided in rehearsal will need adjustment. A separate loudspeaker must be installed in the front of the house for interval music which cannot be heard from a stage speaker as the curtain deadens the sound.

The E.M.I. Company has a very complete library of sound effects likely to be needed. It is sometimes possible to make a recording at home but it is always advisable to do so in a studio properly equipped for sound recording. In London, the Stage Sound Company specialises in theatre effects and can usually supply any effects from West End productions. Copyright exists in commercial recordings and purchase of E.M.I. effects discs permits re-recording on tape for public performances by amateur societies. In the professional theatre a licence is required to play or re-record music, speech or effects from records sold by the recording companies. Application should be made to the gramophone company or to Phonographic Performance Ltd., 62 Oxford Street, London, W.1.

CHAPTER 8

LIGHTING

' But if you need a great light to throw more than the rest, then set a torch behind, and behind the torch a bright basin; the brightness whereof will show like the beams of the sun'—Text-book on scenic design by Sebastiano Serlio published 1547

IN the latter half of the nineteenth century, the Swiss philosopher, Adolphe Appia, revolutionised the staging and lighting of theatrical performances and gave us the basic principles of scene design and lighting in use today. Up to that time, stage design had not developed beyond the ideas created by the early Italian scene painters who merely cut their pictures into several pieces and stood them on the stage. Being painters and not scene designers in the sense accepted today, they concentrated on producing illustrations for decoration of the scene. The backcloth was all-important for here, in many shades of colour and by drawing in perspective, the artist could paint a picture enlarged to a romantic dream. The fact that the backcloth was part of the scenery which had to enclose the acting area of the stage by the addition of pieces of cut scenery did not advance his pictorial fantasy. This was further emphasised when the actor appeared upon the scene. The three-dimensional performer looked absurd against the illusion of three dimensions created by the scene painter's art. Not only was the painted scenery out of tune with the actor, it was also in conflict with the lighting illuminating it. For the picture to be seen, the maximum of light had to be thrown on it, and as the lighting lacked mobility in projection and location, the scenery was set where it could be lit to the best advantage. Consequently the actor became subservient to the scenery and lighting instead of unified with it.

180

Appia was the first to indicate the three-dimensional status of the actor and to insist that the scenery should be designed within this convention. He stressed the importance of lighting to enhance and unify it. The flat overall lighting of a scene without regard to shadows lacked definition, and Appia brought to the theatre the light and shade that Rembrandt and other artists had used as an interpretative medium. Where the scene painters had shown perspective, Appia used lighting and showed that distance could be created as effectively by varying intensity of light. He predicted the two systems of lighting the stage; the general light which flooded the scene and the important focussed or mobile light we know as the spotlight. He emphasised the value of focussing light on the actor to intensify the structure and expression of his features. And depending on the importance of the actor's rôle, lighting could also be employed to increase or diminish his relation to the scene.

His predictions are fulfilled and in the development of the modern spotlight its mobility may be controlled, although it remains fixed in one position. Lenses of different sizes and lamps of various strength are used in spotlights to light areas of the stage overlapping one another. The spotlights are also focussed in concentrated light to illuminate the actor's face. Each spotlight is controlled by a *dimmer* (see p. 188) which can vary its intensity over a large number of positions. In the professional theatre up to a hundred spotlights may be in use for a production, each one being focussed on a particular area of the stage. Their shafts of light, varying in intensity and colour, and subjected to minute alterations during the performance, come from above the stage, from the sides and from positions in the auditorium. The lighting installation found in a London theatre is shown in plan in Figure 36. Although the equipment is comprehensive, the principle employed in devising the

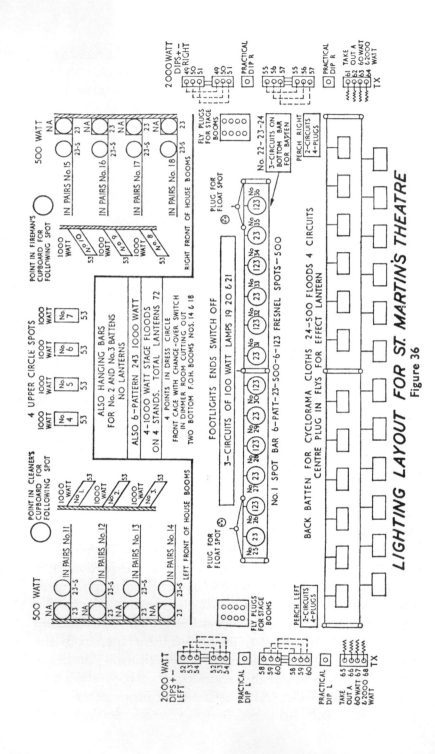

LIGHTING LAYOUT FOR ST. MARTIN'S THEATRE
Figure 36

quantity and location of the spotlights can be used just as well in smaller theatres and halls.

When we see the stage of a village hall or institute, the lighting apparatus will probably consist of footlights and battens with perhaps two or more spotlights in the auditorium. The *footlights* are rows of lamps enclosed in a long metal trough which is placed along the front edge of the stage. The *battens* are rows of lamps in metal troughs that are flown above the stage at the back, the centre and the front of the acting area. They are intended to distribute light evenly over the whole area of the stage. The battens and footlights have individual compartments each containing a reflector and bulb with a frame into which a piece of coloured medium can be inserted. It is usual for the bulbs to be arranged in three or four circuits so that colour alterations may be made throughout the length of the batten. Each circuit is controlled by its own dimmer in the lighting control board.

With this equipment it is a simple matter to light the setting with overall lighting to the exclusion of the actor or to illuminate the actor without lighting the scene. The problem—to preserve the right relationship—is overcome by using spotlights for focussing light on the actor and floodlights for general lighting of the scene.

The equipment in use today is in three forms and includes:

(1) Floodlights.
(2) Soft-edge spotlights.
(3) Hard-edge profile spotlights.

It is hung mainly overhead and the lighting positions can be divided into two categories:

(a) For lighting the actors and the setting.
(b) For special effects.

Lighting for (a) comes from the direction of the audience and is projected from above the stage, the sides and from the auditorium. An actor performing up-stage can be illuminated satisfactorily in a picture-frame stage from positions behind the proscenium and the sides of the stage. Overhead or back lighting is also used to light around the actor's form and separate him from his background. When the actor is close to the audience (that is, in the area down-stage, or the apron) it is essential for lighting to come from the auditorium and these are called front-of-house positions.

FLOODLIGHTS

They provide a wide-angled beam of light and are employed for lighting backcloths, backings etc. They are used on telescopic stands at stage level or hung from bars above the scene. The floodlight is a large single lamp with a reflector enclosed in a metal case attached to a bracket so that it can be tilted to diffuse light over a particular area. A frame with a coloured medium is inserted in the front of the casing. The compartments in battens and footlights are in effect a series of smaller floodlights joined together. The battens are used for lighting backcloths and cycloramas and sections similar to the footlights are employed at the bottom of cycloramas or cloths where they are used behind ground rows. Footlights or ' floats ' as they are sometimes called, still occupy the position of the early ' floats ' being the name for the wicks floating in oil, before gas or electricity. They were used to balance the effect of overhead lighting but nowadays, with the help of spotlights placed at a lower level, are becoming more of an auxiliary part of the equipment. (Figures 37 and 38.)

SOFT-EDGE SPOTLIGHTS

The focussing spotlights mentioned earlier are the most important lighting equipment on the stage. For lighting to be ' plastic ' i.e. giving shape to an object otherwise formless, it must be localised in order to

FLOODLIGHT
Figure 37

BATTEN AND FOOTLIGHTS
Figure 38

emphasise it. It should provide a dominant light to a given area and avoid spilling or dissipating its light elsewhere. The adjustable beam of this spotlight has a soft edge i.e. the beam has no clear outline and the light is scattered. A shutter may, however, be fitted to intercept light spilling on an area where it becomes excessive. The spotlights are mounted on bars behind the proscenium and sometimes attached to part of the scenery.

PATT. 45 JUNIOR SOFT-EDGE (FRESNEL) SPOTLIGHT
Figure 39

PATT. 123 BABY SOFT-EDGE (FRESNEL) SPOTLIGHT
Figure 40

They are also placed on vertical bars and may hang above the scene, in the wings, to provide lighting at a higher level. In many theatres, there are small platforms immediately behind the sides of the proscenium arch and about 12 ft. from the level of the stage. *Perch spotlights* are placed here and shine on to the down-stage area through apertures cut into the tormentors masking them. (Figures 39, 40, 41.)

HARD-EDGE PROFILE OR MIRROR SPOTLIGHTS

They give a concentrated beam of light which is varied by a shutter and focussed by the lens. They are very suitable for front-of-house work and depending on

PATT. 243 1Kw SOFT-EDGE (FRESNEL) SPOTLIGHT

Figure 41

PATT. 23 BABY HARD-EDGE PROFILE (MIRROR) SPOTLIGHT

Figure 42

the wattage and size of the lantern can throw a beam from 30 ft. to 120 ft. controlled so that it does not light the proscenium arch. The smaller 'baby' spotlights are also employed on the stage where they are used for very clear definition. (Figure 42.)

LIGHTING CONTROL

The control of the electrical equipment and the different circuits is performed by the *switchboard*. This has the power to switch on or off all the individual items of equipment and to increase or reduce the light from them either individually or collectively. The spotlights and other equipment will therefore require a switch and a resistance for each circuit in use. The simplest form of resistance, known as a *dimmer* is an apparatus consisting of a coil of wire wound round an insulating material. A slide contact runs over the entire length of the coil and connected in circuit with a lamp it increases or decreases the amount of light radiated. The number of dimmers included in the switchboard will relate to the number of circuits in use.

When the stage has to be darkened or ' blacked out ' it is done by a master switch though sometimes it is required to perform this effect gradually. It is difficult to operate more than three or four dimmers together by hand and one large dimmer sufficient to control all the circuits is used. It is known as the *master dimmer* and includes switches whereby certain circuits may be left unaltered if so required. Portable dimmer boards can be obtained to operate independently and at a distance from the switchboard. They are also very useful when it is necessary to install temporary equipment in the absence of a permanent form of control.

The dimmer is the important element in lighting control and the description given here is of the most elementary form. Much thought has been given to the design of new resistances and in the larger installations all-electric dimmers are used of which the silicon-controlled rectifier is probably the best. Stage lighting is a comprehensive subject and there are several books on the subject obtainable from Samuel French Ltd. who cater for the professional and the amateur stage.

COLOUR

The use of colour in lighting the scene is to reproduce by artificial means the colour we find in life. To appreciate the nature of colour we should understand that colour is the sensation produced by a ray of light separated into its elements. The elements of a ray of sunlight, which may be described as white light, can be shown when it is passed through a glass prism. It

1	Yellow	18	Light Blue	38	Pale Green
2	Light Amber	19	Dark Blue	39	Primary Green
3	Straw	20	Deep Blue (Primary)	40	Pale Blue
4	Medium Amber	21	Pea Green	41	Bright Blue
5A	Deep Orange	22	Moss Green	42	Pale Violet
6	Red (Primary)	23	Light Green	43	Pale Navy Blue
7	Light Rose	24	Dark Green	48	Bright Rose
8	Deep Salmon	25	Purple	49	Canary
9	Light Salmon	26	Mauve	50	Pale Yellow
10	Middle Rose	29	Heavy Frost	51	Gold Tint
11	Dark Pink	30	Clear	52	Pale Gold
12	Deep Rose	31	Light Frost	53	Pale Salmon
13	Magenta	32	Medium Blue	54	Pale Rose
14	Ruby	33	Deep Amber	55	Chocolate Tint
15	Peacock Blue	34	Golden Amber	56	Pale Chocolate
16	Blue-green	35	Deep Golden Amber	60	Pale Grey
17	Steel Blue	36	Pale Lavender		

COLOUR MEDIUMS
Figure 43

becomes divided into seven components i.e. violet, indigo, blue, green, yellow, orange and red known as the spectrum. If we introduce a piece of (say) blue glass between the ray of sunlight and the prism, we shall find that it has the effect of destroying all the colours in the spectrum except its own. The medium corresponds to the colour filter, made from acetate sheeting, used for colouring the stage. The range of colour mediums is formidable and includes fifty different shades, although only about twelve of them are in normal use. (Figure 43.)

Before describing them, there are two important points to note. The first concerns the mixing of colour. When we mix coloured pigments we know that the addition of each colour produces a darker one. This is not so when mixing coloured light. Here the addition of each colour gives a paler effect that eventually produces white light. The second point to observe is the effect of coloured light on the pigment of an object. Any light colour will intensify the pigment of its own colour but will substantially alter the pigment of other colours. For instance, the brilliant blue to illuminate a moonlit scene will be found to turn the actors' make-up to a very muddy complexion.

It is obvious that a knowledge of basic lighting principles is necessary and effective use of the primary colours should be understood. With paints the three primary colours of red, blue and yellow, when mixed in certain quantities, will produce any other colour. However, the primary colours in lighting are the dominant colours of the spectrum, i.e. red, green and blue, which mixed suitably will produce any colour to light a scene. For instance, red plus green will produce yellow light, blue plus green produces blue-green, red plus blue produces magenta, and mixing all three colours produces white light.

The practical application of lighting with primary colours is limited. To mix colours a spotlight or flood with a separate dimmer is needed for each primary colour. The mediums used are No. 6 red, No. 39 green and No. 20 blue with which a variety of colours may be produced. Red and green when mixed and controlled by the dimmer will produce red, orange, amber and yellow. As the red colour is taken out the green will predominate, resulting in pale green and finally the primary colour. Colour mixing of primaries is unsuitable for lighting straight plays as two spotlights are required for each colour and shadows tend to reproduce the primary colour, giving an unnatural effect. It is valuable in lighting backcloths or cycloramas and used imaginatively excellent pictorial results are obtained. Loss of power is a drawback which may be overcome by exchanging the primary colours for paler ones of a

similar tint.   By adjusting the dimmers a wide range of
atmospheric effects are produced.

As the principal object in lighting a scene is to light
the actors it is therefore best to avoid the use of vivid
colours and to choose the softer shades of mediums.
Among those to be recommended are the yellows and
pale golds, pale blues and greys, and pale pinks.   The
numbers of the mediums or filters are:

Yellow and Gold	1, 2, 3, 50, 51 and 52.
Blue	17 and 18.
Grey	56 and 60.
Pink	7, 53 and 54.

Pink with a shade of lavender is No. 36, and used in
place of blue is favourable to make-up.

Observation of natural lighting will also assist in the
choice of colours.   Unlike scenes set in a tropical paradise, the lighting of the English scene alters very little
throughout the day.   The transition from morning to
night is gentle, although it will include the warm after-
math of a sunset and subtle changes in season.   Observation of interior lighting will show that the warmer or
deeper shades of light occur progressively as the light
from a window crosses the room.   If this is taken into
account it will also assist in the 'plastic' lighting of the
actor.   His face, lit on one side with gold, and on the
other side with a salmon colour, gives interesting
texture to his features.

LIGHTING THE PLAY

At first, lighting a scene may be a mystery and it is
difficult to know just where to begin.   But if certain
basic principles are understood, a plan can be evolved
which will serve for a variety of settings.   The equipment for lighting the acting area as shown in Figure 44
will be the spotlights hung on No. 1 bar behind the
proscenium, the front-of-house spotlights, stage floods
and footlights.   It will be seen that there are ten

LIGHTING EQUIPMENT

Figure 44

spotlights on No. 1 bar and four in the front-of-house. With this equipment the scene can be well, though modestly, lit and if funds permit, extra F.O.H. spotlights and vertical bars at each side of the stage with extra spotlights could be provided. Eight of the ten spotlights on the No. 1 bar are of the soft-edge type and they are chosen for their ability to provide an ill-defined beam of light which may be adjusted over a small or large area. The other two spotlights are of the hard-edge variety and are selected for the special purpose of providing concentrated light and clear definition. The F.O.H. spotlights are the hard-edge type and include shutters to cut off light from the proscenium and in the area near the footlights.

We should now try to visualise where the main scenes in the play are performed. There are certain well-defined acting areas in all plays and they are within a space of about six feet running across the stage. In an interior scene, the furniture used by the actors will be found roughly in this area and most of the scenes are played around it. The lighting plan shown in Figure 45 could be employed in the scene illustrated in Plate 6. (In the photograph of the scene, the armchair is moved from its original position in the centre of the stage to provide an uninterrupted view of the door and the exterior hall.) It may appear complicated but when studied in detail certain facts will emerge.

The main acting areas are around the fireplace (RC), the centre of the stage (C) and near the window (LC), and if we arrange our lighting in these areas most of the stage will be lit. It will, however, leave the area up-stage partially lit and as the door is an important entrance, we must also arrange lighting there.

Before setting and colouring the spotlights, let us consider the effect we wish to achieve. In the scene the principal source of light comes from the window and as it crosses the room becomes diffused. An actor standing

LIGHTING PLAN FOR AN INTERIOR SETTING
Figure 45

GARDEN BACKING

ACTORS ENTER

FLOOD ON TALL STAND

WALL

SKY FLOODS

SPOTLIGHT No. 2
COLD

SPOTLIGHT No. 9
WARM

SETTING OF SPOTLIGHTS AND
LIGHTING FOR WINDOWS AND BACKING

Figure 46

in the centre of the stage will be lit on one side of his face by light from the window and the other side will be in shadow. But we should remember that reflected light will also light the side of his face in shadow and consequently we must arrange to provide it. Now let us observe the locality of reflected light in a room. It will frequently be reflected from a white ceiling or wall and will shine on the actor from above and from the side. In other words it provides shadows appropriate to his features and accentuates his expression.

In the theatre we cannot rely on reflected light because this in itself is not sufficient for details of the actor's face to be visible to the audience. So it is necessary for us to arrange lighting which will model his face in highlights and shadows in a natural way. And it will be found in practice that two spotlights focussed from the No. 1 bar on either side of the actor at an angle of about 45° will provide the light and shade we are accustomed to see. (This is shown in Figure 46.)

It is essential to make a lighting plan well in advance of the first lighting rehearsal. Apart from assisting the electrician, who has to prepare equipment and cut mediums for the spotlights and floods, it will provide the director with a general idea of the lighting treatment for his production. So with a plan of the scene and the furniture marked on it, we consider the acting areas. (Figure 45.) The area LC will need two spotlights focussed on the actor who will be lit by beams of light with an angle between them of about 90°. In order to avoid lighting the top of the actor's head, we must choose a spotlight to his side and consequently No. 1 spotlight is the first to be directed into the area. The second spotlight will be further away and if we take No. 7 spotlight and train it into the area, we shall have two spotlights with the angle of light we require.

The acting area C is treated likewise and is covered by spotlights No. 2 and No. 9. The area RC will correspond to the area LC and we can choose spotlights in relative positions which would be No. 10 and No. 4. But here is a point to watch. We shall need light on the door up-stage and No. 5 spotlight is suitable, for it will also light the entrance very well when the door is opened. However when No. 4 spotlight is turned round to shine into the area RC it may be obstructed by No. 5 spotlight directed up-stage. In order to overcome the difficulty, the spotlights are reversed by training No. 5 spotlight into the area RC and No. 4 spotlight on to the door. This problem may occur at any time and the plotting of spotlights should be a flexible arrangement. We have now arranged lighting for the main acting areas and the centre door. There remain the areas up R and L and No. 3 and No. 8 spotlights can be used for these positions. The last spotlight No. 6 is employed for additional light in the centre of the stage.

The colours selected for the spotlights and floods will depend on what the script mentions regarding the season of the year, time of day and whether alterations in light will be required due to change in the state of the weather. For our purpose let us suppose that the play is divided into three acts as follows:

Act 1. Sc. 1.	Summer	Mid-day.
Sc. 2.	do	Early evening.
Act 2.	Autumn	Day, raining.
Act 3.	Winter	Evening, moonlight.

The principle of using two spotlights in each acting area is followed by placing warm and cold colours in each pair of spotlights. (Figure 46.) There are several combinations of colours each of which may have a special appeal. For example, No. 7 (light rose) and No. 17 (steel blue) can between them produce a near approach to white light pleasing to the actor. By dimming one or the other colour, a heightened effect of warm or cold colour can also be obtained. On the whole, the pale golds and

pinks are suitable for most purposes and are kind to the
actor's make-up. In our play it will be observed that we
have to arrange day and evening light from the window
(L) and firelight (R) for the winter scene in the last act.
This means that the colder light will come from the
direction of the window and the warm firelight will
be on the opposite side of the stage. Even in the summer
scenes, when the fire is not alight, the warmer tones of
colour will still be in that area.

The colours chosen for the centre acting area are No.
53 (pale salmon) in spotlight No. 9 and No. 51 (gold
tint) in spotlight No. 2. (Figure 45.) The salmon is a
mixture of yellow and pink which blends well with the
pale gold of No. 51. For the fireside area, we shall need
a deeper pink and No. 7 (light rose) will provide warmth
in spotlight No. 10. And as this is the furthest point from
the window, we can afford to use a pale salmon colour in
spotlight No. 5.

The area LC near the window requires special attention.
An actor sitting at the desk with his back to the window
will appear dark in contrast to the strong external light
and therefore we have to arrange as much concentrated
light as possible. The spotlights employed (No. 1 and
No. 7) are the hard-edge type and they provide concentrated light with clear definition over a small area. To
retain light we use pale colours and the pale rose (54) and
gold tint (51) should be sufficient.

With the spotlights directed upon the acting areas, it
may be asked how it is intended to light the scene. This
is unnecessary because the *spill* or reflected light from the
spotlights will show up the setting. Sometimes an
architectural feature needs additional light and then one of
the spotlights is replaced by a small flood which with the
appropriate colour will enhance the colour of the setting.
It may also be used to gain ' atmosphere ' in evening or
firelight scenes when one side of the stage may be lit with a
shade of blue to accentuate contrasting light from the fire.

When the footlights are used correctly, they can be valuable in balancing the effect of the overhead lighting and adding tone to the painted quality of the setting. Colours should be provided in the three circuits which may be of special value in different scenes. No. 7 (light rose) and No. 52 (pale gold) or No. 3 (straw) are the warm colours and No. 17 (steel blue) will provide a good contrast for the day scenes. For night scenes, although it should be used carefully, No. 32 (medium blue) can replace the gold colour.

The F.O.H. spotlights are intended to light the downstage areas, and as will be seen in Figure 45, are trained across the stage with colours to harmonise with those of the other lanterns. To help lighting actors near the window, the colour is omitted from No. 3 F.O.H. spotlight to provide maximum light.

WINDOW LIGHTING

There is a fairly large expanse of window on the side of the scene which includes french windows and a smaller one above them. The exterior backing is probably a garden scene which is not difficult to light using stage floods. Five will be needed and three of them are set at stage level on telescopic stands to light the garden part of the backing; the other two being attached to the setting at a convenient height to light the sky. It will be seen in Figure 46 that the stage floods are spaced at intervals and arranged to throw light on the two sides of the backing. The flood placed below the french windows should be on a very tall stand to prevent shadows when the actors make their entrances.

The colours to be used will depend largely on what is painted on the backing. And to give contrast to the sky and garden, No. 54 (pale rose) in the stage floods will provide texture to the garden scene and No. 17 (steel blue) will help to bring out the blue of the sky. These are suitable for the summer scenes in Act 1, though it happens sometimes that a scenic artist may have difficulty with his colours, in which case it is best to use the floods without colours. At the end of Scene 2 we may want the effect of sunset and in the scene change between Scenes 1 and 2, the colour in the down-stage flood is altered to No. 9 (light salmon). By dimming the light in the other two stage floods, the salmon will predominate and the sunset effect be obtained. (Figure 45.)

In Act 2 we require a dismal autumn day and this need not mean that we see a torrential downpour of rain which would be distracting to the audience. It will be enough to provide a misty exterior in a sombre colour. No. 56 (pale chocolate) in the stage floods will give the effect and by dimming the two sky floods, the blue will include yellow from the reduced filament in the lamps to balance the overall picture.

The evening scene in Act 3 needs a dark background. The backing must be lit with a suitable colour and it should never be left without light, as reflected light from the stage will spoil it. No. 32 (medium blue) is a good colour to use in the stage floods. When the lamps are dimmed, they produce a deep yellow or red light and combined with the blue medium, mauve light is projected which is realistic. It may be necessary to show evening light fading to night and in this event keep a No. 52 (pale gold) in one of the floods and when dimmed completely it will leave the mauve colour in the other stage floods.

If we rely on the exterior floods to indicate sunlight for the summer scenes, our acting area will seem flat in relation to the light outside. And to provide the illusion of real sunlight would require a considerable amount of equipment beyond the means of small theatres. The larger soft-edge spotlights will, however, give a dominant beam of light which is very effective. They can be obtained in either 1,000 or 2,000 watt size and three or

four focussed through the windows will help considerably in bringing the interior of the setting to life.

Let us assume that in Act 1 Sc. 1 the sun is immediately overhead and therefore at its strongest light of the
day. The spotlights are mounted on tall stands and
directed through the french windows without colours
to give the maximum light. We shall also need sunlight
to balance the window up-stage and a smaller (500 watt)
spotlight is placed on a stand to shine through this
window.

For Scene 2 it is early evening and we must arrange
to show the light at that time of day and also that the
sun has moved to the west. In the scene change between
Scenes 1 and 2, a gold colour (No. 52) is inserted in two
of the spotlights and No. 8 (deep salmon) is placed in
the third. The latter is turned round slightly so that its
beam is focussed on the reveal of the french windows
and the curtains. The light reflected here will indicate
the altered position of the sun and when the other spotlights are dimmed later in the scene, the pink glow on
the window and curtains will be that of the sunset sky.
It will be a matter of choice whether to use the spotlight on the up-stage window in this scene but probably
it will not be noticed if it is taken out.

We have already decided the exterior lighting for the
evening scene in Act 3, and if moonlight is required,
the colour to use is No. 40 (pale blue), which is put
into one or two of the spotlights focussed through the
french windows. In open settings, i.e. those without a
ceiling, the spotlight representing sunlight or moonlight
can be hung above the scene or attached to the fly rail.
The beam of light coming from a high angle is impressive and indicates sunlight as it is normally seen.

DOOR BACKINGS

These should not be overlooked, and even if the door
opens off-stage near the proscenium, some light should

be provided.   There are three methods in use and they
are :

(a) A flood on a stand.

(b) A flood attached to the scenery above the door.

(c) A *length* which is a small batten carrying a number
of white or coloured bulbs.

If a flood is used on a telescopic stand, it should be
extended as high as possible and the shadow directed to
the floor of the stage.   The best position should be
found to avoid throwing shadows of the actors when
they make their entrances.   The arrangement of fixing
a small (500 watt) flood above the door is good, provided it is not too near the top of the door, which will
reflect light if it opens off-stage.   The advantage is that
the flood is out of the way, does not throw shadows
from the actors, and provides even light over the whole
side of the backing.   (Figure 45.)   Lengths are convenient in a scene change as they have a hook at the
end which is quickly slipped over a rail behind one of
the flats.   Colours should be chosen to harmonise with
the acting area, and gold is suitable which may be
dimmed to give a contrasting effect.   The colour of a
length is varied by inserting bulbs which may be amber,
pink, red or blue.   By alternating them with white
bulbs, different shades of colour are obtained.   A length
is used to light the backing seen when the serving hatch
is opened (Up L).

LIGHT FITTINGS

A chandelier, standard or table lamps and wall fittings
are connected to the switchboard and controlled by the
electrician.   By operating them at the switchboard, the
alteration in the stage lighting to correspond with the
lamp is assured.   They should never be switched on or
off by the actor.   He performs the motion of switching
the lamp and waits for a moment with his hand on the
switch until the effect is completed.   The bulbs of light

fittings should be suitably screened in order to avoid dazzling the audience. This can be done by wrapping round the bulb a piece of coloured gelatine. An improved method is to load a 500-watt flood off-stage in circuit with the lamp. In this way the lamp may be set at the correct level by controlling it through a dimmer at the switchboard.

The light switch should be placed near the door on the side it is normally found. Also it should be remembered that there are floor switches for electric fires and lamps. Apart from scenes lit by oil lamps, all interior settings require switches whether they are used or not. The switches are property ones and are not ' practical.'

Gas fittings are improvised by using a 15-watt bulb inside the glass shade. The lamp is wired in circuit with a 500-watt flood off-stage and when the actor holds a lighted match above the globe, the lamp is brought in, fairly bright at first and then reduced with the dimmer. *Oil lamps* are wired similarly and have a pigmy lamp around which a small funnel of gold gelatine is placed to mask its shape. *Candles* are not easy to imitate. Although real ones are sometimes allowed by the fire authority, a candlestick can be made by using a cylinder of white fireproof cardboard to enclose a long shank attached to a bulb holder. A pygmy bulb may be obtained that is shaped to look like a flame and is improved by wrapping a twist of tissue paper around it. *Portable lamps* and candles are wired with batteries. A convenient place, usually in the base, is found to house the battery which is the 4½-volt type. Oil lamps need two or three torch bulbs as one of these small bulbs is not sufficient to indicate the flame. A small switch is included and whenever possible the actor lighting the lamp or candle conceals it with his body.

FIRES

It is not difficult to make a reasonable imitation of a

fire by taking an ordinary grate and fitting one or two electric bulbs covered with a sheet of deep amber and segments of red medium. (No. 33 and No. 6.) Small mesh chicken netting moulded to take coal or coke is built over the filter and the result is quite authentic.

When an electric fire is used, the best kind is the type with a reflector and imitation coal. It frequently contains vanes that revolve in the heat of the lamp to produce a flickering effect and colour in the reflector. The heating elements should be removed as of course they are not required.

A log fire may be made by wrapping linen around chicken wire netting. The linen is painted red and black and a coloured bulb is put inside the log. A few real ones may be added to make up the fire which is mounted on a piece of plywood.

Although the fire will appear real in the fireplace it is not sufficient by itself to give this effect to the audience. And to help the illusion, a baby spotlight is placed on a small stand out of sight to shine through the fireplace opening. It gives the impression of firelight when someone approaches the fire. The spotlight should have colours and Nos. 5A, 6 and 36, if they are cut irregularly, will provide a good combination. In large open fireplaces a small flood is also used to light the fireplace backing and surround. This is placed to shine on the up-stage part of the backing and will give a pleasant glow seen by the audience. (Figure 45.)

The Lighting Rehearsal

When the lighting plan is worked out, a note should be made of all information helpful to the electrician. He will want to know the number and type of spotlights to be used, the floods required for lighting the backings and cloths and details of the F.O.H. spotlights and the footlights with the colours required. The information is taken from the lighting plan and written in the form of a *lay-out plot* shown in Figure 47, and with it, the electrician is able to do a good deal of work in advance which will save valuable time at the rehearsal. He can prepare his equipment, cut mediums and put them in

SPOT BAR   stage left to right.

NO.	1	COLOUR	54	POSITION	L. C.
	2		51		C.
	3		51		UP L.
	4		52		Door Up C.
	5		53		Fireplace R.
	6		52		C.
	7		51		Desk L.
	8		53		UP R.
	9		53		Armchair C.
	10		7		Sofa RC.

Nos. 1 and 7: Patt. 23
Others: — 123

F.O.H.

	1	52	C.
	2	52	RC.
	3	OPEN	LC.
	4	54	C.

FOOTLIGHTS   17 Blue, 7 Pink, 52 Gold.

EXTERIOR WINDOWS L.
  3   1,000-watt Fresnel Spotlights Patt. 243 to cover arc through french windows. OPEN or 52, 40 and one 8.
  3   1,000-watt floods on stands to cover garden backing. 54, 56, 32 and one 9.
  2   1,000-watt floods on brackets above scene to cover sky 17.
  1   500-watt spotlight Patt. 23 on bracket to light through window UP L. OPEN or 52.

EXTERIOR HATCH UP L.
  1   Length amber and white bulbs.

EXTERIOR DOOR C.
  1   500-watt flood on bracket above door. 52.

FIREPLACE R.
      Practical fire.
  1   200-watt flood to light backing. 5A, 6.
  1   250-watt baby spotlight to light through fireplace. 5A, 6, 36.

FITTINGS
      Standard lamp UP R. 2 Brackets at fireplace.
      Anglepoise lamp on table UP L. Switch L of door.

SPECIMEN LIGHTING LAY-OUT PLOT

Figure 47

their frames and he will also know where the stage equipment is used. He provides cables to the dips, mentioned in chapter 5, and arranges circuits to his switchboard.

The first task is to decide the position of the furniture and to mark it on the carpet or stagecloth. This ensures correct placing of furniture at every performance and is vital in relation to the spotlights. A chair out of position can mean that an actor is out of the light focussed upon it.

The spotlights on the No. 1 bar are then adjusted to the positions marked for them on the plan. (Figure 45.) All the spotlights are switched off except the one which is being 'set.' Starting with No. 1 lantern, the electrician takes a ladder and instructs his assistant on the lighting board to switch it on. He loosens the lock-nut and is ready to focus the spotlight. The stage manager, if he is lighting the play, stands in the place marked for the spotlight on his plan and asks the electrician to move the lantern so that it shines directly on him. By looking at the filament and seeing that it is in the centre of the lens, he will know that the spotlight is set in the best position for maximum light. The light is powerful and can be harmful to the eyes so coloured glasses should be used whenever looking directly at the filament. The medium is put into the lantern and the stage manager observes the area on the floor of the stage that is now lit. A wide area indicates a weak projection of light which can be improved by focussing the spotlight. When this is done the electrician tightens the lock-nut so that the lantern is firmly fixed in position.

Sometimes a very concentrated light is needed as, for example, when a spotlight is directed for a special effect on the face of a grandfather clock. The spotlight is focussed to the smallest position and a metal mask with a hole is inserted. This gives a powerful beam directed on to a small area.

Each spotlight along the bar is treated accordingly

and the stage manager moves to all the positions marked
on his plan. Most of the lanterns are set at eye-level,
but sometimes a position will have to be found to cover
an actor when he is standing or sitting. Acting areas
overlapping one another have to be watched for ' dead
spots.' And when spotlights are trained on to adjacent
positions, they should be checked by walking slowly
out of the light of the first spotlight into the second.
If the light is uneven, the position or focussing of the
lanterns will need adjustment.

The use of soft-edge spotlights prevents harsh light
from falling on to the walls of the setting. At times the
light from certain spotlights will be too prominent and
circles of light become evident where they are not
desired. To prevent this, a frosted medium is inserted
with the colour in the frame. It diffuses light over
quite a large area, but strength of light is reduced. To
retain it, a hole is cut in the centre of the frosted medium
which then preserves definition and also softens the
hard edge of the beam.

The spotlights on the stage, in the fireplace and
windows, are the next ones to receive attention. There
may be a chair or sofa near the fire and the stage manager
sits in it while the fire spotlight is trained on him. The
flood to light the fireplace backing is dealt with and the
amount of light decided to give warmth. The spotlights focussed through the window are placed in
position and set to light a certain scene. In the case of
a side window, powerful sunlight across the stage may
shine into the auditorium, out of the acting area, and
the setting of the lantern must be adjusted to prevent it.
Light can also be reflected from mirrors, shiny surfaces
of trays or silver cigarette boxes.

All equipment outside the windows and elsewhere
off-stage should be carefully checked that it is not visible
from the auditorium. The spotlights and floods are
bulky and it is surprising how often we have considered

them safely out of sight when an awkward corner of a flood insinuates itself round the edge of a flat. The scene designer will have considered the space necessary for this equipment and on our plan one flood can be tucked away between the french windows and the smaller window up-stage. Another flood is put above this window, and as it might be in view, it can be hidden behind a small flat painted to resemble an exterior wall.

The actors will make their entrances through the french windows and to avoid shadows the flood down-stage must be on a tall stand. Nothing is more potent in destroying the illusion than if the shadows of actors are seen, particularly on the garden backing, and it takes time before the right position for this flood is found. Shadows may also appear on the backing from the stage lighting. Window panes have a nasty habit of throwing shadows and the way to prevent it is to increase the light on the backing or reduce the stage lighting—often a spotlight that is focussed near the window is the culprit.

The other exterior floods or lengths lighting the door backing are set and points to watch are shadows from the actors, reflection from pictures hung on the backing and light creeping around the edge of the door when it is closed. This may be avoided by attaching a wooden fillet to the back of the reveal which effectively masks light around the architrave.

The various lamps and fittings should be tested from the auditorium for dazzle and smaller bulbs may have to be used. Table lamps should be viewed from the dress circle and if the bulb can be seen through the opening in the top of the shade, a circular piece of frosted gelatine is fitted to diffuse the light.

The F.O.H. spotlights are the last to be set and the A.S.M. stands on the stage while they are adjusted. The stage manager in the auditorium watches his face and has the spotlight focussed for the best position. A shutter may have to be used to cut off light from the edges of the proscenium arch and the black returns masking the sides of the setting. It is also used to over-come the reflection of light near the footlights along the forestage which is often covered with polished lino-leum. Shadows from the F.O.H. spotlights on the back wall of the setting have to be watched and their elevation may need adjustment.

The circuits in the footlights are brought in gradually and there should be sufficient light and no more to balance the overhead lighting on the actors' faces. If the footlights are too bright, the effect is to flatten the other lighting. The A.S.M. should wave his hands slowly above his head, and if shadows from them are seen on the setting, the footlights must be reduced until the shadows disappear. Whenever circuits in the foot-lights are altered, which will occur in different scenes, they are checked for shadows in this way.

The lighting lay-out is now completed, and while the electrician is writing it down, the stage manager looks at the setting to see if anything else requires attention. Does a mirror reflect light in the auditorium? If so, it will need spraying with a strong solution of size. Are there any properties that reflect light? And most important, are there light cracks in the scene? Small pinholes can radiate light surprisingly and canvas on the flats may be thin. If painting the back of the canvas with black paint is not entirely successful, black cloth must be secured to the flat. Where the ceiling meets the top of the flats there is sometimes a small gap which is not seen in normal stage lighting but is visible in a black-out with exterior window lighting. Some canvas attached to the edge of the ceiling to fold down over the flats will prevent light escaping.

All is ready to start lighting the play and the stage manager sits in the auditorium with his script, lighting plan and lay-out plot shown in Figures 45 and 47. The

A.S.M. remains on the stage to convey instructions to the electrician as the lighting board is usually too far away for direct communication to be made. (A hand microphone and long lead in contact with the lighting board is available in many theatres, and see 'remote control console,' chapter 10.) The stage manager asks for a complete black-out and commences to build the lighting for the opening scene. The spotlights are switched on individually and he observes the effect they create. It is useful to do so, as an offending lantern which is perhaps spilling light or causing unwanted reflection is immediately recognised. The exterior floods and spotlights with the F.O.H. spotlights and the footlights are brought in and the stage manager asks the A.S.M. to walk or sit in positions taken by the actors. He should walk slowly from one position to another and the stage manager looks at his face which should be uniformly lit. If there are any dark places, the dimmer of a spotlight may need adjustment, its colour changed or it may have to be reset. There·may be too much light at the window in which case the exterior floods will be adjusted.

Then the general picture of the lighting is considered. Does it convey the lighting at a particular time of day and season of year? It may be helpful to reduce the value of spotlights covering an acting area. Or perhaps the scene appears cold and a warm colour in the footlights is increased or a cold colour reduced. The F.O.H. spotlights also may need attention to give special emphasis to a part of the acting area. When the stage manager is quite satisfied, he asks the electrician to plot what is called the opening or setting light for the scene. Act 1 Sc. 1 is a summer's day and unlikely to need any change in lighting throughout the scene. The electrician is told accordingly which information he notes in his plot.

The day has advanced to early evening in Scene 2 and there will be a change during the scene to suggest sunset.

The colours are altered in the floods and spotlights lighting the windows and the stage manager considers the alteration needed in lighting the acting area to correspond with it. On the whole, the room will have warm or richer shades of colour as opposed to the cold and lighter colour of the previous scene. He will start by reducing the value of the spotlights on the No. 1 bar, bearing in mind that those focussed near the window and on the centre of the stage will be brighter than those at the fireplace. He will, nevertheless, consider that later the sunset effect will occur and therefore he must not dim the lights unduly early in the scene. The No. 7 (light rose) and No. 52 (pale gold) will be the warm colours for the footlights and probably the F.O.H. spotlights will be dimmed just below their maximum light. The A.S.M. can help by taking up important positions that are likely to be affected by the alterations in lighting. Small adjustments may be needed and when completed the opening light for the second scene is plotted by the electrician.

Arriving at the first cue, the stage manager explains exactly what he intends to do. The cue will be a gradual reduction in light to correspond with sunset and the first point to consider will be how long the dim or ' check ' in the lighting will take in stage time. The stage manager indicates a suitable place to start the cue and the A.S.M. marks it in the script with a warning cue a page or so beforehand. If the cue involves much adjustment on the lighting board, the electrician will ask for a fairly long warning so that he has time to prepare his circuits and dimmers. As a rough guide, a page of quarto script plays a little over a minute and unless there are considerable pauses for ' business ' about seven pages will be needed for a cue lasting ten minutes. The electrician is told that the cue should take ten minutes and he plots the change in lighting given to him.

The stage manager may decide to dim the exterior floods lighting the garden backing until the sunset effect is achieved. And the alteration in the interior lighting will be a matter of personal choice. Probably general dimming of the stage lighting will be sufficient although this may make an acting area too dark, in which case the spotlights lighting the area are adjusted accordingly. Alternatively, it may be decided to dim certain spotlights and to follow later with others. The footlights can assist in emphasising the final effect by dimming completely the gold circuit; leaving the pink circuit for extra warmth.

As in all cues of this kind, strict realism is not wanted, but if the lighting ' looks right ' it will be accepted by the audience. When the cue is rehearsed, it is unnecessary to take ten minutes to complete it. It is sufficient to do the cue and leave observation of the exact time to the dress rehearsal. An example of a lighting plot for this scene is shown in Figure 48.

In the following scenes, the electrician consults his lay-out plot, changes the colours in the stage floods and spotlights and plots the opening lighting. For Act 2, the colour change in the exterior floods (No. 56 chocolate) was decided to indicate the autumnal weather and a minor adjustment in the interior lighting will probably be required.

Act 3 is an evening scene and let us suppose that at the beginning the only source of light will be from the small lamp at the work table up-left. If the lamp only is lit, it will not be sufficient to illuminate the acting area around it. And it should be remembered that in the theatre, effects need to be exaggerated in order to appear convincing to the audience in various parts of the auditorium. To overcome the difficulty, additional light is provided from a spotlight covering the acting area. No. 3 spotlight is the one to choose and is controlled with the dimmer to give an apparently natural pool of light which otherwise would emanate from the table lamp. This is an example where strict realism is unobtainable and the illusion provided by the additional source of light is accepted by the audience.

ACT I, Sc. 2.   Summer, early evening.

TO OPEN: SPOT BAR Nos. 1, 2, 3, 4, 6, 7 FULL.
                              5, 8, 9, 10 to 7/8.
                    F.O.H.   Nos. 1, 2, 3 to 7/8.
                              4 FULL.
                    FOOTLIGHTS   Gold and pink circuits as set.
                    EXTERIOR WINDOWS 2 Floods 17.
                                      2   do.   54.
                                      1   do.   9 OUT.
                                      2 Spotlights Patt. 243 52.
                                      1   do.   8 OUT.

                    EXTERIOR DOOR AND SERVING HATCH as set.

                    FIRE   OUT.

CUE 1:   CHECK IN TEN MINUTES.

                    SPOT BAR: Nos. 2, 3, 4, 6 to 7/8.
                              1, 5, 7, 8, 9, 10 to 3/4.
                    F.O.H.   Nos. 3, 4 to 3/4.
                              1, 2 to 1/2.
                    FOOTLIGHTS   Gold circuit to 1/2.

                    EXTERIOR WINDOWS 2 Floods 17 to 3/4.
                                      2   do.   54 to 3/4.
                                      1   do.   9 to FULL.
                                      2 Spotlights 243 52 OUT.
                                      1   do.   8 to FULL.

SPECIMEN LIGHTING PLOT
Figure 48

The lighting may remain for a few moments at the opening of the Act after which a character in the play enters from the centre door and switches on the other fittings. It will probably be done in two parts:

(a) The wall lights on either side of the fireplace.

(b) The standard lamp as shown in Plate 6.

The wall lights indicate the principal source of light at the fireplace and the spotlights covering that area are brought in simultaneously. These will be Nos. 5 and

10 for the sofa area and Nos. 2 and 9 covering the armchair centre. Nos. 1 and 2 F.O.H. spotlights will also be required with a warm circuit in the footlights. The second part of the cue is the standard lamp and with it Nos. 4, 6 and 8 spotlights are switched on. The lighting will now provide conventional realism from the three sources of light in the room. It will, however, leave the area near the windows fairly dark and if an actor is playing a scene in this position, Nos. 1 and 7 spotlights will be needed with the F.O.H. spotlights covering the area. They can be included in the previous cue and if they remain dimmed, the omission of a light source on the stage will not be noticed.

The electrician has to absorb and write down a lot of information during the lighting rehearsal and if time allows, it is good practice to run through the lighting cues again. By doing so, he becomes familiar with them and frequently can find a way of improving his plot by adjustment of circuits and dimmers in the lighting board. The work done at the lighting rehearsal can only really be observed at the dress rehearsal when the actors are moving about the stage and accurate timing is possible. Inevitably there will be alterations and some examples of changes likely to be found necessary are given in chapter 10.

Lighting the Arena Stage

When considering the open stage, it appears that lighting consists in illuminating the centre area from above, rather like a boxing ring, with the lights shielded from the audience. This may be sufficient in theory but something more is needed to emphasise the three-dimensional view of the actor and in practice it is necessary to reproduce as nearly as possible the function of light of the proscenium stage. To do so may seem difficult but the principles used can be adapted to the stage surrounded on all sides by the audience.

In the proscenium stage, lighting is arranged from two divergent sources to give plastic expression to the actor's features. Lighting comes from (a) the front of the house, (b) behind the proscenium from above and the sides; the latter giving the actor increased dimension and (c) overhead or back lighting to light around the actor's form and separate him from his background. By variation in colour and intensity of light, the actor is emphasised in contrast with his fellows and surroundings. It will be seen that four and sometimes five sources of light are in use and equipment is mounted for the arena stage to provide them.

The stage is divided into several acting areas and for each area four or five spotlights in a circle, equally spaced, will light the actor very much as in the proscenium stage. Lighting from above the audience will correspond with front-of-house lighting, side lights will give him increased dimension and lighting from behind will emphasise his form. A centre area is also provided where light is blended in tone and colour from battens mounted in pairs and the flood lighting so provided is particularly valuable when reflected from the acting area.

Spotlights are the Soft-edge Fresnel type with an adjustable beam of from 15° to 45°. The light is gently diffused in the exposed arena stage though in certain circumstances, hard-edge profile spotlights are used when concentrated light near the audience has to be adjusted. For the average size stage, a 500-watt Patt. 123 Baby Fresnel spotlight is recommended with a 250-watt lamp for a smaller stage.

Lighting equipment in full view of the audience is nowadays accepted as part of the open stage technique and the entire area above the stage and audience should be left clear so that spotlights may be mounted to the best advantage. Sometimes the ceiling contains a number of slots through which the spotlights are directed but they are invariably hidden in some positions and the area should be completely free of anything which may obstruct the passage of light to the stage.

One of the advantages of theatre-in-the-round is the ease with which a number of productions may be staged. Without conventional scenery, a repertoire of plays can be interchanged and the stage adapted by refurnishing the acting area. Much therefore depends on lighting and the equipment should be mounted to provide scope for a particular production and at the same time be sufficiently flexible to accommodate others. Personal choice and the architecture of the building will suggest further possibilities but the method illustrated in Figure 49 for mounting the basic equipment can be extended and will give effective and imaginative lighting to meet the requirements of a variety of plays.

An acting area of 20 ft. by 25 ft. is divided into eight lighting areas, each of which is lit independently by spotlights with a ninth area in the centre also covered by battens. The individual area is served by four spotlights around it. This is the basic equipment needed but aisles or gangways in the audience are used for entrances and even for scenes played on them such as a road providing a natural access to a building. When the aisle has sufficient space, an entire scene may be played there and it becomes a form of side stage useful in giving variety to the production. In any event the aisles require additional lighting which is suited to particular needs.

Spotlights are distributed over six bars above the audience and acting area and by arranging them as shown the minimum light will be spilled into the audience. The principle of setting spotlights at an angle of 45° to the actor in the proscenium theatre has to be adjusted. The audience is near to the stage and spotlights directed at this angle from behind will strike the backs of their heads and those in front will shine in their faces. In moving the spotlights to avoid the

LIGHTING THE ARENA STAGE

Figure 49

audience, the new position does not entirely suit the head level of actors playing near the audience. The actor will perhaps be well lit by one spotlight while the other lights his body but not his face. To overcome the difficulty, a third spotlight is directed to reflect light from the floor on to his face as illustrated in Figure 50 and so give the required balance and plastic lighting of his features.

REFLECTED LIGHT FROM 'A' ASSISTS 'B' WHICH HAS BEEN MOVED TO AVOID THE FRONT ROW OF THE AUDIENCE 'D' PERFORMS THE SAME FUNCTION FOR 'C.'

LIGHTING THE ACTOR IN THE ARENA STAGE
Figure 50

The spotlights are set for maximum effect in each area and will not require further adjustment. Lighting can then be spread evenly over the whole acting area; individual areas lit or special areas given a required degree of light using the dimmer control. As the individual areas are relatively small, the four spotlights lighting them may be controlled from one dimmer. However, for improved flexibility one dimmer controlling two spotlights is beneficial, particularly when a subtle effect is required. Additional spotlights will be needed for special effects such as sunlight, light from stage lamps and the varied requirements of a wide range of plays.

Colour is not used in arena lighting to the same extent as in the proscenium stage. The audience is near to the acting area, so colour emphasis of objects and performers is not so necessary. Colour is more generally used for special effects and a three-colour circuit in the battens lighting the centre area will give a colour tone to the entire stage. A further improvement in the basic equipment is in the use of 1,000-watt spotlights directly above the acting area. Downlighting from these helps in providing a change in the mood of lighting and alone can give an ethereal quality difficult to obtain in any other way.

Footlights have not been mentioned as these belong almost entirely to the proscenium stage though the enthusiast could experiment with small sections of the floor removed at the corners of the stage and used to conceal floods or spotlights.

LIGHTING EFFECTS

Many of the effects are projected by a 1,000-watt spotlight converted with a condenser to an optical lantern. A container is attached to the front of the lantern with a glass disc on which the effect is photographed or painted. An electric or clockwork motor revolves the disc and,

OPTICAL EFFECTS LANTERN
Figure 51

as it passes the lens, the moving effect is projected on to a backcloth or cyclorama.   (Figure 51.)

CLOUDS

They are produced by the optical projector and two effects suggesting fleecy or storm clouds may be obtained. By placing grey or straw-coloured filters in front of the lens, an ominous stormy sky is represented.   The effect is projected from the side and is best placed as far as possible from the backcloth.   The speed of the motor can be controlled so that the recurring transit of the clouds is not noticed.   Altering the focus of the lens has the effect of softening the outline of the clouds to give a wind-swept impression.

EXPLOSIONS

They are performed electrically by detonating a number of maroons in an iron tank.   The top of the tank should have strong wire mesh to prevent bits of exploded firework from causing damage.   Great care must be taken in exploding the maroons and the tank placed safely in an isolated place.

FLAMES

Flames are contrived by hanging a small batten with strips of coloured silk near the fireplace backing.   A spotlight is focussed on the silk strips which are kept in motion by an electric fan and the flames are reflected on the side of the fireplace.   For an off-stage effect, a 1,000-watt flood is used with a gold medium and segments of red glued to it.   The flickering is produced by gently shaking a batten with strips of canvas in front of the flood, while at the same time varying the light with the dimmer.   Realistic shadows are made which are projected into a room or on a backcloth.   A method for simulating larger fires is done with the optical projection lantern and revolving slide.

LIGHTNING

A lightning flood giving the effect akin to the photographic flash bulb can be obtained. Formerly lightning sticks were used, consisting of two carbon sticks mounted in well-insulated handles. They were connected to the electric supply and when brought together made excellent flashes of lightning. The fire authorities are not in favour and they are therefore not generally in use. When lightning is supposed to illuminate the interior of a scene, a lightning flood may be attached to the No. 1 spot bar or the flood may be used externally with intermittent flashing of the footlights and a batten. There is also an optical effect to suggest forked lightning.

MIST

Gauze employed to give the impression of mist is described in chapter 6. It is hung in front of a backcloth leaving sufficient room for the floods that are lighting the backcloth from an overhead bar. Lighting for the guaze is provided by floods situated on either side of it down-stage. When the floods lighting the backcloth are on and those lighting the gauze are out, the backcloth will be seen although the gauze is almost invisible. By lighting the gauze, the backcloth becomes indistinct and the impression of mist is obtained.

MOON

This is projected on a backcloth by means of a slide and an optical lantern. If a lantern is not available, the crescent moon is cut out of a fairly large piece of cardboard and glued to the back of the canvas. A spotlight focussed on the aperture from behind the backcloth gives the effect. The cardboard should be sufficiently large to cover the entire area of the beam from the spotlight. Otherwise the shape of the piece of cardboard will be seen.

RAIN AND SNOW

These effects are described in chapter 7 and are also realised with the optical lantern and revolving disc.

SEA

There is an optical projector giving the effect of waves or rippling water and one for submarine effect. It consists of two glass slides, painted with waves or ripples, made to move over one another in reciprocating action and projected through the optical lantern. A simpler device that does not require an effects projector is a case containing a metal tube having small cuts which revolve slowly around a lamp. Intermitting flashes of sparkling water are projected and it is suitable for close projection behind a ground row.

SMOKE

This is produced by placing slow or quick burning smoke powder over the element of a *smoke box*. When the current is switched on, the element is heated and the powder burns, giving off medium smoke or thick clouds. A *flash box* is used in this way for the sudden puff of smoke on the entrance of the magician in pantomime.

SPECIAL EFFECTS

An interesting transformation can be produced by painting a gauze with the same scene as that painted on a backcloth though in a different season of the year. For example, the backcloth may be a view of a street scene in summer and the gauze is painted to show the rooftops and streets covered in snow. In a cross-fade, the floods lighting the backcloth are dimmed out and those lighting the gauze brought in. The effect is quite spectacular when summer is transformed imperceptibly to winter.

Ghosts and the picture that comes to life are produced

in the same way. For a spectre to materialise, the canvas in part of the scene is replaced by gauze. It is painted in colours to match the surroundings and is invisible under normal stage lighting. Black velvet is hung at the back of the gauze, enclosing it, and strip lights are attached out of sight at either side. Whoever is performing the apparition takes up his position in good time and at the crucial moment the strip lighting is brought in. Part of the scene dissolves and the ghost appears in bodily form. It is sometimes necessary for the actor to cover his face which may be visible while awaiting his cue.

In a recent production, the entire scene indicating the interior of a house was painted on gauze apart from the architectural framework. At the end of the play, the lighting was dimmed and in a dramatic finale a magnificent garden appeared enclosing what remained of the original scene.

STARS

A permanent cyclorama sometimes has stars included to be illuminated when required. They can be reproduced very well by attaching strings of low wattage bulbs to the back of a skycloth.

ULTRA-VIOLET LIGHT

This is mentioned in chapter 2 and is light that only becomes visible when projected on an object painted with liquid or clothed in material susceptible to this light. It is used humorously when dancers wearing black tights have skeletons painted on them invisibly with ultra-violet paint. The stage lights are dimmed, leaving the ultra-violet light, and a chorus of skeletons performs a macabre frolic.

Special lanterns are used which must be switched on some time before the Ultra-Violet effect is produced. Details are included in a booklet entitled *Black Light* obtainable from the Strand Electric Co. Ltd.

In lighting as in everything else in the theatre, it is best to avoid elaborate and costly flights of the imagination. Try to visualise clearly what the author had in mind when describing his scene. If his idea is followed and the lighting constructed with integrity, it will do much to enhance the production. And it may be observed that often a work is praised not only for its wealth but also for its economy.

CHAPTER 9

THE WARDROBE

'At this point remind God, who is underneath the hall of
Paradise, to have two angels bring with them two fur robes
which will be ready, to give to Adam and Eve when He returns
to the Earthly Paradise.'—*Mons* script.

THE wardrobe is the centre of that part of the production most intimately associated with the artists—
their clothes. Apart from her knowledge of dressmaking
and repair, the *wardrobe mistress* understands the
importance artists attach to their dress and her personal
attention is of great value. When taking up her duties,
she will need a complete *wardrobe* or *costume plot*. It is
prepared by the stage manager who, at the earliest
opportunity during rehearsals, obtains all details from
the designer. Whether or not it is a failing of human
nature, the fact remains that some designers are sensitive
about revealing their creative ideas at an early stage. It
is up to the stage manager to continue with his enquiry,
for much of the time occupied later in rehearsals may be
saved by early preparation of the costume plot. Figure 52
provides details of the information a costume plot
should contain.

Where costumes are not specifically designed for a
play, they are hired from a theatrical costumier. Here
the stage manager assumes additional responsibility;
sometimes acting as guide to artist and producer. Often
no one has a very clear idea of what is wanted and by
collating the information and discussing it with an
experienced wardrobe mistress, the essential requirements are obtained. Rehearsals must not be interrupted
for artists to be measured and fitted for their costumes.
The stage manager advises the costumier when the artists

Artist	Character	Act I	Act II	Act III
Mr. Lord	The Mayor	Wig, Cravat, Embroidered waistcoat. Georgian silk coat. Breeches. White stockings. Buckle shoes. Tricorne hat. Mayoral chain. Silver-topped black stick.	As Act I with plain coat.	Torn coat. Wig which has not been dressed.
Mr. Roberts	Ernest the Policeman	Country policeman's uniform. Truncheon hanging on belt at back. Whistle on chain.	—	Dented helmet torn jacket,
Mr. Frost	Mr. Growser	Dickensian coat with check waistcoat and trousers. Stovepipe hat. Check muffler. Elastic side boots. Umbrella.	As Act I with yachting cap.	Torn coat.
Mr. de Vise	The Inventor	Dickensian brown coat. Coloured waistcoat. Plain trousers. White collar with cravat. Black shoes.	Overalls. Check shirt open at neck.	Torn overalls used at end of Act II.

etc.

WARDROBE AND COSTUME PLOT

Figure 52

will be free and a rota of appointments is arranged. He
keeps in touch with the costumier throughout rehearsals,
who informs him of progress.

In small productions, where everyday clothes are
worn, there is not much for a wardrobe mistress to do,
but in costume and musical plays her duties are essential.
They are:

(a) Checking the receipt of costumes and wigs to
ensure that all have arrived and arranging for
their return at the end of the run of the play.

(b) Supervision for cleaning and repair of clothes used
in the production and the periodic return of wigs
for dressing to the wig makers.

(c) At the dress rehearsal and every performance,
ensuring that the artists have all the articles of
clothing they require.

(d) Being ready to perform emergency repairs at any
moment during the performance.

(e) When costumes are made in the theatre, purchase
of the necessary materials, engagement of assistants
and supervision of the work in making the
costumes.

(f) Securing the costumes so that under no circumstances are they removed from the theatre during
the run of the play.

The dress or costume can be essential to the success
of an artist's performance and it may be designed for a
special purpose in colour or style to enhance the grouping of characters in a part of the play. The designer
advocates the costume chosen, but it is worn by the
artist—who may know or feel that the colour or proportion does not become her. The wardrobe mistress
with a tactful suggestion often provides a solution
acceptable to all concerned, and if she herself is a former
actress, as many of them are, is worth her weight in
gold.

The success of period costumes does not lie entirely

in the design or the way they are made. How they are worn can make all the difference, and to an actor the ability to wear costume with conviction is just as important as the delivery of his lines. Rehearsal in the costume is often a necessary part of his equipment left to the last moment. In pantomime, when artists take the parts of animals, the costume or 'skin' must be provided as soon as possible. Otherwise the actor may be unfortunate enough to find his face trapped inside the animal mask and he is unable to utter a word of his part. Swords, long sticks, cloaks, crinoline hoops, muffs and parasols are some of the articles essential to rehearsal and if the original is unobtainable a substitute should be provided. An actor wearing period clothes needs more room in which to move than in everyday clothes, and if this is not realised he may trip over his sword, or his spurs may interlock, to a round of laughter in the audience.

Although the stage manager is not expected to have specialised knowledge, it may be helpful to know that line, colour and material are the three basic elements in the design of stage costumes. The line or silhouette of the garment will be noticed by the audience in preference to the material or fine decoration. Each period has its own line and contour to arrive at a particular silhouette and it is worth examining the design closely to discover how it is achieved. A costume merely embellished with trimmings to recall the period will remain fancy dress unless the line is indicated. The colour of the costume is related to the setting in which it is seen and blended or contrasted accordingly. It is also used to emphasise the plot or character in the play. In *The Barretts of Wimpole Street* the father in dark clothes is a sombre figure in contrast with the colours worn by his children.

The colour of materials should always be examined in stage lighting. Blue, for instance, undergoes a considerable change when pink or amber in the lighting is predominant. It should be remembered that costumes are not subject to close inspection and the overall impression should be stressed rather than the relative texture of the material. Rough, loosely woven fabrics with stencilled design that hang well can often vindicate the use of a cheap material which under stage conditions appears rich and beautiful.

THE COSTUME PARADE

During the week before the dress rehearsal, the costumes should be assembled and worn by the artists. It is usual to make a special call for the *costume parade* which is held in stage lighting. If the scenery is not available, the stage manager arranges some form of backing. The dress parade is organised in scenes and individual dresses are approved in addition to the general ensemble. This is important in productions for which costumes are specially designed and affords an opportunity of judging colour so that anything clashing may be altered in good time. Make-up should be used to judge the complete effect. Costumes having voluminous cloaks, crinolines and tall head-dresses should be tried out for the space they need through doors and other entrances. The right shoes must be worn, for frequently an artist has to become accustomed to them; more paces and smaller strides being needed when wearing costume than in everyday attire.

The stage manager notes observations made by the director which he gives to the wardrobe mistress and costumier. His assistant arranges the order in which the costumes are inspected, and if artists are likely to be recalled, he warns them to remain in their costumes until a final decision is made. Costumes that are well designed and made are an asset to any production and the director and designer will be alert to the smallest detail. An actor content with his clothes is able to give of his best in performance.

DRESSING ROOMS

Allocation of dressing rooms is arranged by the stage manager. In professional companies the order of billing (i.e. the precedence artists take in the advertising matter) is a guide to the sequence of rooms. There are times when artists have equal billing and in this event a ruling is obtained from the management. In amateur companies the importance of the parts played by the artists will be the guide. Only rarely are there enough rooms for them to be allocated individually. When they are shared or there is a choice between a large and a small room, the larger room is given to the artist requiring more accommodation for costumes. Each artist should have enough space to make up seated comfortably before a mirror well supplied with lights. An armchair is appreciated and an artist playing a long part often likes to rest on a couch. When the rooms are allotted a list is made out and placed on the notice board. This will include the numbers of the rooms and the names of the artists occupying them. Copies are given to the manager and to the wardrobe mistress. The company and stage manager has a room for use as an office and it is usual to provide one for the musical director. The orchestra is normally accommodated in a room not far from the orchestra pit called the *band room*. Each dressing room should have the number clearly indicated and a small label with the names of the artists using the room is typed and attached to the door.

DRESSERS

They take the place of a valet and apart from looking after his clothes, the industrious ones perform additional duties as personal assistant to the artist. The actor's job is exacting and to be relieved of the worrying small details concerning make-up and dress is of immense value to anyone of artistic temperament. This is especially recognised by leading players who sometimes engage their personal dressers at home as well as in the theatre in order to retain their services. Dressers are valued not only by the artists but also by the management. An expensive dress left lying about a room can quickly become unserviceable unless placed on a hanger and covered with a cloth. The wardrobe mistress often dresses one of the principals and is in charge of the other dressers. In elaborate productions, dressers are shared; one dresser being allocated to six chorus artists. The artists should dress in adjacent rooms so that dressers can save time and energy in looking after them. Amateur stage managers are strongly advised to organise dressers from willing members of the society. Their assistance can greatly help the presentation of the show and will be repaid in the appearance of the artists.

CLEANING AND REPAIR OF COSTUMES

The wardrobe should be a large room with enough space for storing, cleaning and repair of costumes. Duplicates are provided of articles requiring day-to-day cleaning such as shirts, lace collars, ruffs and tights, and a laundry or cleaning firm known to the theatre will collect after an evening performance and return articles the next day. As they are essential to the performance, the wardrobe mistress takes great care of them and in the case of an individual item she washes or cleans it herself. Manufacturers of washing machines, powders and spin dryers, interested in theatre advertising, supply their equipment free of charge for a credit line in the programme.

Wigs are kept on wig blocks in the dressing rooms and the dresser brings them to the wardrobe occasionally for attention. When they require dressing, the wardrobe mistress returns them to the wig-maker. Several measurements are required for a wig to provide

the artist with one of the right shape and size.   The
wig-maker supplies a chart which includes measurements
as follows:

    (1) Circumference of the head.

    (2) Front hair line to nape hair line.

    (3) Ear to ear over the top of the head.

    (4) Temple to temple around back of the head.

    (5) Across the nape.

    (6) Top of the ear to the nape.

    (All measurements from the hair line.)

During long runs, costumes become worn and need
renewal.   The wardrobe mistress repairs them as far as
possible and when a new one is required she advises the
stage manager who informs the management.

CHAPTER 10

THE DRESS REHEARSALS

' Remember at this point to remind a painter to go to Paradise to paint Raphael's face red.'—Mons script.

THE final week of rehearsal arrives and with it an urgency and lively sense of anticipation that was absent during the earlier weeks when moves and business were plotted and the actors were studying their parts. The director and stage manager have previously decided the number of dress rehearsals which depends on a variety of factors. If the play is fairly straightforward, in one setting, it will probably be sufficient to arrange a rehearsal in the setting for the actors to get to know the entrances and position of furniture, then a lighting and effects rehearsal, followed by one full dress rehearsal. However some directors insist on rehearsals in the setting throughout the final week before the first night.

If the play is a musical one or has a number of scene changes involving technical rehearsals, several dress rehearsals will be required. A short provincial tour is normally included before a play is presented in London. With the knowledge that it will be performed before an audience for some weeks, the director often decides that one provincial dress rehearsal will be sufficient. It is of course different for amateur companies, and although the ideal number of dress rehearsals is three, the amateur company frequently has to be content with one, because the hall is booked or it is difficult to assemble the cast.

There are, however, certain preliminary details which must not become part of the dress rehearsal to avoid keeping the actors waiting while they are completed, i.e. scenery must be set and scene changes rehearsed, the lighting rehearsed and time given for rehearsal of effects. There will be a *Band Call* for the orchestra to rehearse the music and if the play has recorded music, the entire repertoire is played for overture, incidental and interval music with the volume of the F.O.H. and stage speakers approved by the director. Finally the head flyman will be told the speeds for the curtain at the beginning and end of each scene by the stage manager.

When the technical side is completed, the company is called and shown over the setting. Special features are indicated such as the way windows open and close, where the light switches are placed, and the position of furniture and location of spotlights in particular scenes. At this time, the actors will get the ' feel ' of the theatre from its size and situation of seats. Don't be surprised if they declaim lines to test their voices. Acoustics vary considerably and the voice sounds strange after rehearsing on a bare stage or in a room.

THE PROMPT CORNER

This corresponds to the bridge of the ship and is where the mechanical side of the play is controlled. It is usually in the down-stage corner on the left of the stage facing the audience. In some theatres, where space was limited, the lighting board was installed on the opposite side of the stage and therefore the prompt corner may also be found there. (See Figure 9.)

It includes a desk for prompting and a small board containing a number of switches with miniature light bulbs by which the stage manager gives his cues. Each switch and light bulb communicates with a distant part of the stage. The switches are labelled and for instance, if the one marked CURTAIN is switched on, a light also appears at the point where the head flyman controls the curtain. There are two switches and two lights for each point. One is marked WARNING and operates a red lamp. The other is marked GO and switches on a green lamp. The lamps are wired in circuit so that a green lamp switched on in the prompt corner also lights a green lamp where the cue is performed. The stage manager is therefore certain that if his lamp is alight, a lamp of the same colour lights up at that part of the stage labelled on his board.

In this manner the two switches and lamps communicate firstly a warning or stand-by cue and secondly the cue on which the appropriate action is taken. The stage hand receiving the signal performs the cues in the order given him in his plot and the system normally prevents any possibility of a mistake. Always remember to switch off the light directly the cue is passed so that it is ready for the following one.

The positions controlled from the prompt corner are labelled as follows: CURTAIN, ELECTRICS, STAGE R, STAGE L, FLIES R, FLIES L, ORCHESTRA and FRONT OF HOUSE. There are usually one or two spare switches with cue lights for positions under the stage or elsewhere used for special effects. Cue boards vary in different theatres and it is advisable to ask the local stage manager to explain his board.

A telephone is installed connecting the stage manager with all parts of the theatre and he can also speak to staff at special positions such as the flymen, the stage door and the orchestra. The latest form of lighting control board is the remote control console which is installed behind the dress circle or the stalls. From this vantage point, the electrician can see the play through a window which formerly he was prevented from doing when the lighting board was built at the side of the stage. The stage manager communicates with him through a microphone and gives his cues verbally. It is a two-way system and the electrician can also speak to the prompt corner.

To warn the audience that the play is about to start, the stage manager announces through a microphone and amplifier connected to speakers in the front of the theatre, or he has a bell-push attached to his board that rings the *Bar Bells*. The theatre manager usually tells the stage manager the number of bells to ring so that those in the bars have time to finish their drinks and return to their seats. Three, two and one minute warnings are normally given.

Although the stage manager is in executive control of the stage, the deputy stage manager 'runs the corner.' He is the member of the stage management team nearest to the performance and consequently one on whom much of the responsibility rests. He (or she) has marked the script during rehearsals, prompted the actors, observed them as they studied their parts and has watched the play grow from the original reading to the ultimate goal of the first night. The D.S.M. is in the prompt corner throughout the performance and, in addition to prompting, gives the signals to the stage departments. The assistant stage manager helps him and later shares the task of prompting.

PROMPTING

The prompt corner is hidden from the audience by the tormentor and in order to see the stage, an aperture is cut in it which may be covered by a hinged flap or gauze. In theatres with a large proscenium opening, prompting is not always possible from the corner which is quite a distance from the edge of the setting. A view of the acting area is needed not only for prompting but also for the timing of cues. Where this is difficult, a small opening is cut in a flat through which the prompter has a better view. It should be made in a position not easily observed by the audience and often can be hidden behind a projection of part of the scene. The hole should be at a convenient height for the prompter to look through when seated. It is made about the size of an envelope and cut on three sides so that the canvas may be replaced when the flat is used again. It is covered with gauze glued to the back of the flat. A small mirror held at an angle to reflect the setting can be helpful when there is an awkward line of sight from the prompt corner.

In complicated settings the prompter may have to move anywhere around the stage. Sometimes he can see through the opening of a fireplace and even may have to hide behind a ground row. Where cues are difficult to operate from the prompt corner an alternative arrangement must be made. The D.S.M. has a length of electric wire, one end of which is attached to his cue board and the other wired to a switch. He looks through the opening in the setting and gives the cue by pressing the switch. Prompting and the timing of cues are important and it is essential for the stage manager to see that any difficulty is overcome before starting the dress rehearsal.

The Call Boy

Towards the end of rehearsals, the D.S.M. enters the calls for the artists in the prompt script. A call is judged to allow the artist sufficient time to get from his dressing room to the stage for his entrance. It is given a number and a line of dialogue to identify it. The calls are copied into the *call book* and show
>
> (a) The number of the call
> (b) The dialogue cue
> (c) The name of the artist to be called.

It is handed to the call boy and the prompter tells him to call by giving him the number. The dialogue cue is helpful as an experienced call boy will pick up the line when he hears it and hurry off to call the artists without being told to do so.

In addition to personal calls, the call boy warns the company at half an hour, a quarter of an hour and five minutes before the beginning of the overture. He walks round all the dressing rooms knocking and calling: 'Half an hour, please,' which warns the artists that the overture will start in half an hour. This is followed by the other routine calls, and if the overture is a short one, the final call: 'Overture and beginners, please,' will be timed between five and ten minutes before the rise of the curtain. This is arranged to allow the artists who begin the play enough time to reach the stage. When they have arrived, the call boy reports to the D.S.M. that the artists are ready. Artists should always acknowledge their calls and the call boy is told to wait until this is done.

Directly the play has started, the call boy makes another round of the dressing rooms calling: 'Curtain up.' During the intervals he waits for the stage manager, who will ask him to call artists beginning the next act. The call boy goes to the dressing rooms calling: Act 2 beginners, please,' which he repeats during the next interval for Act 3. Matinees are called at the end of the evening performance on the previous day and he calls: 'Matinee tomorrow, please.' The stage manager also asks him to warn artists about understudy and other rehearsals.

In many theatres a 'cue-call' system is installed in the prompt corner. It consists of a microphone connected with a loudspeaker in each dressing room and usually another microphone situated near the footlights enables artists to hear the performance. The stage manager can speak to a particular dressing room and with some instruments the artist is able to acknowledge the call by using a switch in the dressing room. A bulb lights up in the prompt corner advising the stage management that the call is heard. The system dispenses with the call boy but adds to the responsibility of the stage manager. Like all electrical equipment it can be erratic; fuses and bulbs are known to fail and sometimes the volume control in the dressing room is turned down and the artist has difficulty in hearing the call. Although there is a saving in expense, it is never a substitute for a good call boy whose assistance is invaluable to artists and staff.

THE ORCHESTRA

To call the members of the orchestra a bell-push in the prompt corner rings a bell in the band room. Access to the orchestra pit is from under the stage and the band room is usually near to it. A stage manager who understands music is fortunate as he can give cues by following the score. Otherwise cues are given him by means of a buzzer connected to a bell-push operated by the conductor. A system is arranged between them indicating one buzz for the house lights to be dimmed and two buzzes for the curtain to rise, and so on. Where the curtain has to rise on a music cue, the stage manager counts the bars of music preceding it and times the cue accordingly.

THE DRESS REHEARSAL

If it is possible to have three dress rehearsals the method of running them is as follows:

1st   A run-through with notes given by the director at the end of each scene, and if a mistake occurs, stopping the rehearsal to correct it.

2nd   A run-through of the whole play with notes at the end.

3rd   Performing the play as if the audience were present. In some cases an audience is invited to this rehearsal.

Before the dress rehearsal, the technical side of the production has been completed and this is the first time that it will be rehearsed with the actors. The play is run through to the end of each scene, and although mistakes are bound to happen, the stage manager only asks the director to stop the rehearsal if he is unable to make an unobtrusive correction himself. When something of the kind occurs the difficulty is examined and put right before the rehearsal continues. In starting again it is usual to choose a suitable place just before the mistake happened and the stage manager has to be quite sure that everyone understands the point at which the play is resumed. To do this he calls out loudly: ' Going back to the entrance of Professor Higgins,' or whatever place is chosen. The electrician checks his cue sheet to decide that the lighting is correct and the actors, the flymen, the call boy and the prompter all start again at the same place. It is important for the stage manager to take action in this way as otherwise someone may be performing his task out of turn, with an unexpected and explosive consequence. When the stage manager is quite content that all are ready, he tells the actor to start once more and the rehearsal continues.

Difficulties that may be encountered are that the presence of the scenery makes it hard for a cue to be heard and an actor misses his entrance. In this event a cue light is attached to the scene near the entrance and connected to the prompt corner. The prompter switches on the light at the right moment and the actor enters. The quick change room on the stage may be too far away for an actor to do a complicated change of clothes and it is necessary to build a substitute nearer to the scene. This is usually made up of two book flats with a table, mirror and a light. A further problem may be the time needed for a change of scene. The stage staff pride themselves in completing a scene change quickly but it may be a physical impossibility to do it in the allocated time. The stage manager must decide and if he considers that the next scene will not be ready when the cue arrives, he arranges with the director to include extra dialogue or music while it is being done.

At the end of each scene, the stage manager should see that everyone concerned in the scene is present for the director to give his notes and if they are likely to involve the staff, the heads of departments including the wardrobe mistress should also be there. The curtain is raised and any part requiring alteration is run again. While notes are being given all activity stops and the rehearsal is only resumed when the director has finished and the stage manager gives instructions for it to continue. If the scene is followed by a quick change of scene, the last few lines are replayed, the curtain rung down and the scene change done under working conditions.

The stage manager should always be aware of safety and this is especially necessary with equipment in use while the cast is on the stage. In a change of scene, space is limited and accidents must be avoided. The artists should be warned in advance of anything that might be dangerous, such as a difficult piece of scenery being moved quickly to the wings, and he does everything possible to help artists and staff by advising them that care is needed.

After the dress rehearsal, the stage manager goes over details with the heads of departments and the company is given the rehearsal call for the following day. Much of the stage manager's job at a dress rehearsal and perform-ance consists of thinking ahead. Some provide them-selves with their own plots and at a glance they can see what comes next and be ready for it. But in any case the habit of being alert to what might happen before it does is a valuable asset and often a mistake can be prevented by being forewarned. At the first dress rehearsal patience is required for everyone has to become accustomed to their task which would prove tiring and exhausting without the co-operation needed in achieving a good performance.

LIGHTING

During the dress rehearsal, the electrician and the prompter giving the cues will be doing their jobs for the first time and technical difficulties are bound to occur. The prompter may not be able to see an actor when he is switching on a light and a solution has to be found. Lighting cues may follow one another too quickly.

The electrician, faithfully dimming the general lighting in ten minutes, finds that the next cue is given before he has completed the first one.   The lighting is being seen in relation to the actors and it may be that a cue is performed leaving an actor in comparative darkness while he is doing something important.

Adjustments will be needed and at the end of the scene the cues are tried again.   The lighting should be considered from the point of view of all seats in the theatre and it is better to have lighting that appears bright from the front rows than that an impenetrable gloom appears to those seated at the back of the theatre.   Finally a decision should be reached with the electrician about the lighting in the front of the house.   The footlights are brought in slowly as the overture starts and when it is finished, the house lights are dimmed gradually and the footlights adjusted for the opening scene.   As the curtain rises, the F.O.H. spotlights are brought in to avoid an unpleasant glare on the curtain which otherwise would make the audience aware of them.   These may seem small details but make for agreeable presentation of the play.

The Time and Report Sheet

Timing of each scene and interval in the play is important.   It is used by the director to confirm that a scene is played at a constant speed.   The catering department need to know when the intervals occur to prepare the bars and there are telephone calls to the box office and the stage door enquiring when the play starts and finishes.   During rehearsals, when scenes are played through for the first time, the D.S.M. begins to time the play by noting the beginning and end of each scene.   He continues to time them during the first dress rehearsal and makes allowance for pauses when dialogue is replayed, though this is not easy as frequently he is busy with his own work.   It is only possible to obtain accurate timing when the play is run through to the end without interruption. His time sheet takes the following form:

Title of Play:　　　　Date and number of performance:

Overture	Up 7.30	Down 7.34	Time 4	Interval
Act i, Scene i	7.34	7.59	25	2
Scene 2	8.01	8.16	15	10
Act ii	8.26	8.58½	32½	12
Act iii, Scene i	9.10½	9.23	12½	1
Scene 2	9.24	9.47	23	
		Total	112	25

TOTAL PLAYING TIME　112
　　　　　　　　　　　　25
　　　　　　　　　　137 = 2 hours 17 minutes.

REMARKS: Miss Worthington absent. The part of 'Honey-bunch' was played by Miss Lightfoot. 5 calls and speech.

TIME SHEET
Figure 53

Although a stop watch is invaluable for accurate timing, there is usually a clock in the prompt corner with the minutes clearly marked, and the stage manager will find that working to half a minute is sufficient for his purpose. The time sheet is helpful in the later running of the play for the evidence of the clock does much to dispel argument when the playing time of a scene or timing of business is disputed. Timing of the play is usually recorded in a firmly bound exercise book which may be consulted as required, although some managements like to see the daily time and report sheet in which case it is forwarded each evening. Clocks and watches used by the stage management are checked for accuracy with the telephone or radio time signal before each performance.

THE FINAL DRESS REHEARSAL

Whether or not an audience is present, this rehearsal is taken as if it were an actual performance. The entire play is performed according to plan and the times recorded. Nothing is allowed to interrupt it, and if a mistake occurs, the play continues and whatever post-mortem may be required is held after the final curtain. The stage manager and his assistants meet when the half-hour is called. In order to be fully prepared, it is called thirty-five minutes before the time arranged to start the dress rehearsal, and the other calls, quarter of an hour, etc., are also advanced by five minutes.

Meanwhile the stage manager looks over the scene to confirm that the furniture and properties are in position and sees that the staff are prepared. By this time the electrician is setting his lighting board and the stage manager asks him to switch on the stage spotlights one at a time. In scene changes, a tall flat taken across the stage can sometimes strike one of the spotlights knocking it out of position. By checking them he will be quite sure they are set correctly and if one is out of position there is time for the electrician to bring his ladder to reset it.

When ' Overture and Beginners ' is called, the deputy stage manager rings the band room bell. Shortly afterwards, the members of the orchestra file into the orchestra pit and the electrician puts on the footlights. The artists beginning the play arrive on the stage and the call boy reports that all are present. At this point the stage manager is ready to commence the rehearsal, but before doing so, he goes into the auditorium to obtain permission from the director. When he returns to the prompt corner, the D.S.M. switches on the ' warning ' signals for the orchestra, electrician and the curtain. After a quick glance round to see that all is well, he puts on the ' go ' signal for the orchestra, who strike up the overture, and he asks the electrician to set the stage lighting.

The D.S.M. records the beginning of the overture in his time sheet and at three, two and one minutes before the end of the overture, he rings the bar bells. He has previously obtained the length of the overture from the conductor and therefore is able to time it as it is played. The overture is finished and after a moment for applause, the D.S.M. says: ' House Lights,' and the electrician dims the lights in the auditorium and sets the footlights for the opening scene. Normally he announces that the F.O.H. lighting is out as it is not always possible to see if this is so from the prompt corner. The D.S.M. warns the artists who are starting the play and then gives the signal to take up the curtain.

The foregoing remarks apply just as well when recorded music is used. Sometimes music is specially chosen as *curtain music*, and whether it is played by the orchestra or recorded, it should not be commenced without a signal from the stage manager. At the last moment an emergency may arise, such as an artist finding that something important has been left in the dressing room and time is needed to collect it. The D.S.M. telephones the conductor or has a pre-arranged signal to flash his warning light a few times. The conductor arranges to play additional music and the curtain music is started only when he receives a further signal from the prompt corner.

CURTAIN CALLS

At the end of the play, the curtain is rung up and

down for the artists to receive their well-earned applause. The *curtain calls* must be organised beforehand and it is usual for the director to plan them with the stage manager. A typed list is pinned to the notice board and for complicated calls the A.S.M. takes a copy to the dressing rooms for the artists to study in advance. The curtain calls may be taken with the whole company assembled in line and the leading players in the centre. To provide variety, they are sometimes rearranged so that artists appear in groups of two or three until the star takes a call alone. Thereafter the entire company acknowledges further applause.

A *picture call* is given immediately following the final curtain as, for instance, when artists are grouped in character to illustrate a particular scene. The curtain calls are rehearsed at the end of the dress rehearsal, and as the stage manager is listening to the applause, the A.S.M. can help by seeing that artists are ready at the side of the stage or other entrances. It is customary to have brighter lighting for curtain calls and the stage manager signals for it to the electrician when the curtain falls on the play or after the picture call.

After the dress rehearsal, the director gives the artists his notes and usually leaves the day of the first night free for recuperation. With all the additional effort of a full dress rehearsal there may be mistakes in the lines and the director calls a *word rehearsal* on the following day for the artists to refresh their memory. It is held in a bar in the front of the theatre where they go through the play mainly for words. Otherwise the stage manager dismisses the company and gives them the time the curtain will rise on the first night. He goes through his notes with the heads of departments and organises the work for the morning, which will probably include retouching of the scenery, adjustment to the lighting and minor alterations to properties and costumes.

THE FIRST NIGHT AND RUNNING THE PLAY

'The actors outdid themselves. The stage was remarkable for its painted scenery . . . and for the great curtain that rose and fell all of a sudden.'—Jesuit theatre 1623.

THE author's idea has occupied the thoughts and efforts of many over several weeks and the presentation of the play is put to the test of an audience for the first time. The performance marks a division in the routine production of the play. The work of the director is finished and the responsibility for running the play is handed over to the stage manager. His duties have taken him away from rehearsals and consequently he needs time to gain an intimate knowledge of the production. The director normally sees the play during one or more performances after it has opened and his presence is helpful to the stage manager in observing details of acting and production. As mentioned in chapter 3, the first night also marks a change in the finance of the play when the production account ceases and the running account begins.

The stage manager entering the stage door on the first night finds the telegrams for the artists wishing them good luck, and those addressed to the company are pinned to the notice board. On the stage he finds everything awaiting the rise of the curtain. The first scene is set, properties are ready on the stand-by tables in the wings and the electrician is testing the spotlights, floods and other lighting equipment. The furniture and properties are checked and the call boy starts to make his calls. The artists are usually in the theatre in good time but the stage-door keeper records their arrival, and should there be any absentees when the half-hour is called, he tells the stage manager, who informs the understudy and the front-of-house manager. The A.S.M. goes round the dressing rooms to confirm that the artists have their hand properties, and the stage manager also visits them to give his personal greeting for their success. The procedure for the dress rehearsal is followed and from the other side of the curtain comes the sound of conversation as the audience enters the theatre.

A first night is like none other. The dramatic critics are invited, there are social celebrities and avid first-nighters with friends of the artists and the management. It is sometimes difficult to get them to their seats and the stage manager rings the bar bells at intervals of one minute until he receives word from the theatre manager that most of the audience is there and the overture may be started.

The artists arrive on the stage and in the prompt corner the deputy stage manager opens his script. Red lights warning the electrician and the curtain shine from his cue board. In a moment he will give the signal for the rise of the curtain and everything else that follows throughout the play will be in his care. It may be the first time he has managed a play in London. The artists rely on him for their cues and effects and many others, from the author to the management, place their trust in his ability to control the production which on this—the first night—must be played at its best. He may be pardoned for thinking about his task and feeling perhaps:

> ' Like one that on a lonesome road
> Doth walk in fear and dread,
> And having once turned round, walks on,
> And turns no more his head;
> Because he knows a frightful fiend
> Doth close behind him tread.'

His reward comes the following morning when he opens

his newspaper and reads that the critic likes the play; even thinks it may run, and he can look forward to some months when he will be happily engaged knowing that his efforts are brought to a successful conclusion.

The first night is of course an exciting event, everyone is keyed to give the finest performance and under these circumstances a small deviation may cause a mistake. When it happens the stage manager must decide if it is wise to correct it or better to carry on. Sometimes mistakes observed by those on the stage are not apparent to the audience whose interest is directed elsewhere and they may be safely overlooked. In any case, it is better to continue than make a correction that is advertised to the audience. The curtain calls are likely to create excitement and the stage manager has to exercise judgement in listening to the applause. They should continue until he decides that the applause justifies one more curtain. At this point it is time to finish and he gives the signal for the house lights. This is the cue for the orchestra to play the National Anthem, followed by a short piece of music called a ' chaser,' played while the audience leave the theatre.

UNDERSTUDIES

Immediately the artists are engaged the question of understudies for them arises. Those understudying the leading players and important supporting artists are engaged to attend rehearsals at the earliest opportunity, and as rehearsals continue the list is completed. An actor may be required to understudy two or more parts and is called a *walking understudy* if he is engaged solely to understudy. Otherwise he appears in crowd scenes or plays a small part. During rehearsals, the understudy carefully notes the director's instructions, writes down the moves and records alterations in the principal's part. Before the first night he should have memorised the part and have a working knowledge of it sufficient to appear.

Every effort should be made to give the understudies at least one rehearsal before the play opens, and after the first night they should be rehearsed regularly in order to become thoroughly confident. The understudy should be encouraged to play the part in his own way but not to be so individual in his performance as to disturb the other players. He must of course adhere to the rehearsal pattern and give a rendering close to that given by the principal.

Regarding clothes, the costume worn by the principal is fitted at a convenient moment and in the absence of major alteration is worn by the understudy. Sometimes parts of the costume are worn and the remainder supplied by a costumier to fit the understudy. In modern dress the understudy may have a suit in his wardrobe that he prefers to wear. Wigs and beards are duplicated as they are personal to the actor and unlikely to fit another performer. Understudies use their own make-up and are allowed to occupy the principal's dressing room whenever they are called upon to play.

An understudy may have to appear at very short notice or he may receive a warning some hours before the rise of the curtain. In the latter event, a notice is displayed at the box office and slips, previously printed, are inserted in the programme indicating the change in the cast. In a sudden emergency, the curtain is rung down and the manager goes in front to announce the indisposition of the principal and the name of the actor taking his place. The understudy must be in the theatre when the half-hour is called and does not leave until the last entrance of the principal. Understudies should be allowed to watch the play from the auditorium, and when doing so, the stage manager is told where they can be found. They receive a weekly salary which is increased for each performance played. A list is attached to the notice board indicating every part in the play with the names of the principal and understudy covering it.

PHOTOGRAPH CALL

Much of the publicity announcing the play depends on photographs of the actors and scenes in which they appear. A *photograph call* is arranged in professional companies as soon as possible after the first night. The notice advising the company is attached to the notice board and the artists in the first photograph are told at what time they are required to be dressed and made-up. Make-up for photographs is lighter than stage make-up and particular attention is given to the joins of wigs and beards. In plays with a large cast involving several changes of costume, the call boy and dressers are also called. The photographer usually sees the play in advance and notes situations he regards as specially effective. With the press representative and producer a complete list of photographs is made and captions chosen from the dialogue with which they are associated. The list is typed and copies given to the A.S.M. and the call boy which are helpful in marshalling the actors as they are needed. A skeleton staff is called to assist with scenery, properties and lighting. The photographer sometimes brings additional lighting equipment to the theatre and gives the electrician instructions as to the stage lighting he requires. When the photographs of each scene are concluded the furniture is replaced and a reference photograph taken of the setting.

WATCHING THE PLAY

For some performances after the first night, the stage manager will be required to keep a watchful eye on the stage. As time goes on, the play settles into a comfortable rhythm and with his team working reliably, he can go in front and see the whole play from the auditorium. This should be done at regular intervals but not so often as to blunt his critical appreciation. A long run can become a tedious business and some actors by reason of temperament find it so exacting that they need relief. It is here that the stage manager can be particularly useful in maintaining the performance.

Unconsciously the actor alters the inflexion or delivery of a line and even his memory may fail to the extent that words are changed. The prompter is able to help by telling the actor but should deviations continue, the stage manager must insist that the actor returns to the author's dialogue. Conscious alterations occur in jokes or ' gags ' in which an actor improvises and although they may give personal enjoyment are hardly likely to be appreciated by an audience paying to see the play. Some artists are especially inventive and like to improve on the moves or business arranged by the director. It can be disturbing and may affect the careful grouping of a scene—a point which may not be appreciated by the individual performer. The artist's costume may be altered and I have known an actress to be complimented by her leading man on the hat she wore at the end of the play. By this time she had suffered a bereavement and was dressed in widow's weeds. She was, however, so touched by the compliment that she arrived next day on the stage in the first act, wearing the hat that flattered her. Needless to say the audience was bewildered, not to say alarmed, when the lady appeared in mourning for no apparent reason. These are the kind of things which call for the stage manager's attention and while watching the play he will also observe the condition of scenery and costumes and any change in the lighting.

THE END OF THE RUN

Towards the end of the run, the parts and scripts are collected from the cast and an exact copy is made of the prompt script. Moves are clearly indicated, cues for lighting and effects and alterations in dialogue included. Plots used by the stage departments and wardrobe are copied and the A.S.M. provides plots of furniture and properties. With the photographs and plans of the settings, everything necessary to show a complete record of the play and performance is assembled and given to the producer.

During the week following the last performance, the stage management is responsible for return of all the furniture, properties, wardrobe and electrical equipment which is hired for the production. The hire companies collect the large items of furniture and equipment from theatres in London or from the station to which the production is returned at the end of the tour. With road transport they are delivered by lorry direct to the owners. Small items of wardrobe and properties are returned by the stage management personally and they are engaged for a few days longer at the end of the run or tour to supervise arrangements in winding up the show. All articles are checked against the lists provided originally so that the management has details of anything broken or mislaid.

What to do with the scenery at the end of a London run remains a great problem. If a tour is arranged the problem is temporarily solved but unless a purchaser is found who can make immediate use of a setting, it becomes a production item involving a charge for storage. Repertory companies occasionally need scenery to replenish their stock and if they can arrange an early production of the play take the setting used in London. Storage accommodation must be clean and dry. Curtains, carpets and wardrobe items should be cleaned and all traces of make-up removed. Metal properties will keep free from rust if they are given a coating of vaseline and wrapped in a dry material. Flats should be stacked with adequate support otherwise they may become warped; cloths and borders are rolled up on their battens. A detailed inventory is made of everything sent to the store which includes the contents of wardrobe baskets, items of furniture and properties bought for the production and the measurement of flats and cloths.

TOURING

Unless a position is obtained with a repertory company, the early experience gained by the A.S.M. will be on tour and a brief description of the routine work of a touring company may be helpful. Touring companies usually stay for one week at provincial theatres, although the time is extended for musical plays and spectacular productions that have enjoyed long runs elsewhere.

The stage manager is required to send preparatory details to the local stage manager and chief electrician. These concern the staff required for the *Get-in and Fit-up*, the time of arrival and the number of staff needed to work the show at performances. 'Get-in' is the term used to describe the conveyance of scenery from the station and unloading at the theatre, and the term 'Get-out' is used when the operation is repeated on leaving the theatre. The cost of getting-in is accepted by the local theatre and getting-out is paid by the visiting company. When the get-in takes place on Sunday, it is customary to share the cost although some theatres require the visiting company to pay for it in full. The stage manager will find the agreement in the theatre contract.

Early in the week, the stage manager should reach agreement with the local stage manager and the chief electrician regarding the number of men required and the cost of the 'Get-out.' An Agreement is in force between the Association of Touring and Producing Managers and the National Association of Theatrical and Kine Employees relating to charges for 'Getting-down,' i.e. dismantling the scenery, effects and properties and 'Getting-out.' In this agreement, towns throughout the British Isles are listed as No. 1 or No. 2 towns and theatres are also named with 'Difficult get-outs' where access to the stage involves difficult handling of the scenery which may perhaps have to be taken up by a lift. The rates of payment are shown with the minimum number of men per load required to handle the scenery. The weight of scenery varies from one production to another; payment is flexible and subject to on-the-spot agreement with the local staff.

The chief electrician should be asked for details of the lighting installation at each theatre well in advance so that equipment is not hired for the tour that can be obtained in the theatre. When this is received, a lighting requisition is forwarded indicating the number of staff required for fitting up and for the performance, with details of the colours of mediums needed, the local equipment to be used and particulars of the equipment travelled with the show. In complicated productions, a complete lighting plot is also sent in advance.

When the scenery travels by rail, it is unloaded at the station and taken by lorry to the theatre. The local stage manager arranges transport and allocates his staff for work at the station and on arrival at the theatre. Otherwise it is sent by road from one theatre to the next. The staff travelling with the company includes a master carpenter and a wardrobe mistress. In the case of productions with considerable lighting equipment and properties, an electrician and property master are also engaged.

The wardrobe, curtains, etc. are packed in wicker baskets with waterproof linings and secured with padlocks. The properties are packed in baskets or tea chests and the electrical equipment is travelled in strong wooden boxes. The flats are loaded first into the lorry and carefully stowed to prevent damage in transit. Built pieces of scenery are constructed in sections to fold wherever possible and are packed flat. Cloths and borders are rolled up on their battens and tied to strong wooden bars called *bearers* to make them secure. Sometimes they project beyond the length of the lorry and need to be covered with canvas. The cartage of scenery is measured in *loads*; one load being approximately the amount of scenery to fill a medium size lorry.

The details sent to the theatre stage manager are as follows:

(1) If the scenery travels by rail the station and time at which it will arrive.

(2) The number and type of trucks used for the production and the number of loads travelled.

(3) The loads will govern the number of lorries required and as the local stage manager attends to this task each week he can advise the most economical transport.

(4) The number of men needed at the station and the number required at the theatre for unloading and fitting-up.

(5) If the scenery travels by road, the time it will arrive at the theatre, the number of loads and description of the lorries.

(6) The number of staff required for the performance in the stage (including flies) and property departments.

(7) The dressers required, stipulating male or female and whether a call-boy is needed.

(8) Any special requirements such as a quick change room with its position on the stage and all information helpful to the local staff, including a description of the scenes and mention of scene changes. In the case of a heavy production, the ground plans and fly plots are forwarded.

On tour, the stage manager can be expected to work for seven days in the week and the week-end is his busiest time. Long distances need to be covered between towns and the time required to fit-up a show has to be considered. For plays staged in more than one setting, arrangements are made to receive the scenery on Sunday and much of the work in fitting-up is performed

PLATE G

Medicine cupboard used in *Dr. Angelus*

PLATE 16

A Clean Kill (Michael Gilbert). Criterion Theatre. London

PLATE 17

A Clean Kill, Model

PLATE H

Lutyens and Masey's first design for a National Theatre
opposite the Victoria and Albert Museum

on that day, leaving Monday for lighting and staff rehearsals. Double time is paid to the staff for Sunday work and consequently the stage manager has to decide on the amount of work done that day. Four hours is the minimum time in which the staff can be employed on a Sunday and expense is saved if the work can be restricted to that time. When the production is a small one, the scenery arrives early on Monday morning and is fitted up during the rest of the day. The three heads of department at the local theatre i.e. the master carpenter or stage manager, the chief electrician and the property master work closely with the touring staff and the procedure followed in building the setting depends on the size of the production. With plays that are not complicated, the last setting is built first and so on through the play leaving the first scene standing for the performance. The stage manager has to decide when to commence lighting the play and it is normally started in the principal setting. Where there are difficult lighting cues and effects, this scene is fitted-up first and the lighting for the rest of the play completed as the other settings are built.

One of the earliest duties for the stage manager is the allocation of dressing rooms. The wardrobe and personal luggage is taken by the property staff to the dressing rooms and the wardrobe mistress then distributes the costumes worn in the play. Meanwhile on the stage, fitting-up is started. Ceilings and flats are battened, cloths are hung and the stage cloth is laid to the setting line. The electrician may need help in identifying equipment and will ask about the practical fittings and probably where to fly a bar for the overhead floods. The method of working the prompt corner will be discussed and the cue lights tested as they may be different from other theatres. An essential task is to ' dead ' the spot bar and border which must be done before the lighting is commenced. The ' dead ' of the spot bar is its height from the stage and it is hung as low as possible for the spotlights to give the maximum light to the setting. The height of the spot bar and border is related to the line of sight from the gallery or upper circle and the local stage manager can indicate the usual position. This, however, may be varied in certain settings when it is necessary for action at the rear of the setting to be seen. The border is deaded first and afterwards the spot bar is lowered to a position from which the spotlights are not in sight when viewed from the front row of the stalls.

A band call is normally held on Monday morning and the conductor will want to know the performance times, length of intervals and scene changes and the type of music to be played. In the case of musical plays or where music is specially composed, he will ask the stage manager for the band parts. The stage manager forwards a call to the musical director giving him this information which will include the band parts. Two sets of band parts are always obtained for the production.

A note with the running times of the Acts, scenes and intervals is given to the theatre manager and the stage manager consults him regarding the length of the over-ture and the time it should commence. Intervals are subject to variation as the theatre manager observes the length of the performance so that the audience has sufficient time to catch the last transport to their homes. Before the artists leave the theatre on Monday evening, the A.S.M. makes a list of their addresses and telephone numbers.

The staff of all departments has to be carefully rehearsed and in the event of quick scene changes, the rehearsal often has to be delayed until an hour or so before the performance. Some of the working staff is employed in fitting-up and can be rehearsed during the day but the full staff is augmented for the performance. Nevertheless, the local staff is well prepared for the trials of a Monday night and it is a tribute to their efficiency that the stage manager can rely on them to follow his instructions at short notice.

On Monday night the stage manager goes to the front of the house and notes the lighting at the beginning of each scene, setting of spotlights relating to the artists' positions and the operation of lighting and other cues. At the start of the play he listens to the actors' voices which may not be projected sufficiently in a strange theatre. This is often evident at the rear of the stalls where the circle canopy projects over the seating and the artists appreciate his opinion as otherwise their performance would be seriously affected.

During the week, the stage manager rehearses the understudies. He sends advance details of the production to the following theatre, completes his accounts and reaches agreement with the local stage manager about the cost of the get-out at the end of the week. The representative of British Railways usually calls at the theatre and provides a time-table for the *train call* which is posted to the notice board. When the stage manager combines the duties of company manager he will go to the station to purchase the rail tickets and confirm the reservation of seats for the company and the scenery trucks.

On Saturday night properties that are not required further during the performance are carried to the property room, photographs of the artists are brought round from the front of the house and the staff commences to pack them. After the show the scenery and lighting equipment is dismantled, the wardrobe returned to the baskets and loaded with the scenery in the lorries which are ordered for half an hour after the fall of the curtain. One member of the stage management attends to packing of the electrical equipment when an electrician is not engaged with the play. As the lighting equipment in theatres is not standard a variety of plugs and wiring is in use and those travelled may not fit the theatre installation.

They are altered during the fit-up and small items can be overlooked on Saturday night which may cause delay at the next theatre. The stage manager makes a final tour of the stage and dressing rooms so that nothing is forgotten and gives gratuities to the local staff. When the scenery travels by rail, the D.S.M. goes to the station to see it into the train.

Touring overseas has additional problems involving travel by air, rail and sea with the observation of passport and customs formalities. The weight of personal and company luggage by plane is restricted and travelling by train through European countries can provide an element of adventure when properties are examined at the border. A detailed list of contents is frequently accepted at face value though I was told that with a travelling circus, the carpenter did most of his smuggling in the lions' cage.

Air travel has made it possible to cover great distances in a short time and a company visiting South America played in eight countries; the tour lasting a little over a month. Not without incident. The minimum of properties were travelled and in each city the furniture and settings were found. Coloured filters caused quite a stir with the local electricians as transparent wrappings from chocolate boxes were often used for their colour effects. In Buenos Aires the theatre was set on fire just before the company arrived and at short notice they were transferred to another theatre; sharing it with a troupe of native dancers. Caracas was on the verge of revolution and they were greeted with bombs, tanks and a stubborn guard around the Government buildings including the National Theatre. A day of earnest negotiation was needed with the Venezuelan Army before obtaining release of the properties. These arrived at an outlying cinema to which they were diverted just before the show and the following day the company was flown out to New York.

The stage manager is concerned with the mechanical side of the production but he can by sympathetic attention relieve stress and give encouragement. Artists relying on public approval for their work quickly respond to praise or criticism and in the tiring repetition of a long run, despondency is never far from the surface. Small occurrences, which otherwise would pass unnoticed are sometimes magnified and the stage manager stands somewhere between a father confessor and the Rock of Gibraltar. Nothing disturbs him; at least if it does, he rarely shows it and while keeping a firm control, tempers his outlook with cheerfulness and a sense of humour.

What a deal of cold business doth a man spend the better part of his life in! In scattering compliments, tendering visits, gathering and venting news, following feasts and plays, and making a little winter love in a dark corner.—Ben Jonson.

CHAPTER 12

THE NATIONAL THEATRE: 'GREAT EXPECTATIONS'

God saw men's wicked ways,
And nipped them in the bud,
He let it rain for 40 days
And drowned them in a flood.

The bad all died but mark!
God saved good Noah's life.
He saved him in a mighty Ark
With his 3 sons and wife.

And 2 of every kind
Of insect, beast and bird—
As He had said. For you will find
God always keeps his word.

So now with you and me—
Be this well understood!
If bad we too shall punished be
But helped if we are good.

——Museum of Childhood,
Bethnal Green.

THE concept of a National Theatre was born in the early 19th century and the debate as to the form it would take, let alone that of building and paying for it, lasted well over 125 years. We are reminded of a quote from Hermann Kahn: ' When the time between conception and the completion of a building exceeds the anticipated life of the building, it is time to emigrate '. The concrete edifice on the South Bank of the Thames, approved by Lord Olivier with his committee and designed by Sir Denys Lasdun has since 1976 prevented us from contemplating any such idea. The panoramic sweep of terraces overlooking a stretch of the river patrolled by Port of London Authority police boats evokes the architect's idea of ' rehearsals on the terraces, kite-flying, music and people just gathering and meeting '. The theatre director also believes in breaking the formality; he looks forward to ' cafes, shops and

THE NATIONAL THEATRE 263

pubs—as well as concert halls, art galleries, theatres and a street market on some days '.

With all these exciting projects, the essential intention of a building where people are offered theatrical entertainment may be overshadowed. It is hoped that authors, actors, musicians and scene designers will continue to create magic of the kind that theatre staging has usually provided.

A character in J. M. Barrie's ' Dear Brutus ' mentions what might-have-been. After years of debate mingled with indecision the deeds for a small triangular site (which today remains empty) opposite the Victoria and Albert Museum were given to George Bernard Shaw in 1937 and an architect was appointed to design the national theatre.

Sir Edwin Lutyens had no personal experience in building a theatre and by a fortunate circumstance he was joined by Cecil Masey, the architect of several cinemas. Their swift collaboration is recorded in *The Making of a National Theatre* by Geoffrey Whitworth: ' Each was the perfect complement to the other. Sir Edwin brought all his genius to the common task, and Masey his talent for inventive adaptability '. On a very difficult site, the auditorium was designed to hold 1040 seats with a restaurant, theatre offices and storage space. (Plate H.) The declaration of war in 1939 interrupted the plans; an appeal for funds was abandoned and the South Kensington site was used by the Government as a fire-fighting reservoir. However, the architects continued with their work until in 1942, like a bolt from the blue, the Chairman of the London County Council brought a proposal which was to change entirely the National Theatre project for the future. The development of London, and in particular the South Bank of the River Thames, was under review and it was thought that the London County Council would give favourable consideration to the offer of land on the South Bank in exchange for the South Kensington site.

The theatre committee was impressed with the offer of a larger site and hoped the project would take shape sooner with the support of the London County Council. Bernard Shaw disagreed and he attacked the proposal with the view that the cultural mecca of London would soon become the Albert Memorial and the right place for a National Theatre was therefore in that vicinity. Meanwhile Lutyens and Masey prepared new plans for a building that included two theatres on the South Bank of the Thames between Waterloo Bridge and Charing Cross Railway Bridge. The design recalled the complete symmetry of the Kensington elevations in a 250-ft. square building. (Fig. 54.) Sir Edwin Lutyens did not live to see his plan accepted and his one-time assistant, Sir Hubert Worthington, was the next architect to be consulted on the design of the theatre. He was trained in the Classical tradition and his riverside elevation resembled the pillar facade of the National Gallery and the church of St. Martin-in-the-Fields. He was never officially appointed and the committee was reserved about his scheme.

There were changes in the London County Council's plans for the South Bank which embraced the future Festival Hall and at this time the Shakespeare Memorial National Theatre amalgamated with the old Vic, with the aim of jointly building a National Theatre. The Australian architect Brian O'Rorke was recommended and he combined with Cecil Masey to design a theatre with two auditoria (one with 1250 seats and one with 500 seats) next to the Royal Festival Hall. The National Theatre Act was passed in 1949 and during the Festival of Britain in July, 1951, the foundation stone was laid by the Queen (now Queen Elizabeth the Queen Mother).

At first the delay in building the theatre was blamed on the post-war ban on building for entertainment and in 1953 the theatre was refused planning permission because of its 'unsatisfactory relationship' to the Festival Hall. In the new plans of that year the site was moved next to

LUTYENS AND MASEY'S SECOND DESIGN FOR A
NATIONAL THEATRE ON THE SOUTH BANK

Figure 54

County Hall. Although the Government agreed in principle on financing, debate was renewed as to whether the theatre was needed at all; if it was, the South Bank was not the place for it and surely the design could be restricted to one auditorium and not two.

Costs were rising and ten years after the National Theatre Act was passed it became clear that apart from the projected cost of between £1,500,000 and £2 million, the theatre would need an annual subsidy of £300,000 to keep it in operation. Nevertheless in 1959 the O'Rorke design was approved in principle by the London County Council. In the following year a second scheme was presented and an open-stage theatre was substituted for the earlier small theatre, with its design including a circular stage on the perimeter of a circular auditorium. The architect's proscenium arched theatre was entirely conventional and the solidity of the elevation aroused criticism at County Hall that the design was not in keeping with the kind of lightness and openness conceived for other buildings in the area.

In March, 1961, the Chancellor announced that the Government had decided not to proceed with the project. However the proviso was added that any obligation to build theatres should rest with local authorities and the Government would support them with financial help. The London County Council then put forward an offer to contribute the estimated £1,300,000 needed for the theatre if the Government would contribute the £1,000,000 it had promised under the National Theatre Act.

The British Government accepted the financial proposal for the National Theatre supported financially by the London County Council in July 1961. At this time a new element was added: the Sadler's Wells opera company was to join the theatre companies to be housed in the project. One architect was to be appointed for the scheme. Denys Lasdun was selected and his design was unveiled in May, 1965. It took up the entire site between the County Hall and Charing Cross Bridge, stepping down to a low area in front of the Shell Tower. Three auditoria, seating 1100, 750 and 220 and an opera house with 1650 seats were set within a series of terraces. It was almost immediately apparent that the Government was not going to contribute to the building of the opera house or increase its subsidy to Sadler's Wells on a move to the South Bank. By 1965 the Government was considering more schemes for opera houses in the provinces. Where the London opera house had been planned to stand, a vacant site would remain. Fearing the unbalanced appearance of the sites if the theatre went ahead, the LCC moved the National Theatre to its present site, and Lasdun's final designs got underway.

The three theatres in the National Theatre complex are the Olivier (open-stage), Lyttleton (proscenium stage) and Cottesloe (studio theatre). The early idea embraced a single adaptable auditorium to house everything from Greek tragedy to contemporary drama and the architect advised the planners that three theatres were necessary to fulfil all that was required.

The Olivier theatre satisfies two conditions; that the audience is assembled in one space and it has intimate participation with the actor. During the time of the Victorian theatre and continuing to the early part of this century, theatres were built which separated the audience into classes. Later the orchestra pit was enlarged and separated the musicians from the audience by the prominent—often shining brass—orchestra rail. Hence the name orchestra stalls which occupied the rest of the auditorium with a few rows of seats called the pit behind them, and these were enclosed with a barrier to segregate the cheaper seats from the orchestra stalls. In other parts of the theatre, there were separate entrances with long uninviting stone steps to the upper circle and the bare board seating of the gallery. Theatres became larger with the desire for larger stages and more audience accommodation. The social division continued and with the increased seating capacity of the theatres good sight lines to the stage were lost. Those occupying the cheaper seats became more and more separated from the performance as the architect tried to please the theatre proprietor with stages to present spectacles and the seating space for the audience which paid to see them.

In the 18th century, the Georgian theatre was a popular theatre with everybody going to the play and mixing without regard to social position. The audience liked to be as near as possible to the stage; they sat in the orchestra pit and required little encouragement to leap on to the forestage and mingle with the actors. So much so, that in France 1760, an arret from the King forbade any persons appearing on the stage besides the actors.

A contemporary English author wrote: ' To the disgrace of common apprehension we have often seen likewise in our theatres two audiences, one on the stage, and another before the curtain; and the battle of Bosworth Field has been fought in a less space than that which is commonly allotted to a cock-match. Mr. Garrick indeed must have called to mind a very ridiculous circumstance that happened on the Dublin theatre when he acted the part of King Lear. When the old King was recovering from his delirium, and sleeping with his head on Cordelia's lap, a gentleman stepped at that instant from behind the scenes, upon the stage, and threw his arms round Mrs. Woffington, who acted that character; nor did I hear that the audience resented, as they ought, so gross an affront offered to them and to common decency; so long had they been accustomed to riotous and illiberal behaviour in the theatre.'

The National Theatre Company was formed in 1962 with Laurence Olivier as director. It played at Chichester and in London at the Old Vic and there was very long and complicated debate about the nature of a National Theatre building. At the Festival Theatre, Chichester, there is an open or peninsular stage arrangement in which the audience is seated on three sides of the stage. The audience liked to be near the stage, as in the Georgian theatre, and Olivier has commented: ' For a very popular play the audience would say: " I want to be here tonight. I want to be near the scene between Miss Plowright and Sybil Thorndike at the end of the row scene, when they have their dialogue together." People used to come two or three times and sit in different places, and they were always very complimentary about the fact that it was pretty good from everywhere.'

Although the design of the Chichester theatre was not satisfactory and other thrust-type stages were difficult, this was the concept for the shape of the Olivier theatre that the building committee led by Lord Olivier thoughtfully pursued. Then there was debate about the choice of architect and it was decided that a competition was impossible as no reputable firm would compete—in case they lost. Secondly there would be surrender to the winner who would be entitled to have control over his or her design and its execution as a theatre building. Eventually the impasse was resolved by the Royal Institute of British Architects who organised a competition to produce 20 winners, all of whom were carefully interviewed. Most of the architects came in groups with their partners and were very impressive in their meeting with the building committee across the table. Olivier continued: ' Denys Lasdun arrived . . . entirely alone. Very theatrical. He just sat there; bright, confident and competent to answer all the questions himself. He didn't have to answer " Well, the majority of us feel . . . " There was none of that, just him and nobody else. That was immensely effective and of course, as he knew perfectly well, quite touching. We didn't want anyone who had designed theatre before, we wanted to find a new soul. During the interview Lasdun put his finger on it, very cleverly. He said that surely the most important aspect of what we were talking about is the spiritual one. Oh, my dear! We all fell for that. Well, he was a unanimous choice, we knew we'd got by far the most suitable man and probably the most brilliant man in England.'

Between 1964 and early 1965 schemes were evolved and from the beginning the architect welcomed a partnership with the building committee. The Olivier theatre took the time, they met once a week and kept it up for about three years. A technical subcommittee of the building committee was formed and a number of journeys to other theatres, particularly in Europe, were made by various members of the team. Many months of distinguished conversation preceded the idea of a theatre as a rectangular space with the stage and auditorium set along a diagonal. The fundamental concept became a bowl-like auditorium facing a corner stage; a form used fairly extensively in the U.S.A. and which dates back to 1914 in this country. Sir Denys Lasdun said: 'The building has to be very dense, heavy, because we are protecting The Word from outside noise . . . out of this came a drawing of a room with a stage in the corner, and seats round it. . . . From this, we sought a place on the stage which every pair of eyes would pass through a single point of command of the actor; and conversely, where that actor would stand so that without moving his head he felt he was addressing and signalling to everybody.'

Whether or not the architect was expressing the ' star ' affection for the centre of the stage is difficult to say and his reference is a reminder of the ' single line of vision ' which was described in an article entitled: *The shape of the Eighteenth-century French Theatre and the Drawing-board Renaissance* by T. E. Lawrenson, M.A., Ph.D. published in the journal of the International Federation for Theatre Research Vol. VII Nos. 1 and 2, 1965 and Vol. VII No. 3, 1966. ' In the broadest possible terms of theatrical development, and simplifying outrageously, the Renaissance set is the consolidation of a single line of vision from the audience to stage, and the optimum point upon this line of vision is the Prince's seat.'

RENAISSANCE THEATRES

Professor Lawrenson mentions that the overall form of the earliest of the ancient theatres was doubtless a circle, and he takes his reader through to the break in that circle which was consummated in the Renaissance courtly theatre. This consisted of a solid *frons scenae* and a semi-circular auditorium which was reproduced, though it was out of date, place and time, in the Teatro Olimpico, 1584. (Plate I.) The false perspective set of small houses in the Teatro Olimpico retreating towards a single vanishing point of perspective demanded ideally a single line of vision. Thirty-four years afterwards, in the Theatre Farnese, Parma, 1618, the prototype of the perspective scene was represented on flat wings, with the stage framed in the proscenium arch, and the seating arranged in a 'horseshoe' auditorium. (Fig. 55.) This style, called the picture frame stage, was adopted in Holland with the new Amsterdam Theatre 1775, when the wings were set at an oblique angle to the proscenium opening. (Plates J and K.)

Early in the 18th century the French Renaissance theatre, having assimilated the classical inspiration of the Italian theatre, was undergoing a change. The growth of lyrical drama, the larger audiences from all parts of society and the transfer of theatres from aristocratic patronage to commercial use demanded a new theatrical and stage design.

However, the Renaissance desire to revert to the classical semi-circular auditorium ran into trouble within the confines of a rectangular building, previously enclosed in a palace or the courtyard of an inn. Moreover, visual interpretation and not dramatic verse was encouraged in France to the extent that one theatre, the *Salle des Machines*, had no dramatic text and it produced little else than visual spectacles on a very long stage.

The home of the Comedie Francaise in the 17th century was a theatre which continued well into the 18th century. It had a rounded end furthest from the stage with two lines of boxes widening slightly towards the stage and it was not an independent theatre building. Probably the first completely independent and free-standing theatre building in France was the *Grand Theatre de Lyon* built by Soufflot in 1754. The auditorium was not only curved at the rear; it was a completely oval figure with the stage intervening at the other end. The rectangle was broken and it set the tone for future projects. However, the design included three rows of boxes, amphitheatre, pit and orchestra, which created problems, especially with Opera, as the hidden cavities below each row gave poor acoustics. (Plate L.)

Following the burning of the Opera Palais Royal, the rebuilding was given to Moreau in 1764, opening in 1770, and his plans indicate the influence of Soufflot. The columns of the boxes were abolished and each of the four storeys formed a continual balcony. The divisions between the boxes, however, faced the centre of the Auditorium and were not directed towards the stage, thereby creating difficult sight lines. Moreau arranged a wider stage opening though he placed boxes on the forestage; an unfortunate practice copied by other theatre architects. (Plate M.) The argument between the theatre as an art form and its commercial utility continued. Improvement in sight lines and exploitation of wall space for greater seating capacity demanded a reduction in the number of boxes. The form of the auditorium varied between a complete semi-circle and a flattened ellipse with seats rising backwards. This was reasonably satisfactory in theatres that were not Opera houses as the rise in seating tended to weaken the resonant structure of the earlier theatre designs.

A surprising reaction to the very long and narrow area

PLATE I

The Olimpico Theatre. Vicenza. 1584

AFBEELDING der NIEUWEN AMSTERDAMSCHEN SCHOUWBURG, van het Tooneel te zien.

PLATE J

The Auditorium of the new Amsterdam Theatre. 1775

PLATE K

Ground Plan of the new Amsterdam Theatre, 1775

PLATE L

Le Grand Théâtre de Lyon,
by Sufflot, 1754

PLATE M

Opera de Paris,
by Moreau, 1764

PLATE N

Project for the Opera de Paris, by Cochin, 1765

PLATE O
Plan of the Amsterdam Schouwburg.
restored by van Kampen. 1637

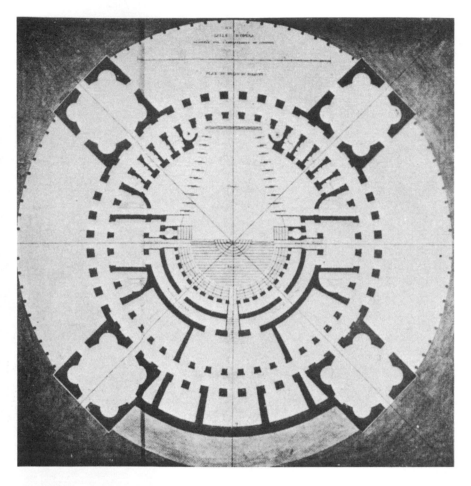

PLATE P

Plan of Boullée's Opera project

Catalogue Request Form

Please tick the catalogues you require and return the form to the address below, along with your remittance.

J. Garnet Miller Limited

All-women Casts:

Short Pieces / One Act / Full Length..............

Mixed Casts:

Short Pieces / One Act..............

Full Length..............

Plays for Youth Groups..............

Kenyon-Deane Limited

Anchorage Press Inc.

Specialist American Publisher   £1.00

of quality dramatic literature for Young People, including adaptations of classics, contemporary works, comedies, dramas and musicals. Over 200 plays to choose from . . . .

I. E. Clark, Inc.

General American Publisher of Plays   £1.00

- sketches, one acts, full length and

musicals for adults and young people. With a special emphasis on challenging plays for teenagers exploring many of the social problems which confront them - AIDS, drink, drugs, how to fit in, sex and others . . . .

Please send me a copy of the above catalogues as indicated. I enclose my remittance for £   as required.

Name _____

Signature _____

Society _____

Position _____

Address _____

_____

_____

County __ __ __ Postcode __ __ __

Cressrelles Publishing Company Limited

10 Station Road Industrial Estate, Colwall,
Near Malvern, Herefordshire WR13 6RN
Telephone/Fax: (01684) 540154

All-women Casts:

    Short pieces / One Act . . . .

    Full Length . . . .

Mixed Casts:

    Short pieces / One Act . . . .

    Full Length . . . .

New Playwright's Network

All-women:

    One Act / Full Length . . . .

Mixed Casts:

    One Act . . . .

    Full Length . . . .

    Plays for Youth Groups . . . .

    Pantomimes . . . .

From Hammitzsch, "Der Moderne Theaterbau," Wasmuth, Berlin.

GROUND PLAN OF THE THEATRE FARNESE IN PARMA.

A typical Italian theatre of the early seventeenth century. The prototype of the "horseshoe" auditorium.

Figure 55

of the rectangle theatre is found in a project for the Paris Opera by Cochin, 1765. The design of a flattened ellipse with the larger axis parallel to the front of the stage, includes three proscenium arches inspired by Palladio's theatre: the Olimpico and its three frontal entrances.

The entire seating becomes curved as opposed to the narrow rows of seats parallel to the stage in earlier theatres. His auditorium brings the spectators much nearer to the actors and for this reason also, he says, the acoustics are improved. The stage has great width and the project is more suitable for a small theatre.

In an aspect encouraged by the French, Cochin observes that in his theatre the viewer is diverted from the stage to the ladies invitingly seated in the boxes. The pit or parterre is arranged as large as possible so that admirers, by turning entirely away from the stage, may contemplate their devotions. (Plate N and Fig. 56.) The design was not new and was acknowledged as such by Cochin. It was used in Holland early in the 17th century for the Schouwburg, Amsterdam 1637. Here was the flattened ellipse with the straight sides of the ' horseshoe ' auditorium and five proscenium openings, probably inspired also by the Olimpico of Palladio with its 3 frontal and 2 side entrances. The large open pit area was surrounded by a row of 10 raised boxes with a gallery above the boxes around the auditorium.

Society in the new Dutch republic was too class-conscious to allow mixing of social position; while spectators in the pit could rejoice in their view of the boxes, the accommodation was separated for the classes. The pit was ' where the people stand ' with the Dutch aristocracy retired in the boxes and the middle class gaining a bird's eye view from the gallery. (Plate O.)

Another drawing board project for the Paris Opera was made by Chaumont in 1766, who criticised both the rectangle theatre and the unsatisfactory acoustics of the boxes. He was the first to visualise his audience in ' a very simple shape whereby every spectator is seated most favourably facing the actor and where the seats form an amphitheatre,' i.e. a round building with tiers of seats. Chaumont was concerned that the actor should perform on the forestage with a rigid division between the stage and the auditorium, leaving the back-stage area merely for scenery decoration. He disagreed with the acoustic value in placing the wings at an oblique angle to the stage and in the auditorium, a compromise was made between the semi-circle of the ancient theatre and the rectangle theatre with boxes. He designed his theatre towards a segment of a circle, the centre of which is the vanishing point on the back wall of the stage. His solution to the problem of the boxes was a compromise leaving the rows of boxes to

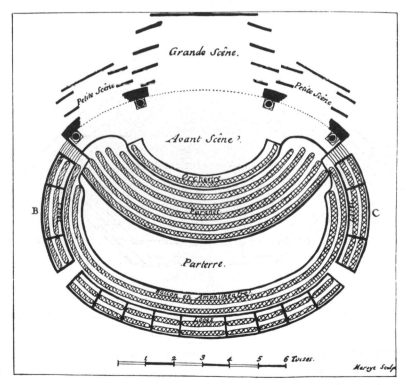

PROJECT FOR L'OPERA DE PARIS BY COCHIN
Figure 56

retreat one behind the other. The blank space of wall round the top of the auditorium helped acoustics and re-called the ancient theatre re-arranged within the confines of a rectangular building. (Fig. 58)

Probably the most important drawing board project was designed by Roubo in 1777, a master carpenter who had received instruction in mathematics, design and theatre mechanics from J. F. Blondel, author of *French Architecture* 1752–1756. The plan is remarkable, coming from a modest man with a carpenter's training and a limited knowledge of architecture. It may endorse the idea of the missing link between the theoretical designer and the practising craftsman employed in working the stage mechanics of a theatre.

Roubo confirms the theatre as a decorated isolated building in the middle of a square and he is original in providing his audience with the additional enjoyment of a promenade or covered walk around the auditorium from which the approaches of the theatre may be viewed in the colonnade.

He acknowledges his tutor, Blondel, and remarks that his design is not original and it is derived from the ancient theatre with a semi-circular auditorium and the greater part of the action taking place on the fore-stage. The stage picture seen through the proscenium arch is mainly decorative and the proscenium opening is made as wide as possible to conform with the semi-circular auditorium. In this way, his respect for the ancient theatre leads almost to the abolition of the proscenium arch.

The reduction in space behind the proscenium arch resembles the area behind the centre opening of the Roman *frons scenae*. The fore-stage also corresponds with the ancient design, though the seats either side facing each other prevent a view of the stage picture.

In the auditorium the semi-circular orchestra has seats parallel to the front of the stage and the open pit area is replaced by the terraced amphitheatre. This is derived also from the ancient Roman design with the centre section at a lower level. Professor Lawrenson continues: ' Apart from the boxes, the remainder of the auditorium is amphitheatrical, the pit, with its noise and disorder, being thereby abolished, and the amphitheatre has no serious differentiation although it is designed at two levels. It is divided into *cunei* in the Roman manner, although Roubo does not call them that; but the passages in between the two halves he does refer to as vomitoires, the Roman *vomitoria.*'

Roubo was an admirable engineer and he produced the advanced idea of a swivel floor in a public building. ' The floor, swivelled along a central axis parallel to the line of the stage edge, can be given a rake when the building is used as a theatre and it can be swivelled back to a level position for other purposes.' His plan for a theatre with its size and decoration was very costly and the large capacity of nearly 2,000 seats could be achieved only in a building of great proportions. Nevertheless, his influence continued until it was employed much later in our history. (Plate S.)

The last Renaissance project of the 18th century French theatre was designed by Boulée, another pupil of J. F. Blondel, who was a painter advised by his family to take up architecture, and although his training as a master builder was undoubtedly sound, the poetry in his work was lyrical in the extreme. His plan was a completion of Roubo and was described as a rotunda or circular building embellished in the Corinthian style. The circle was Boulée's divinity and he was romantic to the extent that the female form was not only to be observed in the theatre seating, it was integrated into the surrounding architecture with female models in bas relief dotted about the building. Acoustics and sight lines were given scant attention and his design was devoted to architectural decoration in a theatre as large as possible. He chose a semi-circular auditorium which stemmed naturally from the circular exterior. He combined, with other theatre designers, approval of the actor in close contact with the audience upon a wide fore-stage. Although he said at one time that all the stage designer required was 2 or 3 flats before a backcloth, his design indicated no less than 10 wings before the backcloth was reached at the perimeter of his circular building. The pit area was filled with seats parallel to the stage line and was a concession to visibility of the perspective set. The small orchestra contained curved seating, probably for the purpose of artistic effect in the plan. The amphitheatre seating surrounded the central area with the seats at the edge of the fore-stage facing each other and his human female figures in the architecture above were given a better view by lovingly facing them towards the stage.

Boulée was unconcerned about the acoustic, visual or social problem of the boxes and his interpretaion was more concerned with artistic effect, to the inclusion of two rows of heavenly figures worked into the ceiling of his theatre. (Plate P.)

OLIVIER THEATRE

The Architectural Review, January 1977, describes this theatre: 'The Olivier was designed under the influence not only of individual theatres from Epidaurus to the Globe, but of Classical and Renaissance theories of the theatre as a microcosm, a little model of the world connected by its architecture to something bigger than itself. There are Classical and Renaissance echoes in the five entrances to the stage, the shape of the auditorium, and the upper-level gallery behind the stage. . . .'

Lord Olivier, with 17 members of the theatre building committee and Sir Denys Lasdun with 35 collaborating architects, were engaged in approving and designing the National Theatre. Lord Olivier has said that the Olivier ' took the time, we all met once a week and we really kept it up for about three years '. This may not be surprising when the technical description is studied: ' The open-stage theatre, the OLIVIER THEATRE, has seating for 1,160 people in two main stepped tiers visually linked by intermediate tiers on each side to give a bowl-like configuration focusing downwards and partially surrounding the stage, which is in the corner of the audience room. Little or no scenery need be used to set the scene, it being possible to extend with screens the walls of the auditorium to meet behind the acting area. However, if scenery is required it can be set and changed in a variety of ways unique to this theatre. First there is a fly tower in which scenery of almost any size and shape can be flown—three-dimensional scenery at any angle to the audience. Second, built scenes can be moved on wagons on to the acting area from any of the three storage areas behind the stage. Third, there is a drum revolving stage built into the floor of the acting area. This enables scenery to be rapidly positioned and re-positioned at the focal point of the entire theatre, as well as allowing exceptional flexibility of the shape and levels of the stage itself. The revolving stage splits into two semi-circular sections. One of these can sink into the service area below, to be replaced by a third section which—complete with scenery and actors—rises to replace the former scene.'

The Architectural Review continues: ' The Olivier Theatre began life as a rectangular space with the stage and the auditorium set along the diagonal: a fixed dynamic space with a strong direction to it, but with action in the same room as the audience. The primary emphasis was on direct communication between audience and actor. Psychological, visual and acoustic qualities were to be paramount. This kept the capacity of the auditorium down and encouraged everyone on the committee to shake off old habits and take risks in suggesting an ideal form. The design process was thus an adventure from first principles. Lasdun had never before designed a theatre. He encouraged the committee to return to primary definitions. The evolution towards the final form continued until 1966 when the curves and side-banked seats came into the design in response to reactions against the constrictive corners of the earlier scheme. The underlying intention of a unified space with focus towards the zone of command of the stage was there from the beginning: the amphitheatre arrangement which matched this intention best was not evolved until late in the process. The proscenium theatre (the Lyttelton) was brought to its final form in the same year.'

It may be questioned sympathetically how the architect, chosen because he had never designed a theatre before, was supposed to satisfy the building committee with novel theatrical schemes, yet lacking the professional knowledge and experience to plan and complete them.

The Architectural Review has referred to Classical and Renaissance theories in the design of the Olivier theatre and these were the views held by theatre designers in Europe described in the ' Drawing-Board Renaissance ' of the French theatre by Professor T. E. Lawrenson. That the greater part of the action should take place on the forestage was a Renaissance desire and the bowl-like configuration of the auditorium stemmed from the Greek theatre of Epidaurus (Plate Q). This was advanced in the Roman theatre with the concavity of the *valvae mediae* or middle section of the seating.

The precepts were demonstrated in the French theatre project of Roubo 1777, and although the design was left on the drawing board, the master carpenter's ideas were sufficiently viable to influence the design of the Olivier theatre unveiled by the architect in 1976, almost two hundred years later to the day. *The Architectural Review* has said that the fundamental dimensions of the Old Vic were used as a yardstick for the overall stage size. However, although there was no consultation by Lord Olivier and Sir Denys Lasdun with the International Federation for Theatre Research, it will be seen from the plans of the Roubo theatre and the Lasdun theatre how well the architect has adapted the master carpenter's designs illustrated by Professor Lawrenson in his article 1965–66. (Plates R and S.)

Although the scale is different, important features of relative proportions are identical with both plans, viz:

(1) Taking the Roubo centre line marked A–B in his plan and placing it over the centre line of the Lasdun plan A–B, the intersecting line marked E–F of Roubo is the dividing line to the rear of the Olivier stage.

(2) The intersecting line of Roubo marked L–L in his plan is the centre line of the Lasdun revolving stage, marked Y–Z.

(3) The orchestra line marked G–H in the Roubo plan is the front line of the 3 sided fore-stage of Lasdun, marked G–H.

(4) The rear line of the Olivier fore-stage marked W–X coincides with the rear of the fore-stage area in the Roubo plan interrupted by the false proscenium.

(5) The line of the Roubo colonnade marked A'–B' corresponds with the foyer line in the Lasdun plan, marked A'–B'.

(6) The fan-shaped seating in the Lasdun plan is a 90° segment of a circle with the poles at the fore-stage turned inwards. This is the architect's solution to criticism of the Roubo plan in which the side seats at the fore-stage were at a right angle to the proscenium line.

(7) When the sections are examined, it will be seen that the classical bowl-like shape is achieved by lowering the centre area of seating in both theatres. (Plates T and U.)

The Olivier theatre is designed for the open-stage form with the audience and acting area assembled in one space. The model shown in Plate V, where the auditorium and stage area are supposed to be fully lit, seems to indicate that the open-stage form succeeds. However, the same model shown in Plate V, with the auditorium lights extinguished for the performance, suggests a distinct separation between the audience and acting area, with the darkened concrete walls completing the rectangular shape of a wide proscenium arch.

The Architects' Journal, January 1977, mentions this feature: ' The concrete fronts to the side seating bays and the concrete panels flanking the acting area form a conspicuous and coherent form of considerable architectural power. They may come, in time, to appear as definitive as any proscenium frame. The theatre may not necessarily be the worse for that, but it may make nonsense of much of what has been written about the open-stage form.' Here the architect has noticed Roubo's respect for the ancient theatre leading almost to the abolition of the proscenium arch. The width of the poles of the auditorium walls, behind the side seating bays in the Lasdun plan, is proportionately the same width as the poles of the circular auditorium walls meeting the false proscenium in the Roubo plan.

The architect has commented upon the bowl-like shape of his theatre: ' A bowl effect . . . when you go into that room it is you and that stage. Personal relationship is unique in the theatre. Make the theatre too big, and you've lost it.' The auditorium of the Olivier theatre seems immense and recalls discussion of the relative merits of the curved stadium seating in the German Littman theatre (Plate W), and the tiered seating with stalls, dress circle, upper circle and gallery in the building formerly called the National Theatre: the Theatre Royal, Drury Lane (Plate X).

The distance from the front of the revolve to the back wall of the Olivier is seventy-two feet and from the proscenium arch to the back wall of the Theatre Royal, Drury Lane eighty-two feet. The Olivier seats 1160 and the Theatre Royal, Drury Lane seats 2283; the capacity is almost doubled with no one more than eighty-two feet from the stage.

Stage Machinery. The *Architectural Review* and the Stage Planning Consultants have described the technical equipment: ' In the centre of the Olivier stage is the Theta drum revolve which is intended to combine the advantage of a revolving stage with wagons and elevators. It is proposed that scenery upon the thrust stage can be quickly positioned and repositioned, lowered into the basement and turned and replaced with new scenery or properties in the same or any other part of the stage.

The revolving stage will split into 2 semi-circular sections. One of these can sink into the service area below, to be replaced by a third section which, complete with scenery and actors, will rise to replace the former scene.

The design of the drum revolve will allow the silent vertical or rotating movement of scenes at an infinite number of speeds. It will allow traps in the surface to be positioned in an infinite number of places. Lastly it will give the freedom to reconstruct the thrust stage shape very rapidly and will even allow the designer the freedom of using the space both above and below the normal stage floor level. The Olivier theatre with its space and equipment will be able to offer varied scenery in repertory economically, it will provide the director with new potential for static or moving environment and also demand from the designer a new scenography, employing three-dimensional space to an unprecedented extent.

The conventional flying system restricting the suspension of scenery to lateral lines across the stage, i.e. the conventional grid, is discarded. Instead motorised spot lines have been installed, running in tracks across the grid, able to cope with almost any contingency for flying three-dimensional objects at any angle to the centre line of the stage.

The front edge of the stage is variable in shape and there is also the possibility of entrances for two actors from under the side tiers. There is no safety curtain but there is a safety barrier that may be raised between stage and audience when the drum elevators are lowered. Behind the stage are three rear stages protected by fire and sound reducing doors on which built scenes will be moved on motorised wagons on to the acting area.'

Lighting Installation. The National theatre will have a repertory of plays and, therefore, it is necessary to change the lighting quickly from one production to another. The lighting system installed in the Olivier theatre may be described as ' saturation lighting ' in which enough lighting equipment with a wide range of angles and with several colours should provide a lighting designer with a selection from the permanent installation for any contingency, allowing for the occasional change of colour.

There are 720 circuits controlled from a ' Lightboard ' situated at the rear of the lower tier of seats which ultimately terminate in stage lighting lanterns (spotlights, floods etc.) At the rear of the upper tier there are facilities for follow spotlights and projection. The circuits controlled electronically by a computerised control board can be grouped, regrouped and controlled at the touch of a button with a Visual Display Unit (like a television screen) to advise the operator about the cue situation and the state of the lighting illuminating the stage picture. (Plate Y.)

The Rank Strand system is described: ' The Lightboard consists of two palettes (one operable in lighting rehearsals from the stalls) which facilitate the preparation of lighting pictures or states through the selection and adjustment of any individual circuit or any pre-recorded balanced or unbalanced group of circuits. Pictures may be mixed on any of eight submasters. In performance, lighting cues are normally performed on the two playbacks, which can be operated manually or to a preset or prerecorded speed. Up to twelve lighting cues may be operated simultaneously at different speeds. Facilities also available include automatic cycling, flashing and memory modification; sound to light control and the operation of remote control colour change, slide change and projector focus and luminaire pan, tilt and focus.'

Sound. A 16 channel mixing desk with 2 echo chains; foldback and monitoring and 3 twin track tape machines with one desk replay unit are operated from the back of the auditorium. The Control desk feeds 15 loud speaker circuits built into the auditorium with additional outputs patched i.e. plugged to 60 loud speaker outlets around the stage and the auditorium. There are outlets for capacitor and other microphones around the stage and the auditorium.

Stage Management. A portable stage management control desk is installed which can be used down-stage left or right, in the rear of the auditorium Control room or in the stalls for rehearsal. There is a Ring Inter communication system (Squawk-box U.S.A.) with 3 separate technical communication circuits mixed with the stage manager's cueing circuit. There are also Radio microphones with further facilities wired to the general intercommunication system. (Plate Y.)

For general communications there is a paging system for artists and back-stage staff from the stage door, the main rehearsal rooms and the theatre; incorporating performance priority. Paging is also communicated from the theatre to the associated foyers and there is paging from the foyers to all public areas. The relay of sound and vision to the backstage areas and to the foyers for latecomers during the performance is installed. There are telephone and radio bleep staff location systems.

In architectural terms, the Olivier theatre is convincing and although the theatrical response may be questioned, the spectator is stimulated as indicated in the extract from *The Architectural Review*: ' It is a curious experience to sit in the upper tiers of the Olivier while the play is on . . . the stage is the centre of a web, drawing its actors in along five lines which stretch (or seem to stretch) outside the theatre: three lines vanish into seemingly limitless backstage, two lines tunnel under the auditorium. And the shell under which one is sitting is a shattered shell; the cave has gaps in it. The balance between feeling shut in, and yet not shut in, is exciting and also very skilful. There is a sense of immensity on tap, yet none of rattling round in an immense space; the scale is human.'

The design of the National Theatre complex with ancillary areas serving foyers and restaurants, dressing rooms for 135 actors, rehearsal rooms the same size as the stages, workshops, offices and a recording studio to match the dimensions of the site, gave the architect the problem of fitting pieces into a jigsaw puzzle. This he achieved while enjoying long deliberation with the building committee who were focused upon the treatment of the three theatres.

Theatre design was not a part of the architect's earlier work and simplicity of form with the use of concrete and glass were his preoccupations directed towards the potential of reinforced concrete. This material, embedded with steel bars to increase its tensile strength, was a product of the 50s employed in building Tower blocks of flats, airports, offices and factories. The German influence in the design of the theatre complex, with large areas of grey concrete relatively unmodified by other colours, except for the welcome row of small trees along the embankment wall, is indicated in Plate Z. Three horizontal terraces or ' streets in the air ' overlooking the Thames on the left of Plate Z are almost identical to those of the Stadttheater, Bonn, overlooking the Rhine. (Plate AA.) *The Architectural Review* has observed: ' As a *national* theatre it is a disappointment in the field of patronage; no artists have contributed to the building in any way . . . our successors may well be mystified by our enthronement of concrete as a thing of beauty and puzzled by the unrefined nature of so many surfaces and the almost total banishment of colour.' It may be interesting to observe the imaginative use of concrete in the structures designed twenty years ago in

South America. (Plate BB).

THE LYTTLETON THEATRE

The Renaissance influence is noticed in the design of the Lyttleton theatre when the plan is examined with that of a theatre described in Professor T. E. Lawrenson's article concerning the eighteenth century French theatre: Chaumont's Opera, 1766. (Figures 57 and 58.)

Although the scale is different, there are features of relative proportions in both plans viz:

(1) Taking the centre line marked A–B in the Chaumont plan and placing it over the centre line of the Lyttleton plan, the width of the proscenium opening, marked by the intersecting line C–D, is the same in both stages.

(2) The line E–F marking the false proscenium of Chaumont coincides with the line of the first false proscenium in the Lyttleton theatre.

(3) The width of the false proscenium in the Chaumont plan corresponds to the width of the side walls meeting the false proscenium in the Lyttelton theatre.

(4) The curve of the seating is similar in both theatres.

(5) Other proportionate measurements may be found in the rectangular size of the two theatres.

The design is described as follows: ' The proscenium stage Lyttelton Theatre has its 890 seats arranged in two tiers in direct confrontation with the stage. Its parallel side walls are heavily modelled to prevent cross reflection of sound. The proscenium opening, which is adjustable in height, width and position, is protected by a two-part safety curtain. The main part of the stage incorporates an elevator which enables its level and rake to be adjusted. A group of smaller elevators in the forestage area can be lowered to form an orchestra pit or can be used in conjunction with the main elevator. Full-sized rear and side stages, separated from the main stage by sound proof

PLAN OF THE LYTTLETON THEATRE

Figure 57

PLAN OF CHAUMONT'S OPERA, 1766
Figure 58

doors, are equipped with motorised wagons to move scenery. The fly tower over the stage has a power-equipped flying system with the conventional parallel bar layout.'

To accommodate the audience in seating almost parallel to the stage, the adaptable proscenium opening has had to be made very wide. The adjustment in width is from 29 ft. 6 in. to 44 ft. 7 in. and in height from 16 ft. 5 in. to 29 ft. 6 in. The width of the proscenium opening normally found in a London theatre is 26 ft. to 32 ft. In the Lyttelton theatre, the actor playing an intimate scene on the centre area of the stage, with the proscenium opening enclosed, is playing above three false prosceniums and as a result he is very distant and there would be difficult sight lines from the sides of the front rows of seats.

The Architectural Review has commented: ' The decision to have long rows unbroken by gangways has led to an inevitable " cinema feel " to this theatre. This is also because there is no messing about with boxes or " papering the walls with people "—it is eyeball to eyeball straight-on confrontation, and very dramatic. The proscenium is strangely undefined by the architecture and much more delineated by lighting and areas of blackness. The front rows A to D are the " ripple " rows—the cheap seats.' (Fig. 59.)

It will be seen from the theatre plans that rows A to D occupy the forestage area in the Chaumont plan, and he was the first to visualise his audience ' in a very simple shape whereby the spectator is seated very favourably facing the actor'. The actor performed on the forestage and the back stage area was left merely as a picture of scenery decoration. The Lyttelton theatre is a simple shape —almost a square block of seats arranged line upon line facing the actor.

During the 18th century theatre going increased in popularity and the larger audiences required more accommodation. The actor was moved further back until in the middle of the 19th century, the actors were confined to the

SECTION OF THE LYTTLETON THEATRE

Figure 59

scenery area of the stage and the opening was surrounded by the proscenium arch. This situation became critical to the extent that the actor was rigidly separated from the audience and a return to the forestage or apron stage has been evident in the design of recent theatres.

Some thought has been given to the forestage area of the Lyttelton theatre and the third proscenium is not only adjustable in width and height, it can retreat upstage to just over 5 ft. from the line of the safety curtain. The stage floor is adjustable and the front edge can tilt to the auditorium floor level or provide an orchestra pit taken from the stage area and not, as is usually found, occupying a part of the auditorium.

The actor playing in the theatre for the first time encountered the wide proscenium opening with the acoustic property of the rectangle theatre and the company was obliged to act in a broad continental style almost unknown in this country. In Renaissance France, the long rectangular theatre led eventually to the abandonment of dramatic text and it was used for spectacle alone, as in the Salle des Machines, 1738. It is to be hoped that the thought given to this theatre will lead to success in time and the situation is summed up in the report of the dramatic critic of *The Times*: ' The place feels like the inside of an expensive camera and we can look forward to displays of advanced technology including a proscenium that opens and contracts like a lens shutter. . . . Besides the larger stage there is also the matter of its proximity to the house. The range of expressiveness obtainable in close-ups is marvellously demonstrated when you witness Peggy Ashcroft against a magnified background of darkness without missing a single blink of her exhausted eyes. Acoustically, however, the company are still feeling their way. . . . At present the indoor scenes are played on a central pocket handkerchief acting area which reduces their scale and pushes them away into the distance; and there is a big aural as well as visual gain when the action swells to take in the whole stage.'

Stage Machinery. Three front elevators in line across the stage are capable of being set at orchestra pit, auditorium, and stage levels as well as raking in conjunction with the main stage elevator. The rear stage wagon incorporates a disc revolving stage. This wagon and the side storage wagon, of similar size but formed of demountable units, can be set on the main elevator at various rakes. The flying equipment consists of double purchase assisted counter-weights and the barrels can be synchronised with 6 spot lines installed anywhere in the grid. The system is controlled from a panel on the down stage fly gallery and the control of the proscenium curtain is duplicated on the stage manager's desk.

Lighting Installation. There are 498 circuits, controlled from a 'Lightboard', identical to that installed in the Olivier theatre, which is situated at the rear of the lower level of the auditorium. Follow spotlights and projection are operated from the rear of the circle seating.

Sound. A control desk situated at the back of the auditorium is similar to the desk installed in the Olivier theatre and feeds 15 circuits of loudspeakers built into the auditorium with additional outputs plugged to 43 loudspeaker outlets around the stage and the auditorium. There are outlets for capacitor and other microphones around the stage and the auditorium. (Plate CC.)

Stage Management. A portable stage management desk which can be used down stage left or right is the same as that installed in the Olivier theatre.

THE COTTESLOE THEATRE

Since the early part of the century, the open stage form called theatre-in-the-round has provided endless variety for the actor and even more so, for the director, designer and technician invited to stage plays within the space enclosed by the bare walls of a converted hall or factory. The scenic end stage, one room end stage, thrust or peninsular stage and the transverse stage are forms which flourish in places where there is difficulty in arranging the conventional picture frame stage and auditorium. The challenge of improvisation and ingenuity aroused by the staging possibilities in these experimental studio theatres has given stimulation to the theatre at the time when existing theatres have suffered from the competition of other entertainment mediums.

The entrance to the Cottesloe theatre is at the Thames embankment level below the dramatic concrete raking struts seen in Plate CC, and the theatre is tucked in between the two L linked main zones of the National theatre complex. It is described in *The Architectural Review*: 'The space on the plan that had to be filled was 66 ft. long and 56 ft. wide —bigger than David Garrick's Drury Lane. The solution that has been adopted has galleries on three sides, each level of the audience consisting of one row sitting and behind them a row of standing (or leaning) patrons. Depending on the stage arrangements the central floor area can take a variety of seating arrangements.

The Cottesloe can be organised inside the space defined by the three walls of galleries in a variety of ways—scenic end stage; theatre-in-the-round; one room end stage and, by raising the auditorium in the central space to stage height and removing the lowest of the three tier fronts, a flat floor over the whole space. A moving " fourth wall " that can vary the volume of the space and provide a completely encircling audience has yet to be installed.' (Figures 60 and 61.)

The theatre consultants mention a second element for future consideration which is a modular elevator system in the central space to allow greater flexibility both in plan form and in the levels of acting and audience areas. Depending on the layout, the seating space of the studio theatre can accommodate between 200 and 400, and the section through the theatre shows the three inter-connected levels on three sides of the central space, available to either audience and performer with flexibility of the floor level. However, it may be said that the portable lighting and sound controls, which may be used in any suitable position, obstruct the main circulation area at the principal gallery level. Using the controls where they are situated, one of the rows is removed where standing (or leaning) patrons are accommodated and the controls block the way across the auditorium.

The acting area is basically an end stage 39 ft. 3 in. wide and 29 ft. 6 in. deep. There is little or no wing space and much ingenuity is needed in the design of settings as curtains are improvised for the actors' entrances with a formidable concrete pillar hindering each side of the acting area. The provision of an acceptable dock or storage area for scenery is not evident in the stage design. There is a dock area off-stage right and it is not at a level with the stage. This is part of the passage giving access to the work-shops from the 'Theta' drum revolve in the Olivier theatre, which is intended as a means of removing and replacing scenery and properties. Scenery stored nearby from the Cottesloe theatre might cause problems in re-arranging the scenery for the Olivier theatre stage. The moving 'fourth wall' has not yet been installed for cost reasons and it is described: 'This will allow either audience or actors to cross between the galleries at higher levels. Movement of the fourth wall varies the volume of the space. Advanced, it completes the audience encirclement for theatre-in-the-round. In other positions it provides either an architectural background to the actor or an access system for multi-level scenery. When not used it is parked upstage.' The fourth wall will hang on tracks against the rear wall of the stage area and be pushed for-ward either manually or motorised electronically to com-plete the square for theatre-in-the-round. The supporting framework to allow either audience or actors to cross be-tween the galleries may be a substantial one and would take away space from the acting area comprising the end

PLAN OF THE COTTESLOE THEATRE
Top: Arena Stage
Bottom: End Stage

Figure 60

SECTION OF THE COTTESLOE THEATRE

Figure 61

© DENYS LASDUN AND PARTNERS

stage.

Lighting Installation. There are five lighting bridges and access bridges and interconnecting walkways above stage level. The lighting positions are on central bridges and gallery fronts and over the end stage areas where minimal scenic suspension on hemp and winch lines is provided. The lighting control is by a portable memory system with the initial installation of 80 dimmers. A portable sound control desk and stage management control is included in the installation.

The Architectural Review comments: ' It is too early to judge this theatre, but it does look a very promising studio theatre. In form and scale it feels like a Georgian playhouse while having an indoor Elizabethan quality that favours non-scenic production. When it is lined by an audience it could well be an exciting cockpit for experimental productions. It is currently painted a stark black all over, which gives it the air of a setting for some grim initiation or ritual. A determination to make it feel like a studio has deprived it of any welcoming warmth and left a great deal of the theatrical atmosphere to be provided by the plays.'

APPRAISAL

The National theatre opened in 1976 with only one of its three theatres completed: the Lyttelton staged a revival of the farce *Plunder* by Ben Travers, and the director said it will be three years before his policy becomes visible and five years before the whole building is properly at work. In 1979 it is possible to observe how his prediction is being fulfilled during the three years since the theatre was opened. The technical side of stage design is intended to support the actor in contact with his audience. There should be good and unobtrusive lighting with speedy handling of scenery, and the design of the setting should illustrate the author's play and provide an agreeable background to support the actor in his performance. It has been said that the artist works in a hostile world and the vast organisation of the National theatre may be in danger of confirming this view.

There are the mechanised revolving stage and power-operated scenery hoists intended for central control by a computer (though without conversion to manual operation) in the Olivier theatre, the power-assisted flying and power-assisted wagon stages with a system of lifts in the Lyttelton theatre and electronically controlled lighting boards with over 1200 circuits for the two theatres. The equipment is intended to assist the playing of repertory and to save labour in a repertoire of 7 to 8 productions in the Olivier theatre, 4 plays in the Lyttelton theatre and 10 plays in the Cottesloe theatre each year.

At the time of writing, the Olivier revolving stage incorporating semi-circular lifts, the power operated scenery hoists and the power assisted wagon stages of the Lyttelton theatre are not yet properly commissioned, and only the main lifts in the Lyttelton stage are working as intended. For a production of *Tales of the Vienna Woods* a temporary manual revolve was installed at the Olivier and mounted on top of the real one. New wheels to support the weight of the ' Theta ' drum revolve have been tested satisfactorily, but it still remains to connect the revolve and the scenery hoists to the complex electronic control system. Similar revolving stages are working in theatres abroad although they are not so complicated as the National theatre system.

There have been difficulties with the Olivier fly-tower in using the secondary emergency brake and in lowering hooks without weights. In the Lyttelton theatre the wagon stages are moved manually until the time they are motorised. Eight men are needed to move the unloaded wagon platform on and off stage. When raked rostrums and scenery are carried the maximum number of men is 22 to move the off-stage wagon on to the acting area of the stage. The additional staff and alternative equipment has increased the production running costs to the National theatre by more than £200,000 in one year.

The wisdom of recommending an all-purpose scenery changing turntable permanently installed in the centre of the Olivier stage has been questioned. When it is working properly labour will be saved and with a repertory system of plays, running costs will be curtailed. However, the design of stage settings is general and covers a great variety of ideas in shape, treatment and colour. A machine is restricted to its design operation which, in the Theta drum revolve, incorporates 2 semi-circular lifts, and the scene designer, accustomed to freedom within the acting area, may find adaptation of his design to the mechanised equipment a restrictive process.

Our country has excelled in the design of fine mechanical engineering; the internal combustion engine, the jet propelled aero engine, the hovercraft and complicated machinery used in factory processes were developed here and are used universally. Just as a craftsman benefits from the quality of his tools, the staff of the National theatre will take pride in and derive advantage from the technology of the sophisticated equipment it is hoped will be operating satisfactorily in the theatre complex.

The power assisted spot-line flying system was designed specially for the Olivier theatre because the audience partially surrounded the stage and the usual lateral grid system of lines running across the stage was unable to provide a flexible arrangement of flying shaped scenery at any angle to the centre line of the stage. There are 127 motorised scenery hooks and 20 point hoists which can cope with almost any flying contingency and they are intended to be controlled centrally by a computer. Although the system has passed stringent safety tests, is silent and is capable of taking the required estimated loads, machinery is not infallible and should it break down there is no provision for immediate manual operation essential to a public performance.

An element of caution has crept into the Olivier theatre

and the staff are entreated not to work on the stage while someone is working in the grid. There is a notice prominently displayed: ' You are advised to wear a safety helmet whenever fit-ups or change-overs are taking place.' What happens to the bare head actor who delays his exit is not disclosed.

The power assisted computer controlled flying system in the Olivier Theatre was handed over by the contractor in October 1978, and the National Theatre company are training staff to accustom them to the new flying facilities available for stage designers. Although the equipment resembles space-age technology, the vast size of the National Theatre complex confirms the need of advanced methods for controlling the machinery installed there. Electronics and the computer do away with flymen loading and unloading counterweights though manual theatrical skill employed in hanging and brailing scenery is still required.

During the last twenty-five years, stage lighting has advanced from the mechanically operated board controlling about 100 spotlights and floods, formerly with liquid dimmers, to the modern sophisticated board with visual display unit and many other facilities designed to control electronically over 500 circuits in the theatre. The circuits can be controlled at the touch of a button though the colour, focus and direction of each lantern has to be adjusted by hand, the electrician mounting ladders to do so, with time spent and added cost of labour.

Due to the improvement in design and manufacture of the equipment, spotlights became smaller in size and consequently more spotlights were installed in the space available. Eventually the installation became so large as to need well-informed technical assistance to explain and use it. At first the Chief Electrician appointed to the theatre took it all in his stride. Later, however, the work became more involved and the Lighting Designer came into being; he was the specialist called in to plan on paper the installation needed and to put it together at the lighting rehearsal. After establishing basic principles, there was a veritable Aladdin's cave of lighting equipment from which to choose, provided by the manufacturers who were enjoying a lucrative business. The temptation was great and stage lighting became brighter with more complicated methods of controlling it.

The Lighting Designer—essentially a technician—then perceived that artistry might improve his function and he embarked on the dizzy ascent of emphasising the plot of the play with his illumination of it. Atmosphere or mood lighting, requiring additional cues, was encouraged and special effects were supposed to be created which, more often than not, were visible to the Lighting Designer and no one else. For moments of sadness or grief in the plot, the lighting was softly subdued and twinkled to brightness again when the heroine was indeed rescued from the the mill stream. This kind of thing became the vogue, to the dismay of the hapless stage manager, who sat up to early hours of the morning carefully adding lighting cue upon cue in his prompt script. When the production account was received the volume of lighting equipment installed gave the theatrical manager second thoughts about the cost incurred and its negative effect on his box office returns.

In the Olivier theatre, there are 720 circuits employing the practice of ' saturation lighting ' in the hope that the lighting designer will be able to choose a selection to suit his purposes from the permanent installation. The solution might be achieved comfortably in about an hour, allowing for any special effects, and assuming that the spotlights requiring exceptional adjustment are accessible without climbing ladders. Afterwards the lighting is set and recorded and the cues necessary to the author's script rehearsed.

The lessons may have been learned and the Lighting Designer accustomed to select a limited number of spotlights from the vast array at his disposal in the Olivier theatre sets them in an imaginative way to produce the lighting already praised in the National theatre. With the disciplined use of his skill he will confirm the observation mentioned at the end of chapter 8 in this book.

A contributor to *The Architectural Review* mentions Charles Dickens' day dream of being in charge of a great theatre and his scepticism about the foundation of a National theatre, which was justified by the 100 years of delay that have preceded the building of the theatre. The lessee and manager of the Theatre Royal, Drury Lane, Augustus Harris, wrote an article in 1885 for the *Fortnightly Review* entitled *The National Theatre* in which he described the history of the Theatre Royal and his experience of triumph and failure in the presentation of plays during the first six years' lease of the theatre. *The Architectural Review* continues: ' Yet the soubriquet of National for Drury Lane was spurious: it might have been merited during Garrick's tenancy from 1747 to 1786, but had long since been abused by those who favoured spectacle in place of drama, scene rather than poem.' The arbitrary dismissal of the title ' National Theatre ' overlooks the reference to Henry Irving in the Augustus Harris article: ' The history of Drury Lane for the past century and a half is not altogether uninstructive. It may be described as a perpetual struggle between the advocates of the legitimate and successive generations of managers who have always come sooner or later (often, alas! to their cost) to realise the truism which Mr. Irving aptly expressed when he said that the drama " must thrive as a business before it can flourish as an art ". In a word, the standing conflict at Drury Lane has been between theatrical theory on the one hand and theatrical practice on the other.'

Charles Dickens mused philosophically on his great theatre in 1870 and it was through the devoted enthusiasm of two people working in modest theatres that the project of the National Theatre was continued. Frank Benson first produced a season of Shakespeare's plays at Stratford-on-Avon in 1886 and continued to perform there for a season in the Spring of each year until 1919.

'Fancy you remembering me!' said Lilian Baylis when she was recognised, and who is likely to forget her? She created three theatre companies; The Old Vic, Sadler's Wells Opera and Sadler's Wells Ballet, which became the Royal Ballet now housed at the Royal Opera House, Covent Garden. In 1914, Lilian Baylis first presented Shakespeare at the Old Vic, the teetotal theatre she acquired from her aunt, Emma Cons, to present Opera in English and Shakespeare at popular prices.

As it happened, the theatre she inherited was admirably suited to simple staging of the classics. It was smaller than the theatres of spectacle such as the Theatre Royal, Drury Lane, and the Covent Garden Opera House. The wrapped round curved seating of the Old Vic comprised the shape of a horseshoe with the poles turned inwards and the galleries around the auditorium ended in boxes at the sides of the proscenium arch overlooking the small forestage and the orchestra pit. The Old Vic and the Stratford theatre struggled with financial problems and from the modest beginning of the Benson touring company and the dedication of Lilian Baylis, who produced plays without subsidies and managed to secure great performers for small salaries, two National Theatre companies were formed. The Old Vic became the nucleus of the National Theatre Company on the South Bank of the Thames and the Royal Shakespeare Company was established at Stratford-on-Avon with a London home at the Aldwych Theatre. The company expects to transfer its production in 1980 to the new Barbican Theatre in the City of London with an appeal of £1 million launched to endow the theatre. (p. 116 and Plate D.)

The fortunes of the two companies treading very much the same ground are different. The Royal Shakespeare

PLATE Q

The Greek Theatre at Epidaurus

PLATE R

The National Theatre: Plan of
the Olivier stage and auditorium

PLATE S
Plan of Roubo's Theatre project
The lettering has been superimposed over Roubo's original

PLATE T

Section of the Olivier Theatre

COUPE PRISE SUR LA LIGNE AB

FLATE U

Section of Roubo's Theatre project

PLATE V

Model of the Olivier Theatre and auditorium
(a) *above*: with auditorium lights
(b) *below*: without auditorium lights

PLATE W

Auditorium of the Prinzregenten Theatre, Munich
Professor: Max Littmann, Architect

PLATE X

The Theatre Royal, Drury Lane

Company, installed in London and Stratford-on-Avon is playing to 86% capacity audiences at the Aldwych Theatre and it is financially successful. Net earned income in 1976–7 came to £1,928,232 apart from an Arts Council grant of £1,100,000, of which £200,000 was a rolling guarantee against loss. Not all that guarantee was called upon, although 5 per cent is the margin allowed for calculations at Stratford-on-Avon. The director's aim is ' to secure the maximum availability of resources for artists to work with and to work quietly within sympathetic controls and disciplines '. The annual repertoire of 32 productions is planned two years ahead and extra responsibilities with concern for detail in all aspects of production sometimes cause late planning and higher production costs. Actors are a favoured race and they must be cushioned from stress; late changes bring disruption throughout the organisation. Play production is dependent upon the availability or whim of actor, director and writer and is the burden carried by every theatrical manager working in a volatile profession. The production of *The Tempest* cost twice the original budget and although the computerised lighting board broke down on the opening night, it was well received.

There is an efficient administration whose policy is that it ' should not be seen and not be heard '. Only 124 actors are included in the 500 people working with the company in four theatres, which has increased its operation with a provincial season and tour, the transfer of plays to other London theatres, and the development of a separate studio theatre.

Two years later in 1979, another picture is shown with national and local government implementing disastrous cuts in the grants given for support of the Arts. At a time of annual rate of inflation exceeding 15 per cent, the Arts Council grants provide only an increase of 7·46 per cent and the grant of £1,800,000 for 1979/80 (against £1,675,000 in 1978/79) includes almost £250,000 which will not be available as cash until after the end of the current financial year. The effect of the higher rate of value-added-tax upon the Box Office also seriously limited companies in their ability to obtain extra revenue by further increasing the price of theatre seats.

The R.S.C. Regional Tour, extended to serve areas where few facilities for live theatre presentation exist, ran into difficulty. The Arts Council was determined to help with the new venture though their financial assistance fell short of the funds necessary to support the tour. Relief came from an unusual source and for the first time commercial sponsorship—established in sport and music— reached the living theatre. The exact sum of £12,000 to allow the 1978 Regional Tour to go ahead was given by Hallmark Cards and the Midland Bank supported the opening production of the Stratford 1979/80 season: *The Merry Wives of Windsor* to the tune of £25,000.

A number of other sponsors are supporting productions during 1979/80 and are gratefully received but these remain commercial ventures subject to the normal business decision regarding their continuation. Grant-aided theatres are not permitted the prudent management of commercial organisations to carry reserves and sponsorship cannot become an adequate substitute for the principal source of Arts patronage i.e. public funding for theatres operating close to subsistence level over several years. It must be the hope of everyone employed in the theatre that those engaged with repair of the national economy will understand the total dependence of the arts on an irreducible level of state support. Without this response there is the risk of permanent damage to our artistic heritage of British theatre and its world-beating reputation.

The National Theatre, with its three stages, is a building spread over approximately 4½ acres and in a television interview, the director emphasised that much of the difficulty in getting the theatre out of the red is the long time it has taken official sources to realise how much a building complex of this stature will cost to maintain. In the financial year, 1977–78 the National Theatre received subsidies of £2,750,000 from the Arts Council and £350,000 from the Greater London Council. The yearly running costs are £3,500,000, of which 33 per cent is required for the upkeep of the building and the staging of plays takes only 4 per cent. The three auditoriums with foyers and river terraces cover an area larger than any other European theatre and are designed to attract 2,000 to 3,000 people every working day in the year. Over the first two years the National Theatre has averaged 90 per cent capacity audiences and the company consists of 106 actors with a staff of 500 to administer the building. For three hundred years the choice of the theatre public has been for spectacle and not the spoken word, which was interpreted in the standing conflict at the Theatre Royal, Drury Lane, between theatrical theory on the one hand and theatrical practice on the other. The National Theatre is a spectacular building and is this the magnet that attracts the public? The audience seen there is content to wander (and lie on the floor) in the foyers and terraces overlooking the Thames. The formality is broken and by keeping the theatre open 12 hours in the day, with the bar, open at public house hours and at public house prices, an additional source of income is assured.

The financial difficulties in the first two years were due mainly to the delay in completing the building which with inflation increased the cost to £17 million and caused the alteration of plans. For the second year running there were no visits by any regional companies and the National Theatre was unable to mount a touring production. The South Bank Theatre Board is responsible for getting the building finished and the technical equipment working, which in the case of the complicated drum revolve in the Olivier theatre was not handed over and has proved an expensive item to the contractors.

A run of artistic and commercial successes has been enjoyed by the National Theatre, though it is estimated that
with the existing subsidy, it will be possible to spend
£1,500,000 on the building and yet present only three plays
in a year. Preservation of the building could be a Government responsibility, as if it were a national monument,
but there is a bleak response to this proposal from official
sources. The theatre complex has provided the opportunity
for architects, technicians and administrators to employ
their skill. In this vast organisation it may be overlooked
that the creation of a theatre is designed for the actor to
play his part and entertain his audience. The company is
liable for the upkeep of a giant building and, in the words
of a technician: ' Time and the further development of the
art of the theatre will prove whether or not all is right and
well for we theatrical people.'

The development of the South Bank site—the largest in
Central London and possibly the most profitable in the
world—continues to be discussed by those examining the
interest of architects, planners and prospective developers
of the site. The Lambeth Borough Council is opposed to
a scheme for the building of substantial office blocks and
desires local community groups to create homes with
gardens on the area adjacent to the National Theatre.
Whether or not this is financially viable on a prime site
planned to accommodate over a million square feet of
offices is a reminder of past mistakes with no commitment
to housing for rental income.

Included in the vanguard of the controversial proposals
is the National Theatre architect: Sir Denys Lasdun with
his contribution of a five-storey office building next door
to the theatre. His Wagnerian concept embraces another
giant complex of uniform terraces with similar character
and features to the National Theatre. Future voyagers up
and down the river may avert their eyes from the prospect
of Isolde and then her Tristan enshrined in concrete and
standing cheek by jowl upon the south bank of Father

Thames.

The National Theatre is one of seven buildings presented with the 1978 award for architecture by the Royal Institute of British Architects and is described by the President as one of the three to become outstanding masterpieces of the 1970s. In the *Architects' Journal* the Technical Director of the Cologne Opera House, West Germany, has mentioned the exterior of the theatre: ' The first thing we saw from the bridge in the dark of a winter evening, was a small lit-up castle mirrored in the Thames and in which apparently, there was already rushing life. This was not one of the usual fortresses; it was a castle with towers and battlements, with balconies and terraces, narrow and wide openings, cool on the outside and warmly lit inside.'

The humble Briton is unaccustomed to a Rhineland castle mirrored in the waters of the Lorelei and for their masterpiece, Lord Larry may have his name and address taken by Ernest the Policeman and Sir Denys be presented with a new silver whistle by the Mayor of Toytown.

A GLOSSARY OF THEATRICAL TERMS

'But there is nothing which delights and terrifies our English theatre so much as a ghost, especially when he appears in a bloody shirt. A spectre has very often saved a play.'—Addison writing in *The Spectator* in 1711.

Not only the ghost but the grave trap and a skeleton are part of the language of the theatre. This glossary contains technical words the stage manager will use and also some of the traditional expressions which he may come across in his work. The description used in the American theatre is given where this differs from the English equivalent.

ABOVE   A stage direction used in describing a position behind furniture, etc.

ACOUSTICS   The science of sound. Qualities of hearing in the theatre.

ACT   The main part of a play.

ACT-CHANGE   A change of scenery. Removing one setting and building another.

ACT-DROP   The curtain or cloth behind the proscenium arch dividing the stage from the auditorium.

ACT-WAIT   The interval between the acts in a play.

ACTING AREA   The stage space enclosed by scenery where the play is performed. As a conventional guide the stage is divided into nine acting areas: down-stage centre, down-stage right and left, centre stage, right and left and up-stage centre, right and left. Centre stage is the most important.

ACTING AREA LANTERN   A round flood without focussing adjustment suspended from a batten above the acting area.

ACTION OF PLAY   Series of speeches, movements, events and dumb show.

ADDITIVE LIGHTING   Primary colour mixing of light. (See Chapter 8.)

AD LIB   The presence of mind by an actor who improvises or 'gags' when the play is held up in an emergency.

AISLE, CENTRE The centre division between the seats in the auditorium.

ALIVE Required during the performance.

APRON The part of the stage from the setting line which extends in front of the proscenium into the auditorium.

ARC A high-powered spotlight used from the auditorium for special effects. It is operated by carbon rods in electrical contact.

ARCHITRAVE The moulding of lintels and jambs around doors and windows, etc.

ARENA Acting area surrounded by the audience on all sides; the stage and audience being contained within the same space.

ASIDE Words spoken by an actor in an undertone to the audience and not supposed to be heard by the rest of the cast.

A.S.M. Assistant Stage Manager.

ASTRAGAL The small moulding which holds together the panes in a window.

AUDITORIUM The part of the theatre with accommodation for spectators.

AUDITORIUM BEAM See F.O.H. lighting.

BABY SPOT A small compact high-efficiency spotlight.

BACK BATTEN The batten used for lighting the backcloth. Also known as the ' Sky Batten.'

BACKCLOTH A cloth painted to represent a distant scene hung behind the setting at the rear of the stage.

BACKGROUND MUSIC Music played to support the atmosphere of a scene.

BACKING A piece of scenery used to limit the view of the audience and placed behind a door, window, fireplace or other opening.

BACK-STAGE The division of the theatre behind the proscenium curtain, which includes the stage, dressing rooms and workshops, etc.

BACK-STAGE STAFF Those employed in working behind the curtain, i.e. Stage Carpenter, Property men, Electricians, Flymen, Stage hands, Firemen, Dressers and the Stage-Door Keeper.

BAD JOIN The gap between flats that do not meet closely when cleated together. Also used in relation to the join between a wig and facial make-up.

BAFFLE Piece of material used to prevent light escaping around scenery.

BALCONY   The seats between the dress circle and the gallery. Also called the upper circle and frequently replaces the gallery.

BALCONY FRONT SPOTS   The spotlights enclosed in a cage and mounted in front of the balcony.

BALSA WOOD   Very light strong wood used in making properties.

BAND   The Orchestra.

BAND ROOM   The orchestra dressing room situated under the stage and near to the orchestra pit.

BAR BELLS   The warning bells in the front of the house to inform the audience when the curtain is about to rise.

BARREL   (1) The steel barrel used for suspending spotlights with the permanent wiring running inside the tube. (2) The barrel used in the counterweight system to which the scenery is attached by snatch lines.   Pipe Batten (U.S.A.).

BATTEN   (1) A long narrow strip of wood fastened to the top and bottom of a cloth.   (2) Part of the frame of a flat.   (3) A steel or wooden bar used for suspending scenery or lighting equipment.   (4) The metal trough with rows of lights flown above the stage.

BATTEN OUT   The method of nailing battens to the back of flats to secure them together.   (See French Flats.)

BATTENS NOS. 1, 2, 3 AND 4   The lighting compartment battens suspended above the stage.   No. 1 is the nearest to the proscenium arch and sometimes is called the ' Concert Batten.'   Nos. 2 and 3 are above the acting area and No. 4 or ' Back Batten ' is used to light the backcloth.

BAY   The division of wall space in a scene dock marked by scaffolding poles between which scenery and flats are stacked.

BEAM ANGLE   The angle of light from a spotlight projected to the stage.

BEAM BORDERS   Canvas borders painted to represent the beams of a mediaeval ceiling.

BELOW   A stage direction used to indicate a position in front of furniture, etc.

BILLY   A single pulley-block and rope used for hoisting scenery.

BLACK   The stage apron which was formerly painted black and is now usually covered with linoleum.

BLACK LIGHT   Ultra-violet light.

BLACK-OUT To extinguish all the lights on the stage. A scene can start in a ' black-out ' when the curtain rises on a darkened stage or a scene may be terminated by switching off all the stage lights.

BLACKS Black velvet curtains and borders used as a stage setting or for masking scenery.

BLOBBY When lighting is uneven it is called ' blobby ' by the electrician.

BLOCK A pulley or mounted set of pulleys used in the grid through which the scenery lines are reeved to the flies.

BOARD The electrical switchboard.

BOARD LIGHT The light on the cue board in the prompt corner or the electrician's board by which the plots are read.

BOAT TRUCK A low-wheeled platform on which a piece of scenery is built so that it can be moved into position. It is used in a scene change when it is wheeled on and off stage.

BOLT A quantity of canvas when purchased for scenery.

BOOK The story and dialogue of the play. The prompt script.

BOOK FLAT Two flats hinged to fold together like a book. Two Fold Flat (U.S.A.).

BOOK WING Two scenery flats hinged in the middle so that they are self-supporting and used for masking open settings.

BOOM A tubular bar mounted upright at the sides of a scene and used for suspending spotlights or floods above one another.

BORDER A length of painted canvas or other material such as velvet attached to a batten and suspended above the scene to conceal the top of the setting.

BORDER LIGHT See Compartment Batten.

BOTTOM LIGHTING Lighting equipment used to illuminate the lower part of the setting.

BOX OFFICE MANAGER The official in charge of the theatre ticket booking offices.

BOX OFFICE PLAN The plan of the bookable seats in the theatre which includes a separate sheet for each part of the auditorium.

BOX SETTING A scene built from flats representing three walls of a room in contrast with the open scene.

BRACE A wooden or metal support, usually adjustable, to prop up scenery. Extension Brace (U.S.A.).

BRACE CLEAT   A small metal plate with a hole screwed to a flat.   The brace is hooked to it and supports the flat.

BRACE RAIL   The corner batten to strengthen a flat.

BRAIL LINE   A line or rope attached to the lines of a piece of hanging scenery for pulling and retaining it up- or down-stage or from side to side.   Guide or Breast Line (U.S.A.).

BREAK   (a) Used to describe a pause when rehearsals are interrupted.   (b) The property master is asked to ' break down ' a property that looks unused, i.e. paint or roughen the surface.

BREAK-UP   Scenery specially designed to collapse on a cue, i.e. a wall shattered by an explosion.

BRIDGE   (1) A platform cut into a section of the stage that is raised or lowered manually or mechanically.   The larger bridges are operated electrically or hydraulically. In addition to moving up and down, a bridge may be moved to the side when lowered and replaced by another bridge which rises in place of the first one.   (2) During rehearsals a platform is built over the orchestra pit with steps to the floor.   It is used by the Director for convenient access to the stage.   (See Elevator, Lift, Runway.)

BRIDLE   Ropes or chains attached at intervals to a lighting or other heavy batten to distribute the weight.   The centre of the bridle is fastened to lines from the grid.

BRING IN   To increase lighting at a cue that is previously dimmed in the stage plot.

BUNCH LIGHTS   A set of light bulbs in the form of a cluster, arranged when it is difficult to illuminate by a normal method.

BURNT SUGAR   Diluted with water is used to represent stage drinks.

BUSINESS   Dumb show.   Actions performed by the artists.

BUZZER   Electrical bell cue.

CAB TYRE   Heavy insulated electric cable used for portable installations.

CALL   A notice in theatre language.   (1) Artists are ' called ' to a rehearsal or for their stage entrance.   Details of a journey are posted to the notice board in a ' Train Call.' An orchestra rehearsal is a ' Band Call.'   A rehearsal for the entire cast is a ' Company Call.'   (2) The ' curtain calls ' at the end of the play when the actors bow to the audience.   When the stage manager takes up the curtain on languid applause he is said to ' pinch a call.'

CALL BOARD   The theatre notice board.

CALL BOOK   The note book used by the call boy for recording the actors' entrances.

CAMEO   A small part so well-written and acted that it becomes conspicuous.

CARPET CUT   A narrow trough with a hinged lid running across the stage near the setting line in which the edge of a carpet or stage cloth is secured.

CAST   (1) Arrange parts for actors. (2) The actors performing the play.

CAT WALK   The narrow platform connecting the fly galleries on both sides of the stage.

CEILING CLOTH   The canvas cloth battened and painted to represent a ceiling set above the flats in an interior setting.

CEILING PLATE   A metal plate with a ring screwed to the battens of a ceiling for bolting together and flying.

CELLAR   The space below the stage.

CENTRE LINE   A line from the centre of the footlights to the middle of the back wall. It is marked on the stage before setting the scenery. Also the middle line of a set of lines for flying a cloth.

CENTRE OPENING   The centre entrance in a scene. (See french windows in Plate 3.)

CENTRE PIECE   Any piece of scenery placed in the centre of the stage.

CENTRE STAGE   The part of the stage actors like to retain.

CHALK A SCENE   In early rehearsals the setting is marked on the stage with chalk lines. Chalk is rubbed on a piece of string which is held taut between two points and snapped on the stage when the chalk will show the line required. (See Chapter 2.)

CHAMBER BORDER   A painted canvas border used in place of a ceiling to mask the top of the scene. Two or three are required, depending on the area of the setting.

CHAMBER SET   An interior set such as a lounge, study, etc.

CHARACTER PART   A part that has a distinctive style, i.e. a member of a profession, the elder relative, etc.

CHASER   The music played while the audience leaves the theatre.

CHECK   Reduction in light.

CHIPS   The nickname for the stage carpenter.

CHOREOGRAPHY   Design of stage movement and dancing.

CIRCLE FRONT SPOTS   The spotlights mounted in front of the dress circle.

CIRCUIT   The path travelled by an electric current. A series of lamps controlled by one switch or dimmer is known as a circuit.

CLAMP   Flats that are warped and do not join properly are held together by a carpenter's clamp.

CLEAR   A clear stage is one ready for the performance. Those artists who are not discovered at the rise of the curtain have 'cleared,' i.e. left the stage.

CLEARING STICK   A long pole sometimes with a T piece at the end, used from the stage for clearing an obstruction such as a border that is not hanging properly.

CLEAT   (1) A metal or wooden hook around which a line is thrown to bind the edge of one flat to another. The line is secured on the tie-off screws. (2) The belaying pin attached to the fly rail for securing the ropes of flying scenery.

CLOTH   A scenic sheet made up of widths of canvas with battens at the top and bottom and suspended on a set of lines. See Backcloth, Ceiling-cloth, Cut-cloth, Stage-cloth.   Drop (U.S.A.).

CLOVE HITCH   The knot used for tying a cloth to a batten.

COLD   When a play is staged in London without a preliminary tour of the provinces it is said ' to open cold.'

COLOUR CIRCUIT   One of the three or four colour circuits in the footlights or battens.

COLOUR FILTER   The medium used as a light filter.

COLOUR FRAME   The frame in which the medium is inserted and held in front of lighting equipment.

COLOUR MEDIUMS   The acetate sheeting and glass used to diffuse light.

COLUMN   A set piece built of wooden cores and covered with three-ply or light plastic material.

COMMONWEALTH   The cast of a play which agrees to accept a *pro rata* share of the takings after expenses are paid in lieu of salary to assist the play over a difficult period.

COMPANY MANAGER   The business manager of the play.

COMPARTMENT BATTEN   The lighting trough enclosing lamps and reflectors with filters in metal frames. They are used above the stage, as sections of footlights and for lighting a cloth or cyclorama. See Battens 1, 2, 3, etc.   Border Light (U.S.A.).

CONCERT BATTEN   See Batten No. 1.

CONNECTOR BOX   Lighting equipment used to connect or adapt electrical circuits.

CONSOLE   A mobile remote control for stage lighting like the key-desk of an organ.   The latest control console incorporates a memory device that stores lighting instructions whereby the operator can execute complicated lighting changes in rapid succession.

COPPER TOE   A strip of copper sheeting attached to the base of a flat to protect it and with which the flat is ' run ' easily when moved across the stage.

CORNER, THE   The prompt corner.

CORNER BLOCK   A small triangular piece of three-ply used to strengthen joints in scenery.

COSTUME PLOT   A list of the characters and artists in the play with details of costumes worn in each scene and act.

COUNTERWEIGHT SYSTEM   The system of flying in which scenery is counterbalanced by weights running up and down in a track at the side of the stage.

COVER   The understudy ' covers ' the part played by another artist.

CRADLE   (1) A board supported by ropes, etc. (2) The casing that holds the weights in the counterweight flying system.

CRASH   A noise effect. A china crash is produced by pouring a quantity of broken crockery from one vessel to another. Also ' Glass Crash.'

CREDITS   Acknowledgements included in a programme to firms who have supplied or lent properties, equipment, etc., for use in the production.

CUE   The line of speech or action in the play that is a signal for another artist to begin speaking or an action to be performed.

CUE LIGHT   A light usually operated from the prompt corner giving a signal to another part of the stage.

CUE SHEET   A list of cues used by the stage manager, electrician and property master for producing effects, etc.

CURTAIN   The curtain behind the proscenium arch raised and lowered during the play.   The end of an Act when the curtain descends is called ' the curtain.'

CURTAIN CUE   The cue for operating the curtain.

CURTAIN LINE   The line across the stage where the curtain meets the stage floor.

CURTAIN MUSIC   The music played immediately before the rise of the curtain to introduce the play and sometimes repeated between the acts.

CURTAIN QUICK OR SLOW   The instruction given to the flyman concerning the speed at which the curtain should descend.

CURTAIN RAISER   A short play presented before the main item to complete an entertainment.

CURTAIN SET   See Drapes.

CURTAIN TRACK   See Track.

CURVED BACKCLOTH   A cloth suspended on a curved steel bar surrounding the back of the stage.   It is used in place of a cyclorama.

CUT   (1) A narrow trough running across the stage.   Cuts are sometimes installed at the back of the stage to drop cloths to the cellar.   They are also found elsewhere and used for entrances from below the stage.   (2) Excision of a part of the play.

CUT-CLOTH   A cloth with the centre cut out, used to frame a backcloth such as a woodland scene.   Several cut cloths painted to represent foliage hanging behind one another complete the setting.   Cutout Drop (U.S.A.).

CUT OUT   A flat profiled with plywood covered with canvas which is cut out in an irregular shape.   Also used for ' Cut-Cloth.'

CYCLORAMA   A curved backing of plaster on a wooden frame shaped like a domed wall at the back of the stage.

DARK   A theatre that is closed before presentation of a play is said to be ' dark.'

DEAD   (1) The term used to describe the exact height at which a piece of scenery is flown.   (2) Properties or equipment no longer required during the performance.   (3) Failure of an electric current.

D.B.O.   Dead Black Out.   An abbreviation for black out.

DECOR   A French word describing stage scenery and decoration.

DETAIL   The statement provided by the box office manager analysing the number of seats sold in all parts of the theatre and the total of money received.   (See Skeleton.)

DIM   To check light slowly.

DIMMER   The electric resistance for lowering or raising the voltage in a circuit.

DIMMER BOARD   The dimmer control board.

DIP   A small trap with a lighting socket in the stage for connecting portable equipment.   Floor Pocket (U.S.A.).

DIRECTOR   He conducts rehearsals, approves the scenery, costumes, lighting and properties and arranges the play for presentation in the theatre.

DISCOVERED   An actor is discovered when he appears alone on the stage at the rise of the curtain.

DOCK   Part of the stage or a space adjacent to it used for storing scenery.

DOCK DOORS   The doors of the scene dock providing access to the street.

DOME   (1) The rounded upper part of a cyclorama. (2) The ceiling in the auditorium that conceals the 'dome' spotlights.

DOMINANT LIGHTING   The principal source of light in a setting.

DOOR FLAT   A flat containing a space for a door unit.

DOOR SLAM   An effect for the sound of a door closing. It may be a door in a frame braced to the stage floor or a box with a heavy lid that is slammed on the cue.

DOOR STOP   (1) A metal plate screwed to the edge of a flat which overlaps the edge of another flat or piece of scenery. It is used when flats are out of line due to warped wood or the rake of the stage. (2) The wooden fillet running around the inside of the reveal against which the door shuts.

DOOR UNIT   A practical door in a wooden frame made to fit into a flat.

DOUBLE   (1) Two parts played by an actor whose identity is disguised by make-up and costume in one and who is recognised in the other part. (2) Properties or furniture used in different scenes by altering their appearance.

DOUBLE CROWN   The usual size of a play-bill: 30 i1. by 20 in.

DOUBLE TAKE   The reaction by facial or physical gesture which an actor makes when he realises something that is said has a double meaning.

DOWN STAGE   A position near the footlights.

DRAPES   Curtains used in place of a stage setting. They are also used with cloths or set pieces such as doors, windows, etc.

DRAW TABS   Curtains suspended from an overhead track which are opened or closed by being drawn from the sides.

DRENCHER PIPE   Used in case of fire to flood the safety curtain from the top and so prevent overheating.

DRESS REHEARSAL   One or more rehearsals in costume with the scenery, lighting, furniture, etc. as they will be seen during the performance.

DRESSING   Stage decoration or properties not used in the action of the play.

DROP   See Cloth, Act-Drop.

DROP-CURTAIN   See Act-Drop.

DROP CLOTH   A painted cloth dropped while a setting is changed behind it, and before which a scene is played.

DROP HOLDER   A metal clip for fastening a cloth to a line from the grid.

DRUGGET   The matting or carpet runner used around the setting to prevent noise.

DRUM   A manual controller whereby the lines operating a curtain track are wound around a drum turned by a handle.

DRY-UP   To forget one's lines.

D.S.M.   Deputy Stage Manager.

DUNGEON   See Cellar.

EFFECTS   On- or off-stage sound effects.

ELEVATORS   Used in the shoes to increase the height of an artist. (See also Lift.)

ENSEMBLE   The general effect of the artists in the stage setting.

ENTR'ACTE   The interval between the acts.

ENTRANCE CUE   The cue for an artist to enter the scene. This may be a 'word cue' spoken by another artist or a 'light cue' operated from the prompt corner.

EXIT   Departure from the stage.

EXIT LINE   The well-written line which provides an artist with an effective exit.

EXIT LIGHTS   Lights in the auditorium and back-stage that by law are never extinguished during the performance.

EXTENSION BRACE   See Brace.

FADE OUT   To check light to a black-out.

FALSE PROSCENIUM   A semi-permanent structure of two wings and a framed border set up-stage of the theatre proscenium.

FEED   The comedian's partner who provides the remark or situation leading up to the line intended to raise a laugh.

FESTOON   A border of leaves used in a country scene.

FESTOON CURTAIN   Curtains that can be looped up to hang in folds.

FILLET   The narrow part of the stage between the bridges carrying the sliders or sections of the stage floor that replace the bridges when they are not used.

FILTER FRAME   See Colour Frame.

PLATE Y

The Olivier Theatre

(a) *above*: Lighting Control

(b) *below*: Stage Management Control

PLATE Z

The National Theatre exterior
(a) *above*: blank rear view
(b) *below*: front view from the river

PLATE AA

The Stadttheatre, Bonn

PLATE BB

(1) (2) and (3) Memorial and Museum, Rio de Janeiro, Brazil. (3) showing coloured mural decorating concrete extension

(4) Airport, Buenos Aires, Argentina

(5) Imaginative sculptural use of reinforced concrete by Eero Saarinen, 1956–62: for interior of TWA Terminal at John F. Kennedy International Airport, New York.

PLATE CC

(a) *above*: Lyttleton Theatre, Sound Control
(b) *below*: Entrance to the Cottesloe Theatre

PLATE DD

New Hall – Eton College: Counterweight System and Safety Curtain

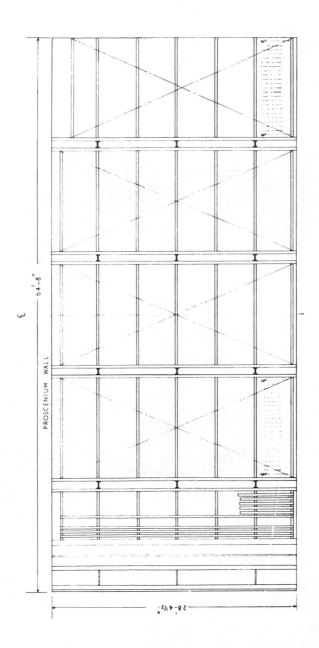

PLATE EE

NEW HALL – ETON COLLEGE

GENERAL ARRANGEMENT OF GRID STEELWORK

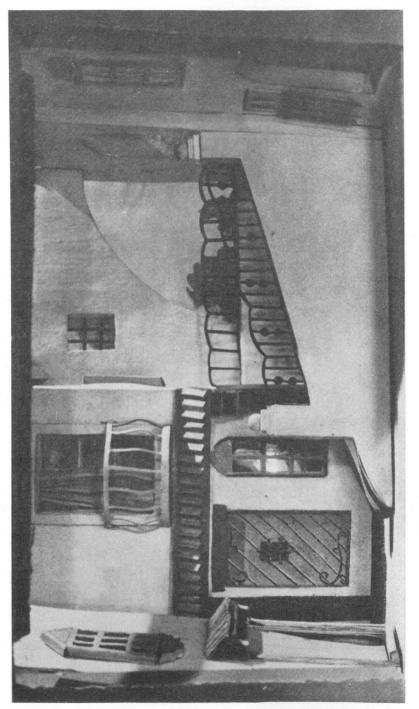

PLATE 18

Spanish Scene, Model

FINALE   The last part of a play, conclusion of an act in opera or the end of a piece of music.

FIREPLACE BACKING   The small backing usually three-fold and painted black that is set behind a fireplace.

FIREPLACE FLAT   A flat with a space for a fireplace.

FIREPLACE UNIT   A wooden frame shaped to the design of a fireplace covered in canvas and made to fit into a flat.

FIREPROOF CURTAIN   The safety curtain that must be lowered once during every performance in sight of the audience.

FIT-UP   A temporary proscenium used with or without a stage that is fitted up in a hall or outdoors and carried round with the company.

FIXING IRON   A metal plate with a fixed ring used in hanging scenic items.

FLASH POWDER   Smoke powder ignited by passing an electric current through it.

FLAT   The unit piece of scenery made of painted canvas on a wooden frame.

FLIES   The space above the stage, including one or two galleries from which hanging scenery is lowered to or raised from the stage.   Wings (U.S.A.)

FLIPPER   A small scenery flat hinged to another one.   The profiled part of a book wing is often hinged in order to display it effectively.

FLOAT SPOT   A small spotlight used for a special effect and placed in the footlights.

FLOATS   The footlights.

FLOOD   A lantern without focussing adjustment which provides a wide-angle beam of light for lighting back-cloths, etc.

FLOOD BAR   A steel bar suspended from the grid for holding floods.

FLOOR POCKET   See Dip.

FLOOR STAND   A telescopic stand used in the wings for mounting a spotlight or flood.   (See Tower.)

FLUFF   To hesitate or nearly forget one's lines.

FLY   To lift scenery from the stage (usually out of sight) with lines from the grid.

FLY GALLERY   The narrow platform some distance above the stage floor running from the proscenium to the back wall.   The working space is used for hauling the ropes in flying scenery.   Also called the fly floor.

FLYING IRON   A metal plate with a hinged ring used for bolting to the stiles of scenery or the sides of a boat truck.

FLY LADDERS   Ladders attached to the walls of the stage for access to the fly galleries.

FLY PLUGS   Lighting sockets in the fly galleries for connecting lighting equipment used above the stage.

FLY RAIL   The two heavy beams running the length of the fly gallery with cleats to which the ropes of hanging scenery are tied.   (See Pin Rail.)

F.O.H.   The front of house, i.e. that part of the theatre in front of the proscenium curtain.

F.O.H. LIGHTING   The spotlights installed in the auditorium to focus light on the down-stage area.   Auditorium Beam (U.S.A.).

FOLLOW   To keep a vaudeville artist in the beam of a movable spotlight.

FOOT A FLAT   A flat lying on the stage is raised by two men, one of whom keeps his foot on the bottom rail, and the other lifts it by 'walking his hands' along the stiles until the flat is upright.

FOOT IRON   An angled metal support attached to a brace or a flat for fixing to the stage with a weight or a stage screw.

FOOTLIGHTS   The rows of lamps with reflectors and frames for mediums enclosed in a metal trough along the front edge of the stage.

FORESTAGE   The small area containing the footlights projecting from the setting line beyond the proscenium arch.

FOUL   A tangled rope.

FOURTH WALL   The imaginary wall in the opening of the proscenium arch.

FRAMED BORDER   A canvas border stretched on a frame of wooden battens.

FRAMED CLOTH   A cloth battened on all sides.

FRENCH BRACE   A triangular wooden brace hinged to a flat with the base screwed to the stage or secured with a weight.   Jack (U.S.A.).

FRENCH FLAT   The flats of a scene which are battened out for flying in one piece.

FRONT CLOTH.   See Drop Cloth.

FRONT OF HOUSE   See F.O.H.

FROST   A white 'frosted' medium used alone or with other colours to diffuse light.

FULL SET   A setting occupying most of the stage, leaving little space in the wings.

FULL UP   All the lighting equipment, i.e. spotlights, floods, footlights and F.O.H. spotlights, etc., switched on at the cue.

GAG   An improvised remark or action by an artist and not included in the script of the play.

GAUZE   A thin translucent net used in mist and transformation scenes.   Scrim (U.S.A.).

GELATINES   See Colour Mediums.

GET-IN   The term used to describe the conveyance of scenery and unloading at the theatre.   Take-in (U.S.A.).

GET-OUT   Opposite of Get-in.   Take-out (U.S.A.).

GET OVER   Successful rapport of an artist with the audience.

GHOST   An actor playing the Ghost in *Hamlet* is said to have cried out in his stage voice that he would not continue unless his salary was paid.   Treasury day is Friday and by tradition the ' Ghost ' walks on that night.

GLASS CRASH   See Crash.

GO OFF   To leave the stage.

GO ON   The understudy is said to ' go on ' when he plays the part of the principal actor.

GO OVER   The rehearsal of difficult lines, cues or business.

GO ROUND   The act of going round to the stage door from the auditorium to visit an artist in his dressing room.

GOING UP!   The stage manager's call warning the artists that the curtain is about to rise.

GRAVE TRAP   A small oblong platform inserted in the floor of the stage and arranged to sink about nine feet below the stage.

GREEN   A vaudeville word for the stage.

GREEN ROOM   A club room for the artists.

GRID   The joists and rafters high above the stage between which the pulley blocks are arranged for flying scenery.

GROMMET   See Grummet.

GROOVES   The wooden fillets between which flats were made to slide on- and off-stage in the traditional theatre.   A long groove suspended above and across the stage was used for a free traverse curtain.

GROUND CLOTH   See Stage Cloth.

GROUND PLAN   The plan of a setting usually drawn to the scale of half an inch to one foot which includes the position and dimension of all parts of the scene and incidental units.

GROUND ROW   (1) A low piece of scenery sometimes profiled or cut out which enhances the effect of distance in a backcloth. It is also used for concealing lighting equipment on the stage floor. (2) The sections of compartment batten used to light cloths and laid horizontally on the stage.

GRUMMET (1) A rope bridle the two ends of which are attached to a batten at the top of a cloth. The centre is fastened to a line from the grid for flying the cloth. (2) A metal fixture on a flat for attaching the throw line. Grommet (U.S.A.).

GUIDE LINES The steel wires each side of the proscenium arch used in guiding the curtain. (See also Brail Line.)

HALF, THE The call warning the company that the curtain will rise in thirty minutes.

HALF UP Lights reduced to half strength.

HANDLING ROPES Ropes that are actually operated by hand in flying scenery, i.e. the free ends of suspension ropes though not the steel wires of the counterweight system. (See Hemps.)

HAND PROPS Properties carried by the artists.

HANGING IRON A hook-shaped piece of steel attached to the bottom rail of a flat for flying purposes.

HANGING LOFT The space below the grid where scenery is flown out of sight.

HEAD BLOCK Two or more pulley blocks framed together above the fly rail. (See Triple Block in Figure 11.)

HEADER A framed border sometimes of architectural shape flown from the grid and attached to flats on the stage.

HEAD RAIL The top rail of a flat.

HEMPS The ropes made from Indian or Manilla vegetable fibre used in flying scenery.

HOT SPOT The lighting is said to be 'hot' in an area where it is uneven.

HOUSE LIGHTS The auditorium lighting.

HOUSE TABS The Curtain or Act-Drop.

INDEPENDENTS A lighting circuit connected to an independent board, i.e. the circuit of a lamp that is alight while everything else is 'blacked-out.'

INGENUE The young female leading artist.

INSET SCENE A small scene placed inside the main setting and often removed in a quick scene change.

IRON CURTAIN The fireproof safety curtain.

JACK A triangular piece of wood hinged to the back of a ground row to support it and fastened to the stage with a weight or a stage screw. (See French Brace.)

JIGGER   A small section of 2-in. batten hinged between two flats in a threefold so that the outer flats may be folded inwards over the centre flat. Tumbler (U.S.A.).

JOG   A narrow flat set back at a right angle to another flat and used to give a scenic wall the illusion of thickness.

JOIN   Flats are ' joined ' where the stiles meet when they are cleated together.

JUICE   The electrician's word for electric current.

JUMP A RAIL   To screw an extra rail to the back of a flat for holding a picture or electric fitting.

JUVENILE   Part for a young person, though not one for a child.

KEYSTONE   (U.S.A.)   A small oblong piece of three-ply used to reinforce joints in scenery.

KILL   To remove or finish with, i.e. (1) Cut out a spotlight. (2) To kill a laugh means interrupting laughter of the audience before it has died down by speaking a line or performing some action.

LACE   Flats that are warped are brought together by ' lacing ' the cleat line around screws on the inner edge of the stiles.

LANTERN   The automatic smoke ventilation in the roof of all stages. It is rather like a greenhouse with windows that fall outwards when a rope holding them is cut at stage level in case of fire.

LASH LINE   See Throw Line.

LASH LINE EYE   See Grummet (2).

LEAD   The star or principal part.

LEFT   A stage direction. Stage left means the part of the stage to the left of the actor when he is facing the audience.

LEG   A hanging piece of canvas used to mask the side of the stage instead of a wing and running up- and down-stage. Leg Drop (U.S.A.).

LENGTH   A few electric lamps fixed to a small batten which may be hung on the back of a flat.

LIBRARIES   The theatre ticket booking agencies.

LIFT   (1) See Bridge.   Elevator (U.S.A.).   (2) Plagiarise another's work in dialogue or business.

LIGHT CHECK   The description of a cue when lights are dimmed. The instruction ' check the lights ' means to reduce lighting to that required.

LIGHT PIPE   See Spot Bar.

LIGHTING BRIDGE   A narrow platform running across the stage above the No. 1 light batten. It is used for special lighting effects.

LIGHTING PLOT   The method of recording the details of lighting equipment and the cues for lighting the play.

LINE   The rope used to fly scenery or the sash line for joining flats.

LINE OF SIGHT   The view of the stage setting from all parts of the auditorium. The line of sight should give a clear picture of the scene and conceal everything that should be hidden from view.

LINES   The dialogue of an actor's role.

LIVE   Equipment connected and switched on to an electric switchboard.

LOADING GALLERY   A gallery above the fly floor used for loading weights in the counterweight system. Also called Loading Floor. Loading Bridge (U.S.A.).

LOFT BLOCK   The pulley block in a frame secured to the grid through which a line is reeved for flying.

LONG ARM   See Clearing Stick.

LOUVRED CEILING   A ceiling arranged like the slats of a Venetian blind. The sections are sloping with the down-stage edge higher than the up-stage edge. It is used when gaps are required in a ceiling for projecting light.

MAKE FAST   See Tie Off.

MARIE TEMPEST   The stage rake sometimes causes a door to swing of its own accord. A metal hinge with a screw lever adjustment is attached to the door and the reveal to ensure that when the door is opened it remains in one position. Named after the late Marie Tempest who asked for these hinges to be fitted to the doors of a setting in which she appeared.

MAROON   An electrically detonated firework used in an iron tank for an explosion effect.

MASK   To hide from view. (1) Stage movement is concerned with 'masking' of one player by another, i.e. when an artist obscures the line of sight from a part of the audience by standing in front of another artist. (2) A piece of scenery such as a backing used to conceal a part of the stage is said to 'mask in' the area that should not be seen.

MASTER SWITCH   See Scene Master.

M.D.   Musical Director.

MECHANICS   The actions and stage movements planned for an artist in early rehearsals.

MEDIUM   See Colour Mediums.

MEN ASIDE   The men in the stage departments working on each side of the stage are described as a certain number of ' men aside.'

MISE-EN-SCENE   The style of arrangement when scenery and artists are grouped together in a scene.

MONKEY POLE   Sometimes it is difficult to ' throw ' a line over a cleat on the top of a tall flat.   The line is threaded through a long stick which is used to guide the line in position and when cleated the stick remains attached to the line.

MOVES   The artists' movements arranged by the director during rehearsals.

MULTICORE   Tinned copper wire with vulcanised rubber insulation the cores of which are twisted together to form one flexible cable in an asbestos covering.   It is used for connecting light battens to the main supply.

NEWEL   The curved part of the handrail at the foot of a staircase.   The newel post is the top or bottom post of the staircase.

NOTICE   (1) The announcement given by the management terminating the run of the play and posted to the call board.   (2) The newspaper criticism after the first night of a play.

OBLIQUE   Scenery that is set at an angle to the centre line of the stage.

OFF   An actor is ' off ' when he has missed his entrance, i.e. he is away when he should be on the stage.

OFF-SET   Scenery set at an angle to another piece of scenery.

OFF-STAGE   (1) Towards the side of the stage.   An actor moves off-stage when he walks to the side of the setting.   (2) Any part of the stage outside the acting area and setting.

OFFER UP   To present a property, piece of scenery, light circuit, etc. for approval, i.e. to show it in position before it is fixed permanently.   ' Offer up the lemon ambers ' means to bring in the pale amber light circuit.

ON   An artist who is playing is said to be ' on ' the stage.

ON-STAGE   Towards the centre of the stage.   (1) An actor moves on-stage when he walks towards the centre of the stage.   (2) A position within the setting and acting area.

O.P.   Opposite Prompt.   The side of the stage opposite to
the prompt corner and on the right of the actor as he
faces the audience.   (See Prompt Side.)

OPEN   A new production is said to ' open ' on the first night.

OPEN COLD   A play that commences a run in London without a preliminary tour of the provinces.

OPEN IN A BLACK-OUT   A scene in which the curtain rises on
a darkened stage.

OPEN ON   A door or window that opens towards the audience
is said to ' open on ' stage.

OPEN STAGE   A setting free from obstruction in the acting
area and used for ballet, opera, etc., where space is
required for a number of performers.

OPENING   The proscenium opening or width of the stage
across the proscenium arch.   It is also used to describe
the open area between scenery or tableau curtains.

ORCHESTRA BELL   The bell operated from the prompt corner
and heard in the band room warning the orchestra to
enter the orchestra pit.

ORCHESTRA PIT   The area in the auditorium immediately in
front of the proscenium where the orchestra plays.

ORCHESTRA STANDS   The stands holding the score used by
members of the orchestra.

PACK   A number of flats stacked at the sides or back of the
stage.   Stack (U.S.A.).

PAGEANT   An adjustable powerful lantern used for off-stage
lighting such as sunshine or moonlight.   It has been
superseded by the Fresnel spotlight.   Parabolic Reflector
Flood (U.S.A.).

PAINT FRAME   A large wooden frame on which canvas is
stretched for painting.   It is found in older theatres
situated at the back of the stage.   A winch operating
counterweighted wire cables raises and lowers it and the
artist paints from a cat walk moving the frame as he
paints each area.   In the scene studios the frame is raised
and lowered through a slot in the floor.

PAN   (1) A panatrope or gramophone sound reproducer used
for effects.   (2) A pantechnicon which is a large lorry
for carrying scenery, furniture, etc.   (3) To criticise or
ridicule an artist or play.

PAPER   Complimentary tickets.

PARABOLIC REFLECTOR FLOOD   See Pageant.

PARALLEL   (U.S.A.)   The collapsible frame support for a
rostrum.

PART   (1) The actor's role.   (2) The typed copy of the lines used by an actor with the cues spoken by other artists.

PASS DOOR   The fireproof door providing access to the stage from the auditorium.   During the performance it may be used only with permission from the company manager or the stage manager.

PELMET   The permanent fixture attached to the top of the opening known as the proscenium arch in order to reduce the height.

PERCHES   The platforms each side of the stage immediately behind the proscenium from which spotlights are directed on to the down-stage area.   The spotlights used there are also known by the same name.   Tormentor Spotlight (U.S.A.).

PERMANENT MASKING   See False Proscenium.

PERSONAL PROPS   Hand properties that are provided by the management but are looked after by the artists, such as a cigarette case, spectacles, etc.

PIANO WIRE   Also called TRICK WIRE.   Cast steel wire used in place of a hemp line when this could not be concealed. Painted black or to match the background, it was virtually invisible.   Now superseded by steel wire cable. (See Chapter 5.)

PICTURE   A dramatic situation or tableau in which the artists are grouped in an interesting situation inviting the audience to picture the event.

PICTURE FRAME HANGER AND SOCKET   A metal hook and socket used for hanging pictures and large objects that have to be removed in a scene change.

PICTURE RAIL   The wooden rail screwed to the back of a flat for holding a picture, mirror, etc.

PILOT LIGHTS   (1) A small low wattage lamp used to light an electric switchboard.   (2) A small lamp connected to a circuit which indicates that the circuit is ' live ' or switched on.

PIN HINGE   Like an ordinary hinge but it has a loose pin holding it together.   The pin is withdrawn when a joint between two pieces of scenery has to be broken quickly.

PIN RAIL   (U.S.A.) Another name for the fly rail.   Derived from the nautical belaying pin, i.e. the cleat to which the ropes for flying scenery are made fast.

PIN SPOT   A spotlight the beam of which is reduced by

inserting in the frame a piece of metal with a small hole in the centre.

PIPE BATTEN   See Barrel, Spotbar.

PIT   The orchestra pit or the rear seats at the back of the stalls.

PLATE   See Keystone.

PLATFORM   (U.S.A.)   The top of a rostrum.

PLOT   (1) The story of the play.   (2) A list of furniture, properties, lighting cues, wardrobe, etc.   (3) To write down, i.e. ' plot a cue,' means to record it.

PORTABLE BOARD   A dimmer board used as an auxiliary to the main switchboard.   It can be moved about the stage and has controls in the form of wheels with handles that can be locked in any position.

PORTAL   (1) See False Proscenium.   (2) The proscenium opening (U.S.A.).

PRACTICAL   Practicable.   Anything fit for use.   A window that can be opened is said to be practical.

PREMIERE   The first performance of a play.   The first or opening night.

PRE-SET BOARD.   An electric dimmer board the circuits in which can be set in advance and operated by one switch at the cue.   The switch is known as a ' Scene Master.'

PRIMING   Preliminary coating of size and paint to tighten new canvas and give it a surface to receive paint.

PRODUCER   Formerly the director of the play.   Now the manager or impresario who presents it and adopted from the term used in the American theatre.

PRODUCTION ACCOUNT   The stage manager's account for all expenses incurred during rehearsals up to the time that the curtain rises on the first night.

PRODUCTION MANAGER   The Producer's technical manager responsible for the organisation of all the stage departments.

PROFILE   A cut-out piece of three-ply or hardboard covered with cloth attached to the edge of a ground row or a wing to show the contour of a landscape, foliage, etc.

PROFILE SPOTLIGHT   Hard-edge spotlight.

PROJECTOR SPOTLIGHT   A spotlight using a moving slide for projection of effects such as clouds, waves, etc., or a stationary slide for projecting a silhouette.

PROLOGUE   Introduction to a play.

PROMPT   To help an actor by giving him the line he is unable to remember.

PROMPT CORNER   The corner of the stage behind the proscenium arch from which the stage manager prompts the actors and where the cue board is situated for running the play.

PROMPT SIDE   In most theatres this is on the left of the stage when facing the audience.   Sometimes the prompt corner is on the right of the stage, and in order to avoid confusion, stage directions indicating a side of the stage are best described as stage left (L) or stage right (R) and not as prompt side (PS) or opposite prompt side (OPS). Stage Left (U.S.A.)

PROMPT TABLE   The table used by the stage manager when prompting and marking the script during rehearsals.

PROPERTIES   See Chapter 7.

PROPERTY MASTER   The member of the stage staff responsible for properties.

PROPS   Colloquial for property master or properties.

PROSCENIUM   The wall in front of the curtain dividing the stage from the auditorium.

PROS BATTEN   The No. 1 lighting batten next to the proscenium.

PROS BORDER   A border immediately behind the proscenium arch used to mask the No. 1 batten and spotlights.   It usually corresponds in material and colour with the proscenium wings. (Another name is the Teaser.)

PROSCENIUM OPENING   The proscenium arch through which the audience views the play.   Portal (U.S.A.).

PROS WING   The semi-permanent wings used to hide the sides of the setting.   They are also called Tormentors. (See Returns.)

P.S.   The prompt side.

QUICK CHANGE ROOM   A dressing room at the side of the stage for an artist who has to change quickly into another costume.   In Figure 9 it is shown next to the exit to the stage door.   A temporary one is built of two or three flats and furnished with a light, table and mirror, a few hooks and a chair.

RAG   Otherwise the Curtain.

RAIL   The horizontal batten in a flat.

RAKE   The slope of the stage running downwards from the back wall to the footlights.

RAKING PIECE   (1) A piece of scenery roughly triangular that is used to mask a ramp.   In Plate 18 the ramp is masked by the raking piece and sloping balustrade.

(2) A wooden wedge inserted underneath a flat to level it on a raked stage.

RAMP   An inclined platform sloping up from the stage to another level and used in place of steps.

REEVE   The ropes of hanging scenery are passed or reeved through the pulley blocks above the grid and down to the fly rail.

REMOTE CONTROL BOARD   An independent lighting switch-board controlling the dimmers.   (See Console.)

REPERTOIRE   Repertory or list of parts and plays that an artist or a company performs.

RÉPITITION GÉNÉRALE   A public dress rehearsal.

RESIDENT MANAGER   The manager (often the Licensee) responsible for administration and control of the theatre.

RESIDENT S.M.   The name given to the stage carpenter per-manently employed in a provincial theatre who is in charge of the stage staff.

RESTING   The sanguine expression for an actor awaiting re-employment.

RETURNS   (1) Flats set at right angles to conceal the sides of a scene.   (2) Tickets returned to the box office and offered for re-sale before the performance.

REVEAL   The board attached at a right angle to indicate the thickness of a door or a window.   Thickness (U.S.A.).

REVOLVE   A revolving stage.   The circular platform on which several scenes can be shown in turn to the audience.

RIGHT   A stage direction indicating the right-hand side of the stage when facing the audience.

RING IN   The stage manager's cue to the orchestra to start playing.

RING UP/DOWN   The signal given by the stage manager for raising or lowering the curtain.   In older theatres a bell was used to warn the flyman operating the curtain.

RISER   The vertical part connecting the treads in a staircase.

ROCKS   Sections of light irregular wooden frames covered in canvas which, if necessary, are built to support the weight of an actor.

ROSTRUM   A collapsible platform.   (See Parallel.)

ROUND   The applause given to an artist during the per-formance.

RUN   (1) The length of time that a play is performed at a theatre.   (2) The time in which an act or scene is played. A scene is said to ' run ' a certain number of minutes.

RUN A FLAT   A flat is moved or ' run ' by holding the forward
stile, i.e. the stile facing the direction in which the flat
is to be moved, with one hand at the toggle and gripping
the stile about three feet higher with the other hand.
The flat is lifted from the stage and, by balancing it, can
be moved easily.

RUNNER   A length of carpet or matting placed around the
scene to deaden the sound of footsteps.

RUNNING ACCOUNT   The stage manager's weekly account of
salaries in the stage departments and petty cash expenses
incurred in running the play.

RUNNING TIME   The actual playing time of a performance,
excluding overture, intervals and curtain calls.

RUNWAY   The bridge from the stage to the auditorium, used
by the director in rehearsals.   It is sometimes extended
in the form of a platform built around the orchestra pit
for artists in musical plays.

RUSCUS   Evergreen obtained from a florist and treated to
remain green indefinitely.   It is used to supplement
foliage painted on scenery.

SADDLE IRON   See Sill Iron.

SAFETY CURTAIN   The Fireproof Curtain.

SANDBAG   Used for weighting a set of lines released from a
piece of scenery to prevent them from slipping through
the pulley blocks when hauled to the grid.

SANDWICH BATTEN   Two battens screwed together with the
canvas of a cloth between them.

SAVE YOUR LIGHTS   The instruction to the electrician for
switching off the lights.

SCENE   (1) The part of a play less than an Act.   (2) The
setting of painted canvas and wood.   (3) A piece of
continuous action in the play which is terminated by
the departure of one of the characters or the introduction
of a new one.

SCENE CHANGE   See Act Change.

SCENE DOCK   See Dock

SCENE MASTER   A single switch controlling a number of
dimmers.   (See Pre-set Board.)

SCENE PLAN   See Ground Plan.

SCENE PLOT   The diagrams showing the arrangement of
scenes in a play and the order in which they are set.

SCISSOR STAGE   See Chapter 6.

SCORING LINE   The line where flats meet when cleated
together.   (See Join.)

SCRIM   (1) Gauze used for transformation effects (U.S.A.).
(2) Hessian used in the construction of scenery.

SCRIPT   Abbreviation of manuscript.   The prompt script is
the book of the play.

SEA ROW   A ground row painted to resemble the sea.

SECONDARY LIGHTING   (1) Lighting used to supplement the
dominant lighting.   (2) The auxiliary lighting system
throughout the theatre supplied with batteries and used
in case of failure of the main supply.

SECTION   A circuit in the footlights or a batten.

SET   (1) The setting or a complete scene.   (2) To build a
scene or place furniture and properties in position.
(3) To switch on the lighting arranged for an act or
scene.

SET OF LINES   A group of three or four lines from the grid
used to fly scenery.

SET PIECE   An individual piece of scenery such as a porch,
balcony, tree, etc., which is set by itself on the stage
floor.

SETTING LINE   The imaginary line across the stage giving
the position from which scenery is set.

SHEAVE   The groove of a pulley wheel fixed in a block
through which a rope is threaded.

SHEET   (1) A part of the box office seating plan.   (2) A
'Six-Sheet' is a large poster six times the size of a
double-crown.

SHOE   (1) The support for a toggle rail in a flat.   (2) An
electrical plug board enabling several circuits to be
connected to one supply.

SHUTTERS   Attached to a spotlight whereby the area of the
beam is reduced.

SIDES   The pages of an actor's part which are typed on one
side of half sheets of quarto paper.

SIGNAL   The cue by a light or a bell from the prompt corner
giving a signal for a cue or effect to be performed.

SILENT CUE   A cue provided by stage business or by a signal
from the A.S.M.

SILL IRON   A narrow piece of metal replacing the bottom
rail of a door flat or other entrance in order to strengthen
it across the opening.   Saddle Iron (U.S.A.).

SILL RAIL   The bottom rail of a flat.

SIZE   A thin solution of glue which, mixed with paint, is
used to strengthen canvas in scene painting.   Sizing
(U.S.A.).

SKELETON The single figure denoting the total of receipts for a performance and provided by the box office manager. (See Detail.)

SKIN The animal costume worn by an artist in pantomime and children's plays.

SKIP The actor's travelling basket also used for the wardrobe and properties.

SKY CLOTH A cloth painted to give the impression of the sky.

SLIDING STAGE See Chapter 6.

SLOAT BOX A long wooden box containing a roller on which a cloth may be wound. It is used for lowering or raising a cloth when it is impossible to do so through a cut in the stage floor.

SNAP LINE See Chalk a Scene.

SOAP OVER A mirror or other shiny surface is painted over with a strong solution of size. Soap can be rubbed over but is not so effective.

SOFFIT The downward surface of an architectural border which is stiffened to give a thickness at the lower edge.

SPARKS The nickname for the electrician.

SPILL Light spreading from a spotlight or a flood. Acting area lanterns have 'spill rings' behind the medium frame to prevent this.

SPOT (1) A spotlight the beam of which can be concentrated or dispersed. (2) Colloquial for an engagement or a part of a performance. (U.S.A.)

SPOT BAR OR BATTEN The steel barrel from which spotlights are suspended. Light Pipe (U.S.A.).

SPOT BLOCK A pulley block fixed to the grid through which a single line is reeved to fly an object which cannot be handled by normal lines. The line is reeved through another block at the side of the grid and carried down to the fly rail.

SPOT LINE See Spot Block.

SPREAD To broaden the beam of an adjustable spotlight.

SPRING FOOT IRON A spring hinge attached to a flat or a french brace for fixing to the floor of the stage.

SPRINKLERS A series of water pipes in the roof of the stage and other ceilings with valves that open automatically to spray water in case of fire.

SQUARED PAPER Drawing paper ruled in inches and twelfths for plans of stage settings where the scale is half an inch to one foot.

STACK See Pack.

STAGE BOARD   The stage electrical switchboard.

STAGE CARPET   A carpet sufficiently large to cover the acting area.

STAGE-CLOTH   A large sheet of canvas covering the acting area on which the setting is built. It is painted to represent boards, paving stones and also carpets. Ground Cloth (U.S.A.).

STAGE DEPTH   The measurement from the setting line to the back wall of the stage.

STAGE DIRECTOR   (U.S.A.) Production stage manager.

STAGE LEFT   See Prompt Side.

STAGE MANAGER   He controls the artists and performance and unites the work of all individuals and departments engaged in the production of a play.

STAGE SCREW   A large screw with a hand-grip for securing a brace to the stage floor.

STAGE TRAP   The principal or grave trap used in pantomime.

STAGE WAIT   An interruption in a performance when an artist misses an entrance.

STAGE WEIGHT   See Weights.

STAGE WHISPER   A whispered remark that nevertheless can be heard throughout the auditorium.

STAGE WIDTH   The measurement between the side walls of the stage.

STAND-BY!   See Going Up.

STAND-BY TABLE   The table in the wings where artists pick up their hand properties.

STANDING SET   A setting that is not struck during the performance. It remains standing for the run of the play.

STAR   (1) The principal actor or actress who is so well known that his personal following enhances the value of the production. (2) The wooden segments hinged with leather that open like the points of a star over a star trap.

STAR TRAP   One of the two kinds of traps inserted in the floor of the stage, the other being the grave trap.

STAY   A wooden wedge used to make a flat secure after it is erected on an uneven stage.

STEPS   They are normally constructed in portable sections and known by the number of treads or horizontal parts, i.e. three-tread, four-tread, etc.

STILES   The long upright side pieces in the frame of a flat.

STRIKE   To take down and remove a setting from the acting area after it has been used. Also to take an unwanted property, furniture or piece of electrical equipment off-stage.

STRAP HINGE A long tapered hinge attached to the back of the reveal of a door, or other frame which, bent down, secures the frame against the opening in a flat.

STRINGER The side of a stairway to which the treads and risers are attached.

STRIP (1) Another name for a length. (2) A strip of canvas used to prevent light leaking through the join between flats or behind a flat where the canvas has worn thin.

SUB Part of an actor's salary given in advance.

SUDDEN DEATH In a cue system with only one light, i.e. on or off, the 'warning' is when the light is switched on and the 'go'—called sudden death—is when the light is switched off.

SUPERS The extra artists or supernumeraries engaged for a crowd scene who do not speak lines.

SURROUND A set of legs—often velvet curtains—to hide the sides and back of the stage. They are hung from a curved bar or from battens.

SWAG Curtains that are looped up and allowed to hang in folds.

SWIVEL ARM A movable batten attached by a ring to a pivot thus allowing a leg to hang at an angle to the setting line.

TAB (U.S.A.) A small sheet of canvas battened and hung like a cloth, used for masking awkward areas off-stage.

TABS (1) The curtain or act drop. (2) Tableau curtains divided in the centre, enabling them to open outwards.

TAG The last line of the play. There is a theatre superstition that it is unlucky to speak the tag line before the first night.

TAILS Borders attached to the fly rails or hung at each side of the stage to mask the top of an open setting.

TAKE-IN/-OUT See Get-in/-out.

TAKE THE NAP A clap of the hands either on- or off-stage to deceive the audience when a blow is struck.

TEASER See Pros Border.

THICKNESS See Reveal.

THREE-FOLD Three flats hinged together which are self-supporting when opened and fold inward when closed.

THROW The distance and area of a beam of light projected from a spotlight.

THROW AWAY (2) A line delivered casually, rendering it unimportant. (2) A box office brochure.

THROW LINE   The sash line attached to one flat and thrown around the cleat on another flat to hold them together. Lash Line (U.S.A.).

THUNDER SHEET   See Chapter 7.

TIE OFF   To fasten.   The line by which two flats are cleated together is pulled taut and tied off on the tie-off screws or cleats.

TIES   Pieces of canvas used to tie around cloths that are rolled on battens.

TOGGLE RAILS   The inner rails of a flat between the top or head rail and the bottom or sill rail.   The method of securing them is by a Keystone (U.S.A.).

TOP BATTEN CLIP   See Drop Holder.

TOP LIGHTING   Lighting equipment suspended higher than the top of the setting, such as spotlights, battens, acting area lanterns and F.O.H. spotlights.

TORMENTORS   See Pros Wing.

TORMENTOR SPOTLIGHT   See Perches.

TOWER   (1) A movable stand on castors with a number of lights suspended vertically.   (2) A movable platform with a ladder, used for adjusting overhead lighting equipment.

TRACK   The rails along which curtains move suspended from wheels or bobbins.   The track may be attached to the setting or flown from the grid.

TRAIN CALL   The notice posted to the call board giving the times of departure and arrival between towns on a tour.

TRANSPARENCY   A painted gauze undetected as such when lit from the front.   It becomes transparent when the front lighting is reduced and lighting behind is brought in.

TRAPS   The trapdoors in the floor of the stage.

TRAVELLER   A slotted steel or wooden track used with draw curtains.   The curtains are hung on metal or wooden bobbins that slide inside the track when the curtains are opened or closed.

TRAVERSE CURTAIN   Traveler (U.S.A.).

TREAD   The horizontal part of a step where the foot treads. See Riser.

TREASURY CALL   Salaries are paid on Friday and in a large company a notice is posted to the notice board indicating the time at which they will be paid (usually mid-day). The artists call at the company manager's office to receive their salaries.   Otherwise he brings the salaries to the dressing rooms before the evening performance.   See Ghost.

TRICK LINE   See Chapter 7.

TRICK WIRE   See Piano Wire.

TRIM   (1) The architrave around a door or window. (2) To level off a piece of hanging scenery at the right height for use during a performance.

TRIM CHAIN   A short length of chain used with a counter-weight bar to hold the top batten of a cloth.

TRIP   To raise a cloth so that it occupies half its height by attaching lines to the lower batten.

TRIPE   Electric cable.

TRUCK   A low platform on ball-bearing castors used for mounting set pieces and small scenes. The truck may be moved freely about the stage or it is run in a track. See Boat Truck. Waggon (U.S.A.).

TUMBLE   To raise a cloth with a roller sandwich batten attached to the foot of the cloth.

TUMBLER   The roller used in tumbling a cloth.

TWO-FOLD   Also called a wing. See Book Flat.

TWO/THREE/FOUR-HANDED SCENE.   A scene in which two, three or four artists take part.

ULTRA-VIOLET LIGHT   See Chapter 8.

UNIT SETS   A collection of built rostrums, etc., which can be interchanged to provide a variety of scenic arrangements.

UP-STAGE   The part of the stage furthest from the proscenium and any position away from the footlights. The rake in older theatres caused an actor to walk up the stage. An actor who stands above a colleague is said to be ' up-stage,' i.e. haughty or vain.

VAMP   (1) To use old material as a make-shift for the real article. (2) To improvise a piece of music.

VAMPS   Spring double doors used in pantomime and lined with rubber for the quick appearance of an artist.

VELARIUM   A canvas canopy or awning used in place of a battened ceiling cloth.

VELVETS   Velvet curtains and borders used as a setting for revue or a concert.

WAGON STAGE   Also called platform stage, rolling stage. (See Trucks, Chapter 6.)

WALKING UNDERSTUDY   An artist engaged solely to under-study and who does not take any further part in the performance.

WALK-ON   A super or extra artist who does not speak lines.

WALK THROUGH   To rehearse a scene mainly for movements.

WALTER PLINGE   The traditional name substituted for the name of an actor doubling a part.

WARDROBE (1) The clothes worn by the artists. (2) The dressing room where they are cleaned and repaired.

WARDROBE MISTRESS She is in charge of the wardrobe and dressers and is responsible for maintenance of the costumes.

WARM (UP) (1) An audience is said to be warm when it is appreciative and generous with applause. (2) The beam of a spotlight is 'warmed up' when the focus is narrowed and the light intensified.

WARNING AND GO The cue signal system from the prompt corner to various parts of the stage. Red is the 'warning' light and green is the 'go' on which the cue is performed. (See Sudden Death.)

WEIGHTS Used in place of a stage screw to keep a brace steady and to give stability to a spotlight or flood stand.

WINCH A mechanism used for hauling weights that are too heavy for ropes, i.e. the safety curtain and electric battens. It is manually or mechanically operated and includes a brake.

WIND MACHINE See Chapter 7.

WINDOW FLAT A flat containing a space for a window unit.

WINDOW UNIT A casement or sash window frame made to fit into a flat.

WING (1) Two or three flats hinged together for masking the side of the stage. (2) To play a part without memorising it, thus relying on a prompt from the 'wings.'

WING NUT A butterfly nut which may be tightened by turning the wings with the fingers and thumb.

WINGS The stage space to right and left of the acting area. (See Flies.)

WING SET A setting consisting of backcloth, borders and wings or cut cloths.

WITH BOOKS To rehearse with the parts or scripts before the lines are learnt.

WOOD BORDERS Foliage borders used in pastoral settings.

WORKING LIGHT A single electric bulb above the stage giving enough light for rehearsals or in the auditorium for cleaning.

WORKING LINE A rope which is used throughout the performance.

WORKING SIDE The side of the stage, including the fly gallery, where the ropes are worked or hauled and tied to the fly rail.

APPENDIX TO THE SECOND EDITION

When this book was written, I intended it as a guide providing information on most aspects of the stage manager's work yet sufficiently compact that it could be carried in his pocket. Of necessity, some of the details are brief and I am grateful to many who have read the book for their observations. The following notes are designed to improve the significance of those terms which will benefit from a fuller description.

Page 46. THE PROMPT SCRIPT. The abolition of censorship in the Theatres Act 1968 has removed the authority of the Lord Chamberlain but there is now the possibility of prosecution for offences such as obscenity, defamation, incitement to racial hatred and provocation of breach of the peace. The Police have rights of entry into a theatre for establishing the nature of an offence and they can demand a copy of the prompt script including any stage or other directions for performance of the play.

It will be seen that the stage manager has an important legal responsibility to have available a complete and accurate prompt script incorporating all instructions, moves and business and calls to the artists. The script may be called as evidence in a prosecution to establish either that the script is offensive or that the performance deviated from the script thereby making it offensive. The stage manager, therefore, must ensure that fidelity to the script and direction is maintained at every performance.

Those liable to prosecution are the producer or director or a performer who without reasonable excuse deviates from the director's instructions. Consequently the stage manager is responsible for warning the artist about any alteration in his performance likely to cause offence and he must inform the producer should this occur.

There may be difficulty in establishing an offence when the play includes improvisation by the artist. However, the stage manager should be sufficiently knowledgeable to realise that an improvisation goes beyond the instruction of the director.

Another important responsibility regarding the prompt script is the copy forwarded to the British Museum. When a play is presented and the script has not been published or performed in the United Kingdom, a copy of the script—which need not be the prompt script—must be given to the Trustees of the British Museum for their archives. The producer usually agrees that a complete copy of the prompt script also is kept by the House Manager of the theatre for production in case of legal difficulty.

Page 48.   Another method for use with a printed play is to cut pages of a loose-leaf folder or stiff exercise book like the opening in a photograph frame.   This should be a little smaller than the printed page, the margin of which is pasted to the cut page of the folder.   One copy only of the printed play is required, the text being read on both side of the page.   Alternative pages of the folder are used leaving a blank sheet facing each printed page for recording during rehearsals.

Page 67.   METRICATION.   The conversion from Imperial to the Metric system of measurement will cause problems in scenery and theatre planning.   References describing the change-over to decimal measurement are numerous and although specific problems need detailed information, the following table indicates the current measurements used in scene design and the nearest metric equivalent:

Imperial	*Metric*
$\frac{1}{8}''$ to 1' 0" (1 : 96)	10 mm. to 1 m. (1 : 100)
$\frac{1}{4}''$ to 1' 0" (1 : 48)	20 mm. to 1 m. (1 : 50)
$\frac{1}{2}''$ to 1' 0" (1 : 24)	50 mm. to 1 m. (1 : 20)

For example, the scale of ground plans of $\frac{1}{2}''$ to 1' 0" (1 : 24) used now will be replaced by the closest metric measurement 50 mm. to 1 m. (1 : 20) or 20 mm. to 1 m. (1 : 50).

There will be a variety of new measurements relating not only to scenery but also to electrical equipment and stage machinery. The A.J. METRIC HANDBOOK published by The Architectural Press contains sections about Theatres, Lighting, Sound, and Drawing Office Practice. Although intended for Architects, the book has information which will be useful to the stage manager. Two free publications are THINK METRIC published by the Ministry of Public Building and Works, which is helpful in understanding the units of measurement, and TIMBER GOES METRIC published by the Timber Research and Development Association. The Association also publishes METRIC POCKET NOTES and METRIC SIZES FOR SOFTWOOD, HARDWOOD AND BOARDS. For electrical notes, The National Inspection Council for Electrical Installation Contracting publishes THE ELECTRICIANS HANDBOOK (CHANGING TO METRIC). There is no information at present on stage machinery but The British Steel Corporation is considering publication of metrication documents.

Page 90. SECTION OF A MODERN THEATRE. (See Figure 62)

Page 93. To simplify stage terms, a platform raised or lowered in the stage area is now called a LIFT. A platform above the stage, used perhaps for lighting equipment, is known as a BRIDGE.

Page 97. Modern theatres are built with methods employing all-steel construction of the grid. The wooden main beams supported by the side walls of traditional theatres are replaced with large steel girders from the rear wall to the proscenium arch. Steel supports are installed between them and the lattice work of wooden rafters formerly running across the stage is replaced by steel strips running up and down the stage. (Figure EE)

At the Theatre Royal, Drury Lane, London, the grid is seventy feet above the stage. In America this is much higher and some theatres include a grid one hundred and forty-five feet from the stage. The high grid is useful when lighting a cyclorama. Scenery that is lifted to the grid does not obstruct the light from floods which are hung down-stage (and not crowded near the cyclorama) to light it effectively.

Page 100. The weight of a cloth that is lowered to the stage may cause the ropes to travel fast when the flyman releases them from the fly rail. He should take care that friction of the ropes passing through his hands does not chafe them.

Page 103. SAFETY. Self preservation is the first law of life and safety in the theatre is essential in the stage manager's responsibility for artists and staff. Everything that is used in flying above the stage must be secure and all knots for the suspension of scenery, pulleys, hanging irons, sandbags, etc., tied safely.

When stage space is limited, it is possible to fly furniture and properties but the grid must never be overloaded. Cloths should be flown with sufficient clearance so that the batten of a cloth does not collide with another one whereby it would be torn away and fall to the stage. Serious accidents have occurred through items falling from the grid that were not properly secured.

Ropes should be examined at least annually. After prolonged use, a rope will tend to chafe and fray which has more effect on the strength of small ropes than on large ones. The main causes of weakening of hemp ropes are Wear, Chemical attack, Heat, Water and Overloading. They have poor resistance to acids and alkalis; heat may cause them to fail without visual warning, and they will rot if left about on wet ground.

A rough guide to the Breaking and Safe Working Load of a hemp rope is to square the size of the rope and divide it by 3 and 18. For instance for a three-inch rope:

Breaking Load	*Safe Working Load*
$\dfrac{(3)^2}{3} = 3$ tons	$\dfrac{(3)^2}{18} = \frac{1}{2}$ ton

or by rule of thumb, the load should never exceed one-sixth of the breaking strength of the rope. The working life will be shortened considerably if loads approaching its breaking strength are placed on a rope.

The grooves of the pulley block used in flying must be the correct size and shape to allow the rope to seat properly. There should be no sharp edges to chafe the rope and the minimum pulley to rope diameter is never less than 5 : 1. Although hanging irons are used for scenery, a piece of furniture may have to be flown in a sling. If there are any sharp edges, the rope should be packed to avoid cutting it.

For examination, the rope is coiled down and disposed of in concentric circles which are as large as possible. Coil the rope clockwise for Right-hand laid ropes and anti-clockwise for Left-hand ropes. (To test the lay of a rope, point your fingers along the rope with the palm upwards. The right- or left-hand thumb which points in the direction of the lay indicates which hand-lay it is.)

The rope is run out on a table and examined by rotating it between the hands, about a foot at a time. External wear may be seen in the fibre breaking up or the rope may have been cut. Internal deterioration, such as rot, can be found only by putting a fid into the rope to examine it inside.

At any time when in doubt, scrap the rope; it is better to be safe than sorry when artists and staff are concerned.

Legislation concerning the safety of theatres in London is published by the Greater London Council in PLACES OF PUBLIC ENTERTAINMENT TECHNICAL REGULATIONS and RULES FOR THE MANAGEMENT OF PLACES OF PUBLIC ENTERTAINMENT. There are separate rules applicable to smaller premises accommodating an audience with a maximum of about 300. PLAY SAFE is another G.L.C. publication and the booklet is a guide intended for play presentation in local halls and similar premises. It provides notes about safety on a traditional raised-end stage and a temporary stage. Scenery, properties and lighting are mentioned with diagrams of seating arrangements for an audience of about 200 in 'theatre-in-the-round' performances.

Extracts from the Regulations are given at the end of this Appendix. They are notes only for which no responsibility is accepted and the Licensing Authority in London or elsewhere should be consulted direct when there is any uncertainty.

Page 104. In small theatres the counterweight system is worked at stage level and if the cradle is filled with weights from the stage, some form of loading arrangement should be made. Otherwise the unused weights, which take up room, lie unprotected and litter the space on the floor. A loading gallery is constructed near to the stage where the weights are kept out of the way. When the operation is carried out from the flies, the loading gallery is built under the grid with access by a ladder from the fly floor. (See Figures D D and 62.)

Scenery, such as a french flat, is attached with steel wires and ' trim chains ' to the counterweight barrel allowing it to hang level. However, it may not be possible to counterweight it exactly whereby the scenery does not meet the stage floor. Overhauling is performed by taking weights out of the counterweight cradle to release the barrel. Tension on the trim chains is reduced and the scenery stands firm on the stage.

Unlike the older method of hemp ropes, the steel wires of the counterweight system cannot be altered independently as they are fixed at one end to the counterweight cradle and the other to the barrel. It is advisable whenever possible to install both rope and counterweight systems. Some work is done better with the rope method and there is more flexibility in combining the two systems.

Page 106. Difficult lines of sight are also sometimes found when the setting is viewed from the back of the stalls and from behind the circle. The architectural projection of the balcony and the dress circle above other seats will mask action at the rear of the stage, especially with different levels in the design of the setting.

Page 108. THE ARENA STAGE is also called Island and Centre stage.

Page 110. THRUST STAGE is the term now generally used for the Peninsular stage.

Page 114. THE ADAPTABLE STAGE. The commercial theatre used for three hours per day or for limited seasons is becoming increasingly less viable with the rise in costs. In recent years, theatres have been turned into cinemas to pay their way and it seems unlikely that new theatres will be built that are not designed to be adapted to a variety of productions and other activities.

The stumbling block in the design of the adaptable stage has been the proscenium arch and when this was incorporated to preserve the traditional atmosphere, the result has been an artistic compromise that was not a completely designed entity.

Under the Greater London Council regulations, the iron safety curtain in the proscenium arch was necessary to isolate the audience from the fire risk of the stage. However, these regulations have been relaxed and consequently theatres may be designed without the safety curtain and the proscenium arch.

The new Winter Garden Theatre, Drury Lane, London dispenses with the proscenium arch and in its place are movable wall panels which can be used to provide a proscenium opening when required. The panels are the same width and texture as the fixed panels which line the curving wall of the auditorium. It is hoped with this arrangement to maintain the flow of the walls from the auditorium to the stage and to avoid the break between stage and seating to help contact between the actor and audience.

Of paramount importance to a commercial adaptable theatre, the change from one form of staging to another should be easy to operate. The alteration must be quick and, therefore, redistribution of the seating accomplished with mechanical ingenuity.

The first six rows of seats in the Vivian Beaumont Repertory Theatre, Lincoln Centre, New York, are built on a lift which can be lowered and revolved from the auditorium to below the stage where they remain hidden from view. The additional space provided in the auditorium is used for extending the acting area of the stage or to accommodate a large orchestra.

Shifting banks of seating by anything other than mechanical means is wasteful in space and seating capacity. At the Winter Garden Theatre, London, a revolve will be installed which is 60' in diameter and carries 206 seats in eight tiers. The revolve includes the main stage acting area which when revolved through 180° will redistribute the eight tiers of seats behind the acting area to form the seating for ' theatre-in-the-round ' performances. The tiers of seats will be raised mechanically until the pitch of the steps matches the fixed seating tiers in the auditorium giving a harmonious arrangement for island stage presentation.

There will be three orchestra lifts in the revolve to provide orchestra pits or a projecting forestage when raised. A smaller revolve 23' in diameter is included in the acting area to interchange with a grid of traps. The main revolve, driven electrically, takes two minutes to travel through 180° and raising the tiers of seats is performed in one and a quarter minutes.

This commercial adaptable theatre will be used not only for

stage presentations but also for conferences, lectures and trade shows. Concerts, band music and light classical music with singers will be well suited to the island stage arrangement. Cinema shows can be screened and there are ancillary areas with banqueting and restaurant facilities.

The theatre was designed to solve the problem of an adequate return on the capital invested in the building. It may have only a limited application but by keeping the theatre in use for a variety of activities many hours of the day throughout the year, it becomes independently and financially secure.

The project for a National Theatre to move Britain into cultural parity with Europe and other countries has been debated for sixty years since 1910. Government support over the last twenty years has inevitably caused postponement by stimulating large committees to argument and delay of the final achievement. Nevertheless, some of the blame must rest with those who did not know what was wanted and even if they knew could not plan to complete it.

The architect was distrusted as a building expert more inclined to design a pleasing exterior than concerned with the purpose to which the building was intended. However, when the director and theatre planners had the idea of a single adaptable auditorium to house everything from Greek tragedy to contemporary drama, the architect established that three auditoria were necessary to fulfil all they required in the National Theatre.

There are therefore three theatres in one complex. The largest will be an upper theatre with an open stage and auditorium for 1,165 spectators suitable for Greek and Elizabethan drama requiring close audience participation. (Plate V.) The thrust stage will be the first in the world capable of using and changing scenery as the overall full height grid covers the projecting part as well as the main stage. It can be modified in its front areas by moving seating blocks outwards so that actors can exit towards and under the audience. Both in this theatre and the proscenium one, scenes will be assembled rear stage and at the sides. With the latest electrical and mechanical equipment the wagon stage setting will be rolled into place at the touch of a button.

As will be seen in the illustration, the auditorium takes a stadium form and not a single floor. Avoiding solid rows of seats resembling a football stadium, it will have terraced levels ingeniously grouped around the thrust stage. The discipline always of the right angle to the circular stage, excellent sight lines across acting areas, and a stage whose shape can be modified will provide atmosphere and scope for the imaginative director.

A lower theatre for 895 spectators will separate actors from the audience with a 'picture frame' proscenium arch. Instead of removing seats to create space for a forestage, the false proscenium technique will be used. Thereby the number of seats will remain constant and provision of a forestage is an extension of part of the main stage area. The stage can be made 50′ wide and a tower and bridge structure will provide the adjustable frame from this opening to 32′ and establish a proscenium.

The third auditorium is a small rectangular studio hall seating 200 and designed for flexible use.

It is thought that the cost will rise to £10 million. But it should be remembered that overtime is paid to staff who often work through the night and running costs will be less in a theatre designed to operate a repertory system of plays with mechanical change of scenes. The impressive site of the National Theatre overlooking the river Thames has offered design possibilities denied to the commercially sponsored theatre often confined with adjoining buildings. While the old and new meet in the three-in-one shape of the complex, it is spectacular twentieth-century design retaining the traditional magic of the theatre.

Page 124. Additional descriptions for the components of a flat are:

B: Head Rail	C: Toggle Rail
G: Foot or Sill Rail	H: Brace Rail (Corner Brace U.S.A.)

Page 125. When a flat is set at a right angle to another flat, i.e. to make a corner, the keystone is set in 1″ from the edge of the frame of the flat. This allows butting up of one flat to the other and provides room for the 1″ thickness of the stile.

Page 127. For additional security, grummets are fastened to the top of a french flat. The steel wires or rope slings are run underneath the battens and through the grummets for attaching to the bar flown from the grid.

Page 144. The pack of flats are usually arranged on the O.P. side, the back wall and the prompt side of the stage. For easy recognition, the flats are numbered with a stencilled mark on the rail starting from the O.P. side of the setting with No. 1 et seq.

Page 191. Vivid colours, however, are used effectively in open settings for ballet and musical plays when one side is lit with a colour that is contrasted with another colour from the opposite side of the stage. This accentuates the folds in a costume and also can intensify the atmosphere of the scene.

Useful contrasting colours are:

No. 35 Deep golden amber and No. 19 Dark blue
    34 Golden amber   and   41 Bright blue
     4 Medium amber   and   17 Steel blue

Rich pools of light are obtained with the deep pink colours: Nos. 7, 8, 9 and 10.

Page 234. THE PROMPT CORNER. So much of the stage manager's work is controlled from the prompt corner and much of the deputy stage manager's time spent there that clarity of operation and comfort are essential in its installation and equipment. Unfortunately in the design of some new theatres, the prompt corner is given slight attention and tucked away in a small space without due regard to the person using it or for the object of its use.

The ideal prompt corner will have adequate lighting to see under normal circumstances and an additional dim blue light for use when the stage lighting is dark or in a black-out. The switches for the cues should be easy to operate and identifiable quickly under all working conditions. It should be constructed to the stage manager's best advantage and not installed more or less as an afterthought to the design of the stage. A clear view of the acting area should be obtained and there is maximum benefit in a position for the prompt corner down-stage of the curtain line. A mirror should be arranged permanently for adjustment of the line of sight under difficult conditions.

In musical and other productions on a large scale, the prompt desk may be built on a movable trolley with the cue board using a multi-core flexible cable that can be plugged in on both the prompt and O.P. sides of the stage.

Open stage performances need different control and the stage manager usually operates from a room behind the auditorium. Although he has a splendid view of the stage, he is out of active touch with the play and relies on his assistant stage managers who attend to the mechanical side of the performance near to the stage. Reliable communication between the stage manager and his assistants is of paramount importance. He cannot see the off-stage areas and his assistants near the stage carry out his instructions. Cue lights should be provided for all positions where artists make their entrances.

The West End Stage Management Association has provided extensive notes on the lay-out of the prompt corner and its equip-

ment. All stage managers should join the Association which is
concerned with their welfare not only in London but also in the
Provinces. Monthly meetings are held with discussion on aspects
of the stage manager's work. The Association has obtained a
valuable improvement in their status and contractual situation by
negotiation with the Society of West End Managers and British
Actors Equity Association.

SECTION OF A MODERN THEATRE WITH LIGHTING EQUIPMENT

Figure 62

APPENDIX TO THE THIRD EDITION

During the ten years since this book was published, the theatre has seen many changes with the building of new theatres and the advance of technology adapted to the need of the entertainment industry. There is evidence of the traditional conflict between artist and poet in the restoration of conventional picture-frame theatres and the design of new acting areas for intimate audience participation with the actor performing ' lines well writ '. The long-awaited National Theatre opened without ceremony in 1976 with only one of its three stages completed. All are now operating with some of the stage machinery working and the three theatres include the open stage, proscenium stage and a studio theatre. See Chapter 12 for details.

Early Victorian theatres have been renovated and a London cinema was restored as a theatre for open-end stage production. The tide of the theatrical stream is seen in the novel adaptation for smaller acting areas of converted factories, the conversion of a circular railway engine marshalling shed: the Roundhouse in London and the successful creation of a theatre exclusively for the production of Shakespeare's plays: the St. George's Theatre, Tufnell Park, London, inside the main body of a church which is circular in shape. The important developments in the field of the integrated circuit industry with the silicon ' chip ' microprocessor have contributed to the simplicity in design of the new smaller cost-saving lighting control boards.

The following notes are intended to supplement the information given in the Appendix to the second edition.

Page 43. THE PICTURE FRAME STAGE. The atmosphere of the Victorian theatre with proscenium arch and wrapped round curved seating to give greater audience involvement is demonstrated in the restoration of the Theatre Royal, Nottingham. The theatre was purchased by the Nottingham Corporation after it was auctioned by the commercial owners and with an investment of three million pounds (since written off) sets an example of the support a civic authority can give to the theatre. The structural alterations include a new proscenium arch with adjustable draped pelmet supported on each side by single Corinthian pillars at an oblique angle to the stage. They replace the somewhat barren four pillar decoration of the original design. The proscenium opening has been reduced from 31 ft. 6 in. to 30 ft. 2 in. and the maximum height from 30 ft.

to 23 ft. 8 in. The stage has been refloored with the normal rake 1 : 25 and preserves sightlines from the gently raked stalls. The stage projects 3 ft. 3 in. in front of the decorated safety curtain. Beyond this there is a lift providing, when it is raised, a forestage extending 7 ft. 9 in. into the audience and when lowered there are two positions for the orchestra pit with either 2 rows (32 seats) or 5 rows (90 seats) removed.

The theatre seating on four levels has been made more comfortable with the stalls arranged in the Continental style without a centre gangway. The wooden benches holding 400 in the gallery have been replaced with individual seats and the total seating capacity of the theatre is reduced from 1,467 seats to 1,133 seats. A new fly tower and grid has been installed with the counterweight system using ropes of synthetic material to replace the traditional hemp ropes now difficult to obtain. Unusual handling and stretching of the synthetic rope has been experienced which probably will settle down in future use. The lighting control room with Modular Memory System is situated behind the upper circle and front of house lighting, directed from several positions in the auditorium, is concealed behind mechanically operated hinged plaster sections which open for the performance.

There is a sound control room at the rear of the upper circle and on stage, cue lights and verbal call cues are given from the mobile stage manager's desk which can be used down stage left or right.

After construction some lessons were learned which might have been avoided if the Manager with professional knowledge had been engaged early in the building operation. For instance, no commission period was arranged in the contract and the theatre opened to the public within a few hours of completion during a time when 4000 patrons were queueing for seats. It is a tribute to the staff, including those not trained in front of house and stage practice, that they have continued to manage performances in the best theatre tradition.

The Theatre Royal was re-opened on the 7th February 1978, the day after the anniversary of the birth of Sir Henry Irving; the Victorian actor who would have rejoiced in this restoration by the architect of the Victorian theatre in which he performed. The building, with restful William Morris design green papered walls, gold paint and large sweeping foyer, is a handsome civic addition to the city.

Other Victorian theatres which have been restored are the Grand Theatre, Blackpool, owned by E.M.I., which company is discussing the purchase of the theatre by a local group of people who are trying to raise £350,000 to preserve the theatre's traditional identity.

The New Tyne Theatre, Newcastle, has been restored by an Amateur Trust at a cost of £50,000. The theatre is the only 19th century theatre still surviving in this country where the original Victorian stage machinery exists intact and in excellent condition.

Page 56. It is usual to number lighting cues 1 to say 50 from the beginning to the end of the script. In this way a particular cue is identified by the stage manager and the electrician working the switch board. To emphasise the cue the word ' Go ' may be written in the script where the cue is required and it is used verbally for lighting and effects cues.

Page 84. Fibreglass is a modern substitute for papier mâché. Various properties are made from this strong and lasting material of woven glass fibre soaked in polyester resin.

Page 104. Overhauling, or transfer of the counterweight from one set of lines to another is also performed by fastening a bracket below the cradle counterweighting the scenery. The bracket engages the adjacent cradle and the counterweight is transferred. When rope lines are installed a block and tackle or a sandbag is used to hold or counterweight the barrel for the scenery to be released. A useful tip when overhauling the counterweight barrel is a mark with white paint on the top weight of the set in the cradle which counterbalances the barrel. This acts as a warning to stop unloading the cradle.

Page 107. There is bound to be conversation when artists and staff are assembled for a rehearsal or before the performance and the stage manager gives the instruction ' Quiet Please ' to obtain silence.

Page 108. There are good reasons for the popularity of studio theatres with adaptability from proscenium type staging to the acting area of theatre-in-the-round. The traditional theatre has suffered from the competition of colour television which with almost unlimited funds has brought spectacular entertainment to the small screen in every home in the country. Nevertheless man is a gregarious animal and fondness of company has attracted young people to the friendly experience of performances in the studio type theatre. This has become an important part of community life and developing out from the acting area, the actor has become part of the community.

The experience of designers who have had to invent new

methods of staging plays has indicated the great variety of settings that are possible for the arena type of acting area. At first the architectural plan of the house or building is examined and important entrances are arranged as near as possible to suit the entrances in the open stage layout of the theatre. To provide variety from one scene to another, the axis of the setting is altered. For example, in Act 1 the layout may be L shaped with the axis travelling diagonally across the stage, and in Act 2 the axis travels diagonally across the stage in the opposite direction in a layout that is square.

In some plays there is an essential piece of furniture described in the action and it is placed as near as possible to the audience. The spectator looks over it and the audience is not especially conscious of it during the action of the play. To avoid confronting the spectator with something on the stage immediately facing him, the designer endeavours to set items at an angle to the audience. It is achieved by placing furniture etc. on the diagonal axis of the setting and in this way the spectator sees the edge of what otherwise might be an obstructive flat surface.

When an advertisement is considered, there is usually an important element which compels interest towards the picture. Likewise in the open-stage setting, something may be arranged in or above the setting to arouse attention and to focus the interest of the spectator. Staging of the ship carrying Captain Cook on his ' Voyages Round the World ' is conveyed by ropes suspended overhead and festooned with other nautical items on the walls or the galleries of seats surrounding the open-stage acting area. The audience takes it all in good part and occasionally something is recalled in the performance which was not there; it is inspired by an item placed in the setting to focus attention and stimulates the imagination of the spectator to greater pleasure in the performance.

The close proximity of the audience gives the actor considerable power and this applies to everything which he uses or which accompanies him on the stage. There is much less in the way of furniture than is found in the traditional stage setting and consequently every object in use has a potent effect on the spectator. Whereas in the proscenium stage setting the properties may be made to look like the real thing and are often enhanced by the lighting, the genuine object only can be used in the open-stage setting and every item is carefully chosen and displayed for a specific purpose. The audience has a close-up view and can observe details of carved furniture, properties and the design of costumes.

Almost the first impression the spectator has as he looks down at the stage is the floor of the acting area and much attention is given to this aspect of the setting. By clever painting the floor can consolidate the appearance of the setting and accentuate the situation of furniture or properties placed on it. There are no sides to an open-stage setting for doors, windows and pictures and when it is essential to establish the situation of an adjoining room, a skeleton door in a door frame is screwed to the floor of the stage. The sound of voices from the other room is recorded and controlled through a loudspeaker whenever the door is opened and closed.

The problems encountered with sound effects are numerous and require thoughtful consideration for each production. By convention the sound has to come from the acting area and a central speaker system is normally installed above the stage incorporating sufficient response to reproduce the full effect from sound effects records. Often if the sound is kept at a sufficiently low volume, the actor can help by indicating in speech or with gesture where the sound is supposed to originate. In some theatres loud speakers are installed in favourable positions around the walls of the auditorium. This is all very well when the sound level is low and the speakers can reproduce quite acceptable sound to envelop the audience. When the sound volume is increased the illusion is lost and the spectator seated near the loud speaker becomes aware that the sound is just behind his head.

Theatre-in-the-round has the great advantage of involvement between the actor and his audience, and the actor needs a special technique of audibility for the open-stage theatre. The actor schooled in the proscenium theatre was able to involve intimately the spectator seated at the back of the gallery with his clear diction and voice projection. The style of acting is not in favour today, though a good actor has no difficulty in adjusting his voice production to the arena stage.

Page 112.   THE END-STAGE.   At one time the open-end stage was greeted as an original theatre concept where acting area and audience are contained in the same space. However, it would seem that the end-stage design of the Mermaid Theatre—492 seats—(and other theatres which have followed this example) was not a new theatre form but was derived from the plan of the existing walls supporting the shell roof of a disused warehouse with a useful working height of about 20 ft. There is no proscenium and no fire curtain and the theatre does not have the grid for flying and wings for off-stage space of the proscenium theatre. Furthermore, it was thought that scenery would not be required and only essential furniture and properties would complete the theatrical illusion. In practice, scenery has been designed and built with difficult fire-resisting problems and although the initial building cost was low there is a heavy running cost in the productions staged at the theatre.

The lighting installation is complicated and time plus labour costs are expended for the adjustment of a variety of spotlights in positions. with limited headroom and the visible presence of the equipment.

A patch or plugging panel used for interconnecting dimmers and outlets was installed at the Mermaid Theatre and is recommended when the difficulties of lighting end-stage productions are encountered.

The audience is seated in a steeply raked single tier down to the stage between walls which are 49 ft. wide. When it is considered that settings in the proscenium theatre are 25 ft. to 30 ft. wide, there is a large expanse of stage floor in this end-stage design. Scene designers have reduced the size by using a raked stage with alternative pieces to build a stage within a stage.

The situation of the Stage Manager and his communication with artists and staff are mentioned on page 285. In the control room behind the auditorium, he cannot see the stage setting when there are light changes with a black-out, and a solution may be the construction of a box in the side wall of the theatre near to the stage. He can see the performance with the audience and also he has quick access to the acting area.

Reliable communication is essential and although verbal instruction is best, it is not always possible. (There is a flexible two-way speech system called Q-Comm which is portable and ' hands free ' in operation. Although it is connected to a ring circuit the 2-metre lead allows operator movement and the Stage Manager can give important individual instructions.) At the time of writing, the Mermaid Theatre is closed for two years, to be rehoused in a building to be constructed by the freehold owners of the site.

On the whole, the open-end stage is a novel method of theatre presentation but it suffers from the rigid stage and its open space. Other theatres faced with the problem of converting four barren walls into a theatre have decided to use a proscenium and build a fly tower. The Concordia Theatre, Hinckley, Leicestershire, converted from a factory, has a tiered raked auditorium with 400 seats and a modern lighting control room behind the audience. There is a 30 ft. wide proscenium opening between walls that are 42 ft. apart and a fly tower capable of flying items up to 18 ft. A very good transformation is achieved with limited cash resources.

The competition of the motion picture closed many theatres and with the advent of television, cinemas in their turn were closed and re-opened as supermarket stores or places for Bingo sessions. The wheel seems to have turned full circle with the welcome conversion of a central London theatre from a cinema to a theatre providing live performances.

This is the reconstruction of the Astoria Cinema which has been converted from a cinema to a theatre with an end-stage and without a proscenium frame. The stage is 55 ft. wide and 37 ft. deep and the auditorium holds 1,180 seats. There was an idea to build a proscenium with a safety curtain and this was discarded in favour of the open-end stage suitable for spectacular productions, within the limitation of the stage area and equipment. There is no off-stage space for scenery to be stored and there is only modest flying equipment. Consequently, the scenery designed for the theatre requires special consideration and will stimulate the designer to contrive an original and clever stage setting. The reconstruction of the cinema is bound to be observed elsewhere as a good solution is found for the use of a building failing as a cinema and its conversion to a financially productive theatre.

The Astoria opened as a theatre with the spectacular musical production around the life of Elvis Presley. As may be imagined, the subject attracted large audiences and the stage presentation adapted to the informality of the novel theatre design probably contributed to its success and was appreciated by the young theatre audience.

Page 113. Until the time of the Victorian theatre, scene changing in full view of the audience was part of the performance which those paying for admission enjoyed. Contemporary theatre has put the clock back and again the mechanics of change of scene with lighting equipment are exposed, though some have regretted the loss of theatre magic when auditorium lights were dimmed and with a faint rustle the curtain rose on the brightly lit scene. Competition with film and television has spelled doom to the living theatre and it is encouraging to see the invention of young stage designers who are restoring theatre magic under moden staging conditions. There was evidence of this trend in the recent exhibition of the best British scenery design at the Riverside Studios, London. Television and film have the edge on theatre staging and the new generation of designers were quick to observe that the film technique of back projection could be employed handsomely for theatrical staging effect. Several of the models showed the advantage gained from stylised reproduction of a stage feature i.e. a flight of steps or a well decorated section of a period interior with interesting profiled surround. The changes of scene are accom-

plished in full view of the audience by slide projection on gauze or
on the cyclorama behind the central structure which is also subject
to alteration. The method with other lighting techniques confirms
the international reputation for writing and acting our country
has always enjoyed and is now enhanced by the invention of
younger stage designers. They are in line with nineteenth century
artists and the tricks they were up to described in a programme
note of: MANKIND (or Beggar Your Neighbour) in 7 Acts. Written
by Paul Meritt (1881): ' Entirely New and Realistic Scenery has
been painted from sketches made at the various places illustrated.
Elaborate Mechanical Effects have been invented and executed;
and no expense, trouble, or pains whatever have been spared to
make this Production by far the most important ever presented at
the Surrey Theatre.'

Page 114.   The adaptable stage is complemented by the variable
capacity auditorium installed recently at the Picadilly Theatre,
London. A moving ceiling is incorporated which when lowered
closes off the Grand Circle and reduces the theatre seating capacity
from 1,132 to 792 seats. The ceiling, driven by motors above the
original dome, and suspended on cable at four points, can transform
the auditorium in either direction in about three minutes and is
operated by one man.

Page 145.   The marks with paint or adhesive tape to indicate the
position of scenery or furniture are called ' Spike Marks ' in the
U.S.A.

Page 151.   Door locks with keys or sliding bolts are mounted so
that they do not engage when used. (I remember an artist of ample
proportions squeezing through the small space below the tormentor
and into the prompt corner when the down-stage door failed to
open.)

Page 161.   Another method for the visual effect of broken glass is
obtained by using sugar and water which is heated and poured
in a form of the size required on a sheet of formica. The solution
crystallises quickly; is translucent, and can be broken.
    When an object such as a vase on a mantelshelf is the target of
something aimed at it, the vase is first scored with a glass cutter
and with ' split-second timing ' is pushed off the shelf with a straw
inserted through a hole in the canvas of the flat. The scoring prevents too much destruction as the vase hits the stage floor.
Scenery which is broken during the play is broken and prepared

for the effect. It is reassembled with light dowels so that the identical breakage can be repeated for each performance.

Page 203.   An auto transformer will dim any size lamp without using a load off-stage in circuit with the lamp. The transformer is large and difficult to use in small switchboard areas. Ghost or Phantom Load (U.S.A.).

Page 221.   In a moonlight scene blue green mediums may be chosen with a pale gold filter to strengthen the acting area. The costume designer should be informed about this lighting which can alter the colour of the artist's costume.

Page 222.   A Fog and Smoke machine providing a trouble-free vapour is supplied by manufacturers of stage equipment. For a special effect crushed dry ice lowered into warm water will give smoke or fog which rises only a few feet from the stage floor.

Page 223.   While on the subject of fluorescent paint for ultra-violet light effects, it is useful to mention phosphorescent paint which, as its name describes, glows faintly in the dark. The paint has this property after being exposed to light and can be used to guide actors in a black-out and to indicate the position of furniture and properties.

Page 254.   TOURING.   The stage schedule of the National Theatre Company with two productions and eight performances during one week of their Autumn tour is shown below. It should be noted that in order to complete the fit-up of scenery, lighting and the mid-week changeover from one play to the other, all-night working is necessary on the Sunday and Wednesday nights.

> *National Theatre of Great Britain—Autumn Tour*
> *Proposed Stage Schedule*   *Theatre Royal, Brighton*
> Sunday 28 September

	09.00	Get in Three Sisters and commence fit up
	13.00	Lunch break
	14.00	Continue fit up and rigging
	19.00	Stage available for rehearsal
	22.30	Resume fitting up and rigging Focus and light to completion
	Note:	This will involve all-night working—possibly into Monday morning.

Monday 29 September	13.30	Set for Dress Rehearsal
	14.30	Dress Rehearsal Three Sisters
	18.30	Full Crew for rehearsal of Scene Change Act 3 to 4—then set to open
	19.45	*Performance* Three Sisters
Tuesday 30 September	10.30	Stage available for rehearsal
	18.45	Set scene 1 and Stage Check
	19.45	*Performance* Three Sisters
Wednesday 1 October	10.30	Stage available for rehearsal
	12.30	Set scene 1 and Stage Check
	14.30	*Matinee* Three Sisters
	19.45	*Performance* Three Sisters
	23.00	Strike and get out Three Sisters Get in, Fit up, rig and focus The Way of the World
	Note:	This will involve all-night working
Thursday 2 October	09.00	Continue Fit up and lighting The Way of the World
	13.00	Lunch break
	14.00	Complete lighting
	15.30	Stage available rehearsals
	18.45	Set to open and Stage Check
	19.45	*Performance* The Way of the World
Friday 3 October	10.30	Stage available for rehearsal
	19.15	Set scene 1 and Stage Check
	20.15	*Performance* The Way of the World
Saturday 4 October	10.30	Stage available for rehearsal
	16.00	Set scene 1 and Stage Check
	17.00	*Matinee* The Way of the World
	20.15	*Performance* The Way of the World
		After performance—Strike and Get Out all National Theatre Scenery, equipment etc.

N.B. Subject to rehearsal requirements it may be necessary to strike to a bare stage after the performances on Monday, Tuesday, Thursday and Friday. If no rehearsal is called the resetting will be done in the morning.

Page 310. A stage direction in Elizabethan plays was ' Enter Above ' when actors (and spectators) used the gallery above stage level in the Tiring House. (Figure 3.)

Page 316. The stage manager's instruction ' Clear please ' is given a moment or so before the curtain rises as a precaution that the stage is ready for the performance.

Page 322. Concentration of light when using a ' frosted ' medium is obtained by cutting an irregular pattern in the centre or by smearing a drop of oil on the rough side of the medium.

Page 343. Flymen with nautical knowledge take a turn of the rope around a cleat on the fly rail. The friction delays the speed of the rope that is lowered and prevents chafing the hands.

Page 343. *Electrical Safety.* ' Safe Sound ' is a pamphlet published by the Association of British Theatre Technicians (price 20p.) which provides information on the cause and effect of electric shock. Safety measures are recommended when using electrical musical instruments and sound equipment. Electric guitars and hand-held microphones are known to become ' live ' suddenly and the precautions advised prevent the occurrence of serious accidents.

Page 384. *The Staging Handbook* by Francis Reid (Pitman, London and Theatre Arts Books, New York 1978) contains extra knowledge of other forms of entertainment—much of which was gained from the author's own experience. There are concise chapters about the staging of musical, opera, dance, light entertainment, tours, one night stands and amateur production which should prove valuable especially when a form of staging is encountered for the first time.

Page 384. An indispensable book for anyone working in the theatre is *Theatre Backstage From A to Z* by Warren C. Lounsbury, the revised edition published by the University of Washington Press 1972. Lighting and the construction of stage settings are covered in great detail and the information about stage practice in the U.S.A. is equally applicable to this country.

The introduction includes a historical survey of stage scenery and lighting practices from the beginning of strolling players, the first recorded theatre built in Williamsburg, 1716 and the arrival of the first professional company from London: ' In 1752 William Hallam, bankrupt manager of the Goodman's Fields Theatre in London, decided that the New World was ready for professional theatre. A newly formed company of twelve adults and three children, under the management of William's brother, Lewis Hallam, set sail in *The Charming Sally*, replete with scenery, properties, and a repertory of plays to be rehearsed during the forty-two-day voyage. The busy little company arrived in Williamsburg, Virginia, in July, bought and remodelled a warehouse, and opened to the public on September 15. This event marks the first professional scenery to be seen in the colonies.'

The sub-title of the book is ' A concise encyclopaedia of stagecraft . . . from Alternating Current to Zoom Lens ' and apart from interesting reading, the information gathered together must be of great value whenever a stage problem is encountered. The terms are grouped under general headings with a system of cross references. Often there is more than one method of doing the same thing and the author has researched the subjects in such detail that the reader can weigh up the alternatives and choose the solution that is best suited to his purpose.

In the theatre history there is a pictorial reference to remarkable double stages that were operating in New York's Madison Square Theatre during the latter part of the 19th century. Each stage, using heavy realistic scenery, weighed 48 tons and counterweighted they were controlled by a cable running to a drum operated by four men. The time allotted for changing from one stage to the other was forty-five seconds. The stages were 25 ft. apart and housed in an elevator shaft 114 ft. high. They were suspended by cables at the four corners and each of the two stages contained its own set of traps. The designer, Steele Mackaye, also devised rising theatre seats, sliding stages, adjustable proscenium, fireproofing for scenery and complicated lighting effects.

The well illustrated book progresses to the modern miniaturised technology employed in lighting control boards and mentions an intriguing method of moving wagon stages on air castors using the Hovercraft principle on a cushion of compressed air.

The British company: Rolair Systems (U.K.) Limited has produced an air-borne method of moving normally immovable objects under licence from the U.S.A. Using urethane diaphragms inflated with compressed air, a large audience-bearing structure was made to glide during the Science Fiction Theatre of Liverpool presentation of ' The Hitch Hiker's Guide to the Galaxy ' produced at the Institute of Contemporary Arts, London, in the Spring, 1979.

Holography

David Garrick, writing a letter of advice to a young actor, said: ' I would have you endeavour to read other books besides those of the theatre. Every additional knowledge to that of your profession will give you importance.' The three-dimensional photography created by laser beams is a subject not immediately associated with the theatre. Nevertheless, the stage manager who wishes to be informed of an area of technology which may in the future have a theatrical application, might consider the experimental work undertaken in the production of Holograms.

The principle of Holography involves the method of creating a photographic image without the use of a lens and the photographic recording of the image is a Hologram. When the Hologram is illuminated by a laser beam, the light is organised into a three-dimensional representation of the original object and the spectator can see different views as he moves, just as he would of the object from which the Hologram is made.

While awaiting a game of tennis in 1947, the Hungarian-born scientist, Dr. Dennis Gabor watched the ball travelling in space across the net. Suddenly the idea of a Hologram came to him and the three-dimensional image apparently frozen in space was born. It was a by-product of his work on improvement of the electron microscope and his search for three-dimensional realism was the same as the problem encountered by photographers in their search for three-dimensional photography. For several years, his work was of only theoretical interest until the development of lasers in the early 1960s changed the situation.

Lasers produce an intense beam of light of a very pure single colour and they fulfil one of the oldest dreams of technology: a light beam of sufficient intensity to vaporise the hardest and most heat-resistant of metals. To achieve three-dimensional realism, the light streaming or reflected from the source must itself be photographed. If the waves of this light can be frozen for an instant and photographed, the wave pattern can then be reconstructed and will exhibit the same three-dimensional character as the object from which the light is reflected. Holography accomplishes this by recording the content of the reflected light waves of a laser beam. The scale of the early images comprised a depth of three to four feet and this has been improved so that images can now appear to extend back fifteen feet into the wall. The reconstructed image is no larger than the original object and is seen through a glass screen. It can also be made to appear in front of the screen. Holograms have been made of film and stage settings for novel publicity in advertisements. A magic effect is produced when a hologram is made of a model stage setting and the reconstructed image used in television as a three-dimensional illusion with actors.

Recent advances using a pulsed laser enable Holograms to be

made of moving objects. The pulsed laser emits an extremely intense short flash of light that lasts only a thousand-millionth of a second, and it will freeze the movement of any object into a three-dimensional image. This aspect of Holography recalls the early work of Edward Muybridge, the English photographer living in America who analysed human and animal activity. On the 4th May 1880 at the San Francisco Arts Association, he demonstrated moving pictures of animals on a screen to an audience.

Although other inventors may be credited with the invention of movies, Muybridge was certainly the first man to succeed in taking moving pictures. He made 100,000 pictures of human and animal activities and every time he made a sequence of some activity such as playing cricket or running, he was the first man to show the way in which humans and animals really move. The three-dimensional Hologram images already produced analyse the movement of ballet dancers, a bullet at the time it is fired from a gun, and water running from a tap. It is too early to say that Holography will lead to three-dimensional television and the present theatrical use is in illusion and the storage on a flat surface of a photographic recording of an object which can be reconstructed into a three-dimensional image.

Micro-Electronics

The miniature world of micro-electronics, where everything is becoming smaller and smaller, is probably the most important industry in this country and will be for the remaining years of this century. The rapid development of the industry is likely to change the habits of society almost beyond recognition and the key to many of the advances is the tiny wafer or ' chip ' of polished silicon which measures a quarter-of-an-inch square. Electronic circuitry is incorporated in the chip with the photographic technique used to etch circuits and cells on to silicon. The minute device can store as much information as a computer in a large room filled with vacuum tubes and wiring twenty-five years ago.

A chip containing all the functions of the central processor of a computer is called a *Microprocessor*. It has the ability to fetch instructions and data from memories; it can recognise and execute instructions for logical and arithmetic operations and it sends results to memory or display. *Micro-Electronics* are the systems of electronic circuits incorporated into a chip of silicon and a *Micro-computer* is a computer based around a microprocessor with interface chips to enable them to work as a system.

The microprocessor is becoming smaller, faster, and more intelligent and cheaper to produce each year. This is evident from the history of the first of the new products of micro-electronics which became well-known during the last ten years: the pocket calculator. A revolutionary micro-electronic TV camera will be marketed shortly in this country. It is about the size of a matchbox and the silicon chip contains nearly 400,000 circuit elements in an area the size of a finger nail. Apart from the use for military surveillance, it has important application in mining as it can be pushed through a small borehole to inspect an accident area. The camera can be lowered to check oil installations rigged below the surface of the sea.

The photographic process used to etch circuits on to silicon involves as many as eight masks overlaid with amazing precision. Each layer of a circuit diagram resembles a duplicate pattern of hieroglyphics. It can be held stretched between a man's arms and is reduced 200 times to a miniscule wafer a quarter-of-an-inch long. There is a limit to the photographic technique and a different method will be required for the next generation of microprocessors. The micro-circuit memory device will store electronic data in 64,000 tiny cells and the information in such a device is equivalent to two pages of a National newspaper.

Electronics and microprocessor techniques have advanced lighting control systems in the theatre from the expensive machine-made products to the simple memory lighting control systems which perform important tasks at a much lower cost of the equipment. They were used in America during the last two years and the system comprises a computer-memory console board with minimum operational controls and a video display screen. Cues can be stored in the memory and recalled; additional cues can be inserted at will and cues can be cancelled. Manual control is incorporated to increase or decrease the intensity levels of selected lighting channels or groups of channels. Readings of all the dimmers are viewed on the screen and a cue in storage can be recalled at any time without changing the stage lighting. The Rank Strand Electric Company has combined essential stage lighting experience with advanced electronics and microprocessor techniques to produce a memory control system called DUET for the lighting needs of small to medium sized stages. The basic system is a table-top Console with a single keyboard, providing access to both channel and memory numbers, and the Console by itself is a complete and self-contained memory lighting control. A mimic display is optional, because on a small-scale installation the operator can assimilate the contribution of each channel to the whole by direct view.

As an alternative, there is a free-standing Visual Display Unit for screening of the percentage intensity of every control channel and the content and state of all master functions. The number of channels controlled can be varied in multiples of 12, up to a maximum of 120, similarly the number of fast-access memories built-in, is also variable up to 199. Both the number of channels and the number of memories can be extended by plugging-in extra printed cards. For bulk memory storage and recall during a performance, or for library storage for repertoire, a free-standing Floppy Disc Unit can be added. This provides the means of storing the contents of the Console memory onto a small, flexible magnetic disc, thus allowing the fast-access memory of the Console to be used for new recordings. Discs can be used to re-programme the Console memory as often as required. There is other optional equipment and the Company has produced a brochure with comprehensive instructions for operating the Console.

Although memory discs about the size of a gramophone record are still made, they are being overtaken by new technology with considerably greater capacity to perform access memory function. The new system incorporating silicon chip devices no larger than a matchbox is already illustrating information received from signals transmitted to earth by the satellite probe travelling an incredible distance into outer space.

The silicon chip is mainly imported from America where there is a thriving industry near San Francisco of firms producing applications for its use and a simple chip bought wholesale for £10 a hundred goes into equipment costing hundreds of thousands of pounds.

In Britain, too, several companies are engaged in finding new marketing opportunities and a device created eleven years ago with a £1,000 bank loan in a bedroom-laboratory of a mortgaged house was the foundation of a business now turning over £10 million a year. The company: Micro Consultants Ltd. has taken the lead throughout the world in the design and manufacture of computer-controlled systems.

Sophisticated electronic and computerised equipment going into television studios, radar installations and North Sea oil rigs, use the device called an ADC—Analogue to Digital Converter—without which the equipment would not operate. The television signal or an electronic current is ' read ' electronically by the ADC which it converts into a series of numbers, or digital code for analysis by a computer. A memory device coupled to the ADC enables information it derives to be retrieved, corrected, and synchronised.

Stage managers working in television studios will in future experience a development likely to change radically the opportunities created in producing television programmes. The new equipment, combining the ADC with a digital framestore and called: Digital Production Effects System, has been sold to American television companies and is being installed in television studios in this country albeit slowly. The DPE 5001 system is electronic magic to the extent that it gives a computer ' eyes ', and simultaneous signals from four or five different sources are fed into the control room mixer for use at will by the producer.

Already we have seen a television screen for a news bulletin divided into segments, each one providing a different motion picture. Film production that occupied many weeks of specialised camera work is now performed quickly with accurate photography. The system can zoom into a picture without any action by the camera, it can change and magnify the picture shape, ' freeze ' it, compress it with much more besides, and the equipment with ADCs, microprocessors and mini computers fits conveniently into the Alice in Wonderland compartment of an average size estate car.

CONCLUSION

Throughout its history, the theatre has relied on the most advanced mechanical skills to assist the actor in his performance. The rope rigging found in sailing ships supplied the method of flying scenery from the grid. Candles and oil lamps were replaced by gas illumination with the burner enclosed in a wire safety screen to protect dresses from catching fire. Electric light was introduced alongside the gas lighting, and massive control boards were installed for dimming the intensity of the stage lanterns and the lights in the auditorium. The sound effects provided by cannon balls released down a wooden thunder-run, transformation scenes in pantomime, with hydraulic lifts and revolving stages, were all used to arouse the interest of the audience. Today the theatre can employ the most recent technology which may be essential to the production of the play or be applauded by the theatre-going public. It is, however, incidental to the work of the artist and although the actor requires a proficient technique, the technician need not be an actor in any way.

> ' The drama's laws, the drama's patrons give,
> For we that live to please, must please to live.'
> Samuel Johnson.

APPENDIX TO THE FOURTH EDITION

The changes in the theatre with advance in technology and its application to lighting and stage equipment have continued since the previous edition of this book was published. There is the knowledge obtained in working the stages of the National Theatre using computer controlled equipment and the following brief notes are given in the hope that they will provide up to date information of the difficulties encountered and the way in which some of the problems were resolved.

Page 186/7.   Since the spotlights illustrated in Chapter 8 were in normal use, their design is improved with corresponding efficiency. The details will give an indication of the spotlights used today relative to those described.

1) PATT. 45 Junior Spotlight is replaced by the MINIM F 500w Soft-Edge (Fresnel) Spotlight.
2) PATT. 123 Spotlight has become the PRELUDE F 650w Soft-Edge (Fresnel) Spotlight.
3) PATT. 243 lkw Spotlight is now found in the CADENZA F 2kw Soft-Edge (Fresnel) lantern with the beam adjustable from a spot focus to a very wide floodlight.
4) PATT. 23 Baby Profile Spotlight and probably the best used spotlight ever produced, is replaced by the MINIM 23 500w Hard-Edge Profile Spotlight.

Page 189.   The existence of the modern high power spotlight has caused a change in the manufacturing process of colour mediums to provide colours that last and do not fade when exposed to strong light. There are now three ranges of colour filters named CHROMOID being the top quality for high temperature conditions, CINEMOID an economical choice of colours and CINELUX a comprehensive list of colour and correction filters.

Included in the CINEMOID range are popular colours some of which are described with the suffix 'A' signifying a change from the original colour as follows:

1 Yellow	10 Middle Rose	22 Moss Green	48 Bright Rose
2 Light Amber	11 Dark Pink	23A Light Green	50 Pale Yellow
3 Straw	16 Blue Green	24A Dark Green	52 Pale Gold
4 Medium	17 Steel Blue	29 Heavy Frost	54 Pale Rose
Amber	18 Light Blue	32 Medium Blue	64 Medium Red
5 Orange	19A Dark Blue	36 Pale Lavender	66 Pale Red
6 Red	21A Pea Green	41 Bright Blue	73 Straw Tint
7A Light Rose			78 Salmon Pink

The following colours are deleted from the list of colour mediums given on page 189: 8, 25, 33, 55, and 60. Other filters not shown in the CINEMOID range can be found in the CHROMOID and CINELUX range of colour mediums.

Page 298.   The variety of productions on the three stages of the National Theatre provides an opportunity to discuss the experience gained in presenting them since the theatre opened in 1976.

OLIVIER THEATRE. Whereas the design has aroused criticism from architects and theatre planners, the theatre has proved exciting to the audience, though exacting for the designer creating the scenery to be staged there. The unusual bowl shape of the auditorium has attracted an audience who enjoys contact with the actor in the open stage concept while the designer faces the challenge of working in a situation totally different from the proscenium theatre.

When the theatre was opened, the Theta drum revolve in the centre of the stage was hailed as the piece de resistance of the machinery installed. Great hope was centred on its achievement quickly to position and reposition scenery upon the thrust stage, lower it to the basement to be replaced with new scenery or properties. However, the complicated arrangement of a revolving stage split into semi-circular sections for sinking into the service area below, with traps in the surface, has proved a long ordeal before completion. It has taken seven years to become mechanically sound and the revolve has since been used extensively. For the first time in public, the elevators were used also for production of 'The Shaughraun' in May 1988. Work is in hand for eventual computer automatic control and until successful the drum will continue in manual operation.

There is the danger element with a large cast assembled, some of whom could be exposed to the open area of the stage with no protective barrier around it, when the drum descends. During the tenure of the Greater London Council, a safety certificate was not obtained and the situation is now resolved by the Lambeth Council who inspect each production for safety before giving their consent. While there should be acknowledgement for the design on the drawing board, it is sometimes difficult to foresee how it will work with hindsight of subsequent knowledge.

The system of the motorised spot lines installed is probably the most advanced of its kind with the ability to lower a powered line almost anywhere on the stage. However, the claim of economy made originally seems to be defeated by sophisticated machinery which for rigging of scenery is slower in operation than conventional means employed in other theatres. The computer system is controlled by one operator and only one bar at a time can be dropped to stage level for the rigging of flown scenery. In older theatres, the manual system allows several bars to be lowered together with time saved.

There is a great reliance on flying and flown pieces of scenery for 4 plays in the repertoire are left permanently rigged which creates a problem for the designer of a new production. He has to be sure that sufficient flying space is free for what he has designed and no other demand will alter his requisition. An electrical fault may be caused by a slack wire or a hoist not moving and the system is stopped automatically. There is no provision for control by the staff who might be able to anticipate and correct a fault before it occurs.

The open stage concept of the Olivier Theatre presents the designer with further difficulties. Instead of the usual safety curtain between stage and audience, there are fire and sound reducing doors at the back of the stage giving access to three rear stages where scenery is assembled and moved to the acting area. Due to stringent fire regulations, the doors remain closed throughout the performance and the designer is unable to bring his scenery to the stage. He has to contrive his setting with everything installed within the stage area from the beginning of the play and in view of the audience.

Consequently the scene changes need careful planning and are a reminder of the time when scene changing in the traditional theatre was done in full view of the audience and was something that every spectator was there to watch. History may repeat itself and in the Olivier Theatre the scene changes have already become part of the performance. During a musical play, the actors used the trucks carrying the scenery; a novel solution that increased the pace and excitement of the show.

A puzzling feature is the difficulty of giving actors good entrances to the stage. The dressing rooms accommodating up to 135 actors, are placed between and behind the main stages of the National Theatre. There are corridors leading to an interior street which in turn provides access from the rehearsal rooms, carpentry and paint shops to the rear of the Olivier stage. The actors arrive on stage from several routes and create a problem for designers in getting them on and off the stage. There is little side space and to arrive quickly to a good position down stage, there is the possibility of entrances for 2 actors from below the side tiers. Another solution consists in removing end blocks of the front rows of seats with steps for the actors to the down stage area.

The 'saturation lighting' was intended to offer the Lighting Designer sufficient spotlights fixed in position from which to make his choice. From experience it has proved difficult to limit him to a small number of instruments from the 720 circuits available and many more are selected causing additional time and expense in lighting the play. The theatre provides a challenge and excitement for those working there although the full capability of the stage remains to be explored. This must wait for easing of the financial situation when experiments may be tried out to discover other uses for the variety of equipment installed.

LYTTLETON THEATRE. The stage of this theatre has been plagued with more mechanical and other problems than it deserved since it opened in 1976.

The scenery was flown manually for the first four years while work continued on the double purchase computer controlled flying system designed in 1970-2. When it was eventually offered for acceptance by the contractors, tests revealed snags and shortcomings in equipment performance. Over two years modifications were made without complete success and the system was abandoned in 1980 when it became ten years out of date.

The contractors were successful, however, with the larger and more complex Olivier Theatre flying system.

During the ten years, there was considerable progress in the design of hydraulic flying and electronic control equipment which has made possible more straightforward and less costly methods of powered flying. Hydraulic operation known in the traditional theatre for a long time, allows both manual and electrical control. The important asset for the design of stage equipment is the exceptional torque i.e. the system of forces producing rotation at standstill developed by hydraulic equipment. It can also provide a range of speed greater than that of electrical motors.

The flying system of the Lyttleton Theatre is now converted to the less cumbersome single purchase manual system and the House Tabs are operated by hydraulic power controlled by a push button in the prompt corner. Major technological advances in hydraulic flying will be applied to the rest of the flying system in due course with the lighting bars early in line for adaptation.

The historian may like to know that the Lyric Theatre, Shaftesbury Avenue, opened in 1888, was one of the first London theatres in which hydraulic stage machinery was used to work a set of bridges by water power.

Another problem needing attention was the condition of the stage floor which was designed with pallets or traps about 6ft × 3ft whereby traps could be used almost anywhere on the stage. The traffic of heavy trucks wheeled over it disturbed the traps leaving an uneven stage surface. The entire stage has been resurfaced and if traps are required in future, they can be constructed individually.

COTTESLOE THEATRE. The smallest of the three National Theatre stages is probably the most interesting and the inventive solution to the staging of productions in the arena and end stage forms has aroused considerable public support. Yet the theatre was closed for three months following the Arts Council decision to increase the National Theatre grant by only 2 per cent to £6,705,200 for 1985/86.

Maximum revenue each year from the Cottesloe box office produces one third of the annual cost to run the theatre. The Greater London Council came to the rescue with a special grant of £375,000 which was in addition to their annual grant of £750,000 for the whole of the National Theatre. The Cottesloe was reopened and following the end of the GLC, the Arts Council is now responsible for funding of the National Theatre.

Before a play is even staged, it costs £2½-3 million a year to run the National Theatre building, which is distorting the theatre's grant. A solution put forward is the separation of the building upkeep expenditure from the costs of running the three auditoriums.

The argument for and against an increased subsidy continues with both sides: the National Theatre and the Arts Council presenting their view. The Council recalled that with £6 million annually, the National Theatre remains the best funded theatre and it was essential to obtain the maximum value for every pound spent. The National's administrator forwarded a report to the Arts Council asking for an increased grant of £1½ million (a rise of about 23%) in 1985/86. The box office revenue was £1,847,000 in 1979/80 and improved to £4,042,000 in 1983/84. In this year the theatre has only received an increase of 2.9 per cent when inflation was ruhning at 5 per cent.

Page 304.   The second National Theatre company: the Royal Shakespeare Company opened in the Barbican Theatre in 1982. They play in the main stage theatre, seating: 1,166 and a studio theatre called The Pit which are part of the Barbican International Arts Centre in the City of London. The main theatre resembles the Olivier auditorium and has about the same number of seats within a smaller space giving an increased sense of intimacy.

The theatre's financial situation was examined in a Government initiated report which said that the company was well managed and under-funded. The scale of grant was increased from £3.6 million in 1983-4 to £4.9 million in 1984-5 thereby recognising that the company performs both in London and Stratford-on-Avon.

In Stratford, the RSC performs on 2 stages: the Main theatre and a small one called: The Other Place with only 150 seats. A progressive policy is indicated with news of a third stage: The Swan Theatre, seating 430 opened in 1986 and built within the auditorium shell of the original Memorial Theatre destroyed by fire in 1926. It is intended to produce a Summer season performing 4 to 5 plays of the period 1570 to 1750. The theatre will be financially self-supporting and construction has cost over a million pounds.

The cost is provided from an unrevealed private source and came about in an unusual way. A model of the proposed Swan Theatre was taken around America in a fund-raising exercise which proved fruitless and subsequently, the model was placed on show in the Stratford Theatre's Art Gallery. On a wet afternoon in 1982, a visitor pausing at every exhibit because the rain continued, was taken up with the model. They enquiried about it and when told the sad story said they wished to talk about it.

Shortly afterwards the visitor made known that they were willing and able to pay for the conversion. There was one proviso, that the visitor did not want their name, address or why they made the offer to be disclosed.

The theatre was opened by H.M. the Queen on 13th November, 1986 who unveiled a Royal plaque and the name of the benefactor was disclosed with a second plaque giving his name Frederick R. Koch, the American art collector.

Two reasons exist for the new stage. Previously the Company produced Jacobean or non Shakespearean plays in the main theatre and overseas visitors travelling long distances were disappointed to find that a play by Shakespeare was not in production. Secondly, the number of popular Shakespeare plays is dwindling and may be repeated more often in the main theatre. Looking towards the future with competition from video and renewed life in films, a theatre devoted to the classics may find itself in recession unless something is done to ensure survival.

The policy of the RSC at Stratford-on-Avon and taking it to the end of the 20th century is to perform the more popular Shakespeare plays in the main theatre; the Swan Theatre will house classic or neglected plays by Shakespeare's contemporaries and new plays will be offered on the small Other Place stage.

Page 362.   A new municipal entertainments centre opened in North-ampton in 1983 uses the Hovercraft principle of moving large objects on a cushion of compressed air. The auditorium can be adapted from a 1200 seat proscenium theatre to a 1500 seat concert hall; a 1700 seat sports arena and an open space floor for community entertainment.

To alter the auditorium, the stall seats and some of the boxes are moved in sections or towers on pallets of compressed air; a considerable gain over the time and money expended with manual labour. The modern invention of the Hovercraft first used at sea in 1959, has found a theatrical use which probably will be followed elsewhere.

Page 364.   In the theatre, the computer age is developing from its use in stage lighting and power flying to creative use for designers and technicians. The time-consuming effort in making three dimensional objects such as a detailed model with furnishings of a stage setting can be frustrating when the process of critical analysis begins. Instead of reconstructing the model to accept different sight lines, the questions raised about sight lines and the ability to view the design from alternative vantage points may now be solved by the Computer Aided Design system called CAD.

The first step is to feed the computer with accurate details of the stage ground plan. Subsequently the front elevation with section and details of flying arrangements are added and at a touch of a button, the computer will model an outline of the stage in three dimensions on the small screen.

When measurements of the scene design are also recorded with objects such as chairs, trees, platforms etc they will be screened by the computer relative to sight lines from various parts of the auditorium.

In other words the computer will draw the design and screen it from an audience view point. The sight lines can be confirmed and when the model is constructed it will be with advance knowledge that the setting is correct for the stage on which it will be presented.

Page 365.   Memory lighting control systems have shown considerable development since the last edition of this book to the extent that a different approach, various prices and a different kind of technology brought confusion to the consumer market. Following market research in broadcasting and theatre lighting design with the technology available, the Rank Strand Lighting Company obtained information for the design of equipment based on the customer requirement and current electronic technique.

The DUET system described previously is discontinued and replaced by the GEMINI memory control system which provides for the need of theatres, clubs and touring companies of all sizes. Although more elaborate with a large range of control functions and effects, the basic system is a compact table-top Console with a colour Visual Display Unit giving details of the operation.

180 channels control up to 384 dimmers with dual playbacks, eight submasters and separate backup equipped with a memory to continue performance in the event of a main system failure. There is a range of options including Floppy disc for memory storage and the Company has produced an instructive brochure with detailed description of individual items for operating the Console.

EXTRACTS FROM
G.L.C. TECHNICAL REGULATIONS

Part 3   (10)   Fire appliances and equipment for the protection of the premises shall be provided to the Council's satisfaction.

Part 5   (01)   All parts of the premises shall be provided with adequate means of illumination and, except where otherwise permitted by the Council, those portions to which the public have access and all routes of escape for performers or staff shall be provided with adequate means of illumination from two independent sources.

(06)   In any premises containing a stage, and in such other premises as the Council may determine, electric light shall be the only illuminant provided on the stage or platform and in the stage basements, the flies, property rooms and scene stores.

(14)   Switches, fuse boards and other control apparatus shall be so installed as to minimise the possibility of interference by the public.

(15)   Provision for the connexion of portable electrical appliances shall be made only in positions approved by the Council and shall be subject to such conditions as the Council may consider necessary.

(16)   Lighting equipment used on stages and platforms shall be of stout construction, encased in rigid, non-combustible material and designed to withstand the temperatures caused by the illuminant without excessive temperature rise on the outer casings and to resist mechanical damage.
(1) Lighting battens and other lighting fittings on stages, platforms, etc., shall be spaced away from any surroundings likely to interfere with their efficient ventilation. Any scenery, drapes or hangings or other combustible material shall not be allowed to approach such lighting equipment to less than 3 in. horizontally or 12 in. vertically, and guards, of non-combustible material and robust construction, shall be provided, where considered necessary by the Council, to effect such spacing.
(2) Any hanging lighting fitting shall be suspended by steel wire ropes which, in the case of battens and similar lengthy equipment, shall be not less than three in number. If required by the Council, suitable self-sustaining winches shall be provided.

(21)   Any lantern or other lighting apparatus installed in the auditorium for stage illumination or special effects shall be enclosed to the Council's satisfaction.

Part 6   (01)   The stage shall be so constructed and arranged as to minimise the risk of fire.

(02)   The means of suspension for scenery shall be to the Council's satisfaction as regards loading, position control and guarding of mechanism and cables. The construction shall as far as practicable be non-combustible.
(1) Flown scenery shall be suspended from wire ropes, attached either to counterweights or self-sustaining

winches, so as to retain full control of the position of the scenery while in use. Any ' barrels ' used for the attachment of scenery shall be of metal and suspended by not less than three wire ropes. Adequate provision shall be made for adjustment to offset stretch of these ropes.

(2) Suspension ropes shall be of flexible steel, shall have a safety factor of not less than six, and shall be carried on pulley sheaves of diameter not less than 30 times the rope diameter and mounted on free-running bearings. Handling ropes may be of nylon, hemp or similar fibre.

(3) Counterweights of scenery shall be guarded and, where possible, shall be carried to the walls and cased in.

Additional requirements for a separated stage :

Part 6   (05)   The stage area in premises designed or arranged for entertainments involving the use of scenery fabricated from materials other than those which the Council accepts for use on open stages shall, except for the proscenium opening, be enclosed and separated from the auditorium and from the remainder of the premises.

        (06)   The proscenium opening shall be provided with a safety curtain.

        (07)   Provision shall be made to the Council's satisfaction for an outlet at high level over the stage, of sufficient area to allow the escape of smoke and hot gases in the event of fire in the stage area.

Construction applicable to smaller premises for the accommodation of not more that about 300 members of the public, of not more than about 1,800 sq. ft. and wherein permanent provision for a closely seated audience is not made.

Part 8   (01)   The construction of the premises shall be such as to minimise the risk of fire involving the structure.

        (3) (a) Any platform or similar superstructure shall be constructed of such material and in such manner as the Council may consider necessary.

           (b) Any proscenium shall be of non-combustible or inherently non-flammable materials.

G.L.C. Rules :

The Rules apply to performances in theatres with a ' picture frame ' stage and also to those using a thrust and arena stage which are defined thus:

PLATFORM means that part of the public assembly space which is arranged for the accommodation of performers and which is not a stage.

SEPARATED STAGE means a stage which is separated from the remainder of the premises.

OPEN STAGE means a stage which is not so separated.

STAGE AREA means, in addition to the stage itself, any scene dock, workshop, stage basement, staff or orchestra room, store or other portion ancillary to the stage.

STAGE RISK means the stage, together with the lobby approaches thereto, the stage basement and any rooms, including the scene dock, flies and grid, open to the stage.

Part II (38) (a) At such premises as the Council may specify, at least one employee shall be a man of practical experience in fire prevention and extinction.

(b) At all premises regularly used for public entertainment the employees shall have allotted to them specified duties to be performed in the event of fire or panic, and they shall be available during the whole time that the premises are open to the public. All employees shall be properly instructed in the use of the fire appliances provided.

On receiving an emergency signal or in the event of failure of the main lighting, the staff should move unobtrusively to their allotted positions and await orders from the licensee or person in charge. The staff should be instructed accordingly.

(41) The London Fire Brigade shall be called to any outbreak of fire, however slight, and details thereof shall be recorded in the log book.

(44) (a) Except with the prior consent of the Council, scenery or properties shall not be kept or used in any part of premises not having a separated stage. (See also Rule 91.)

Provided that scenery and properties comprising the following may be kept or used on a platform or open stage subject to any conditions the Council may impose in any particular case:

(I) Non-combustible material;
(II) Inherently non-flammable material;
resistant by a process of impregnation accepted by the Council;
(III) Timber, hardboard or plywood rendered flame-
(IV) Durably flame-proofed fabric;
(V) Self-extinguishing plastics material having a flame resistance acceptable to the Council.

(b) The platform or stage shall not be congested with scenery or properties and the exits therefrom shall be maintained free from obstruction.

(45) (a) Any hangings and curtains which may be permitted by the Council shall be of non-combustible, inherently non-flammable or durably flame proofed material.

(b) Temporary decorations shall not be used except with the consent of the Council.

(46) Suitable guards to prevent contact with scenery or other combustible materials shall be fitted to all lamps, lanterns, lighting appliances and any other apparatus liable to become heated whether under normal or abnormal conditions.

(48) (a) Real flame shall not be used in an entertainment unless—

The consent of the Council is obtained and—

(A) The use of real flame is essential to the action as distinct from the atmosphere of the entertainment or to its effective presentation; and

(B) An electric substitute cannot be used.

(c) This rule shall not prohibit smoking in an entertainment provided that suitable precautions against risk of fire are taken.

(49) No entertainments involving special risks and no special entertainment for children shall be given until the Council's consent has been obtained thereto.

(53) (b) Temporary dressing-rooms or quick-change rooms shall not be provided except with the consent of the Council.

(c) Candles shall not be used or brought into the dressing-rooms.

Part III (64) Electric kettles, irons and other appliances shall be used only in positions specially approved by the Council for the purpose.

(65) The electrical installation shall be in the charge of a competent person during the whole of the time that the public are on the premises.

(66) (c) Any temporary electrical installation that may be permitted shall be carried out in accordance with the Council's regulations, and shall be maintained to the Council's satisfaction throughout its period of use.

(88) A certificate by an approved firm of safety curtain engineers, to the effect that the safety curtain and its operating gear and controls have been examined and tested and are in proper working order, shall be submitted to the Council once in every fourteen months.

(89) A certificate by a competent lift engineer, to the effect that any stage mechanical installation (e.g., stage lifts and revolves, moving platforms, etc., and any orchestra lift, organ lift and any apparatus of a similar nature, and any scenery counterweighting system installed at the premises) has been examined and tested and is in safe working condition, shall be submitted to the Council once in every fourteen months.

Additional Rules for premises used for stage presentations :
Part IV (90) (a) All scenery including cloths, draperies, gauze-cloths, floral decorations and properties, hangings, curtains and all fabric decorations on the stage shall be non-flammable to the Council's satisfaction, and shall be so maintained.

(91) (a) Scenery or properties shall not be kept or used in the stage basement or in any part of the premises other than on the stage or in the approved scene or property store.

(b) Scenery or properties, other than those required for use in the current production, shall not be kept on the stage, except that consent may be granted for scenery or properties required for use in rehearsals of impending productions to be so kept.

(92) The ropes attached to counterweights shall be tested by a competent person appointed by the licensee at such intervals as may be necessary as a safeguard against failure.

(93) Except as provided by Rule 48 (c) smoking shall be strictly prohibited within the stage risk and notices to this effect shall be prominently displayed.

(94) Fire blankets and such other fire appliances as the Council may consider necessary shall be kept ready for instant use on the stage and in the flies, scene stores and dressing-rooms and in the passages immediately approaching the dressing-rooms and attention shall be directed to them by notices fixed immediately above them.

(95) (a) At all premises regularly used where scenery and/or properties are employed on the stage, at least one employee shall be a man of practical experience in fire prevention and extinction. This employee shall act as fireman and wear fireman's uniform.

(b) At theatres and music halls and at other premises where scenery is kept or used on or over the stage, the fireman shall remain within the stage risk during the whole of the time that the premises are open to the public.

(c) In premises at which a safety curtain is provided to the proscenium opening, the electrician in charge of the electrical installation, or a qualified assistant electrician, shall remain within the stage risk during the whole of the time that the premises are in use for the presentation of a stage production and the public are on the premises.

(96) Explosives or highly flammable substances shall not be used except with the consent of the Council. Explosives and highly flammable substances will only be permitted to be used other than within a 'separated stage' in exceptional circumstances.

(98) (a) The safety curtain to the proscenium opening shall be lowered and raised in the presence of each audience.

(b) In the event of the safety curtain being out of order, the licensee shall immediately notify the clerk to the Council.

(c) Whenever the safety curtain is lowered, sufficient lights shall be immediately lighted, in addition to the minimum lighting, to give good general illumination in the auditorium.

d) No apparatus or scenery or properties or curtains or hangings shall at any time during the performance cross the plane of descent of the safety curtain, and shall not in any circumstances interfere with its descent.

(e) Except with the consent of the Council, scenery or properties shall not be placed on the auditorium side of the safety curtain.

(h) Shutters to openings for the passage of scenery between the stage and workroom shall be kept closed when the public are on the premises.

(99) The sashes and other moving parts of the lantern light over the stage shall be tested periodically to ensure they are in efficient working order.

(100) (a) Explosives or highly flammable substances shall not be used if the desired effect can be obtained by mechanical or electrical means.

(c) No explosives or highly flammable substances other

than a maximum of 500 safety cartridges, 1 lb. of gunpowder, 3 lb. of coloured fire, and 5 lb. gross weight of maroons, shall be upon the premises at any one time. The cartridges shall be fitted with wafer wads.

(e) Firearms shall not contain any article or substance which might serve as a missile and shall not be directed towards any person, scenery or combustible material. If the desired effect cannot be obtained with safety cartridges, maroons fired electrically in a tank or with other suitable protection may be used. The electrical means of firing shall be so arranged that the safety of the general installation is not affected.

(f) Coloured fire shall be used in metal trays which shall be placed at a safe distance from any combustible material.

(g) If it is desired to use petroleum spirit or other flammable liquid for the purpose of any engine or machine, such engine or machine shall not be used until it has been examined and accepted on behalf of the Council.

(h) All explosives, highly flammable substances, petroleum spirit and other flammable liquid shall be stored and used under safe conditions and shall be in the charge of a competent person, preferably the fireman, definitely appointed for the purpose.

(i) Flammable gases for use in airships or balloons, or for any other purpose, shall not be used except with the consent of the Council.

INDEX

SUGGESTIONS FOR FURTHER READING

THE dates of the first editions are given. Several of the books have been reprinted and those out of print probably would be available through the Central Reference Library of the principal Public Libraries.

Acting
THE ART OF THE ACTOR. B. C. Coquelin. (L'Art du Comedien, Paris 1894.) *Allen and Unwin*, London, 1932.
THE ACTOR'S WAYS AND MEANS. Michael Redgrave. *Heinemann*, London, and *Theatre Arts Books*, New York, 1953.
ACTORS TALK ABOUT ACTING. Edited by Lewis Funke and John E. Booth. *Avon Books*, New York, 1961.
ACTOR AND ARCHITECT. Edited by Stephen Joseph. (The relationship between Actor, Architect and Audience.) *Manchester University Press* and *University of Toronto Press*, 1964.

Costume and Wardrobe
A HISTORY OF COSTUME. Carl Köhler. *Harrap*, London, and *Peter Smith*, U.S.A., 1928.
HISTORIC COSTUME FOR THE STAGE. Lucy Barton. *Black*, London, and *Baker*, Boston, 1935. Revised edn. 1961.
DESIGNING AND MAKING STAGE COSTUMES. Motley. *Studio Vista*, London, and *Watson-Cuptil*, New York, 1964.
COSTUME. Margot Lister. (A practical reference book and illustrated survey from ancient times to the twentieth century.) *Jenkins*, London, 1967.

History
THE DEVELOPMENT OF THE THEATRE. Allardyce Nicoll. *Harrap*, London, and *Harcourt*, New York, 1927.
THE THEATRE OF TODAY. H. K. Moderwell. *Bodley Head*, London, 1927.
THE STAGE IS SET. Lee Simonson. *Harcourt, Brace*, New York, 1932. Revised edn. *Theatre Arts Books*, New York, 1963.
WORLD DRAMA, from Aeschylus to the Present Day. Allardyce Nicoll. *Harrap*, London, and *Harcourt*, New York, 1949.
THE OXFORD COMPANION TO THE THEATRE. Edited by Phyllis Hartnoll. *Oxford University Press*, London and New York, 1951.
A SOURCE BOOK IN THEATRICAL HISTORY. A. M. Nagler. (Quotations by contemporary observers.) *Dover Publications*, New York, 1952.
THE STUDENT'S GUIDE TO WORLD THEATRE. E. J. Burton. (Including the primitive origin of the theatre with reference to Egypt, China, Japan, India and Indonesia.) *Jenkins*, London, 1962.

Lighting
A METHOD OF LIGHTING THE STAGE. Stanley McCandless. (A plan for lighting the acting area.) *Theatre Arts Books*, New York, 1932.
STAGE LIGHTING FOR AMATEURS. Peter Goffin. *Muller*, London, 1938. 4th edn. *Garnet Miller*, London, and *Coach House Press*, Chicago, 1955.
LIGHTING THE STAGE. Percy Corry. (How to use light in production.) *Pitman*, London and New York, 1954.

DESIGNING AND MAKING STAGE SCENERY. Michael Warre. *Studio
Vista*, London, and *Reinhold* New York, 1966.
A CONCISE HISTORY OF INTERIOR DECORATION. George Savage. *Thames
and Hudson*, London, and *Grosset*, New York, 1966.

Sound Effects
NOISES OFF. Frank Napier. *Muller*, London, 1936. 4th edn. *Garnet
Miller*, London, and *Coach House Press*, Chicago, 1962.
SOUND IN THE THEATRE. Harold Burris-Meyer and Vincent Mallory.
(Electronic control of sound.) *Radio Magazines*, Mineola, New York,
1959; now *Theatre Arts Books*, New York.

Technical Books
TRUCS ET DECORS. Georges Moynet. (Theatre machinery and methods
employed in the production of traditional stage illusion.) *La Librairie
Illustrée*, Paris, 1893.
BUHNENTECHNIK DER GEGENWART. Friedrich Kranich. (Systems of
stage mechanism in the German theatre.) R. *Oldenburg*, Berlin, 1929.
THE SMALL STAGE AND ITS EQUIPMENT. R. Angus Wilson. *Allen and
Unwin*, London, 1930.
STAGE-SETTING FOR AMATEURS AND PROFESSIONALS. Richard Southern.
Faber, London, and *Theatre Arts Books*, New York, 1937.
ESSENTIALS OF STAGE-PLANNING. Stanley Bell, Norman Marshall and
Richard Southern. (Basic principles of stage architecture with modi-
fications for smaller theatres.) *Muller*, London, 1949.
TRAITÉ DE SCÉNOGRAPHIE. Pierre Sonrel. (History and technique of
staging scenery.) *Librairie Théatrale*, Paris, 1956.
AN INTERNATIONAL VOCABULARY OF TECHNICAL THEATRE TERMS IN
EIGHT LANGUAGES. Kenneth Rae and Richard Southern for The
International Theatre Institute. *Éditions Meddens*, Brussels. *Bodley
Head*, London, and *Theatre Arts Books*, New York, 1959.
PLANNING THE STAGE. Percy Corry. (Including adaptable stages and
theatre in the round.) *Pitman*, London and New York, 1961.
THE IDEAL THEATRE. Eight concepts from the Ford Foundation
Program for Theatre Design. *American Federation of Arts*, 1962.
NEW THEATRE FORMS. Stephen Joseph. *Pitman*, London and New
York, 1968.

General
THEATRE MANAGEMENT. Sanford E. Stanton. A manual of the business
of the theatre. *Appleton*, New York, 1929.
VOICE AND SPEECH IN THE THEATRE. J. Clifford Turner. *Pitman*,
London and New York, 1950.
THE BUSINESS SIDE OF THE AMATEUR THEATRE. Alan Nelson-Smith.
Macdonald and Evans, London, 1953.
MUSIC IN THE THEATRE. Ronald Settle. *Jenkins*, London, 1957.
HANDBOOK FOR THEATRICAL APPRENTICES. Dorothy Lee Tompkins.
French, New York, 1962.
THE PENGUIN DICTIONARY OF THE THEATRE. John Russell Taylor.
Penguin, London and Baltimore, U.S.A., 1966.
PRACTICAL STAGE MAKE-UP. Philippe Perrottet. *Studio Vista*, London,
1967.
TECHNIQUE OF THE STAGE FIGHT. William Hobbs. *Studio Vista*,
London, and *Theatre Arts Books*, New York, 1967.

THEATRICAL LIGHTING PRACTICE. Joel E. Rubin and Leland H. Watson. (Including lighting for Arena, Open-Air Theatre, Television, Ballet, Puppetry and Ice Shows.) *Theatre Arts Books*, New York, 1954.
LAMPS AND LIGHTING. The Research and Engineering Staff of British Lighting Industries Ltd. (A manual of lamps and electric lighting.) *Edward Arnold*, London, 1966.
THE ART OF STAGE LIGHTING. Frederick Bentham. *Pitman*, London and New York, 1968.

Production
PLAY PRODUCTION. Henning Nelms. *Barnes and Noble*, New York, 1950.
DIRECTORS ON DIRECTING. Edited by Toby Cole and Helen Krich Chinoy. *Peter Owen* and *Vision Press*, London, and *Bobbs-Merrill*, U.S.A., 1953.
THE DIRECTOR IN THE THEATRE. Hugh Hunt. *Routledge and Kegan Paul*, London, and *Hillary*, New York, 1954.
THE PRODUCER AND THE PLAY. Norman Marshall. *Macdonald*, London, 1957.
THE CRAFT OF PLAY DIRECTING. Curtis Canfield. *Holt Rinehart and Winston*, New York, 1963.
SENSE OF DIRECTION. John Fernald. *Secker and Warburg*, London, and *Stein and Day*, U.S.A., 1968.

Properties
STAGE PROPERTIES. Heather Conway. *Jenkins*, London, 1959.
STAGE PROPERTIES AND HOW TO MAKE THEM. Warren Kenton. *Pitman*, London and New York, 1964.

Scenery and Design
STAGE DECORATION. Sheldon Cheney. (Illustrations of stage forms and decoration from the Greek Theatre to today.) *Chapman and Hall*, London, and *Dodd Mead*, New York, 1928.
SETTINGS AND COSTUMES OF THE MODERN STAGE. Theodore Komisarjevsky and Lee Simonson. *The Studio*, London and New York, 1933.
DESIGNING FOR THE STAGE. Doris Zinkeisen. *The Studio*, London and New York, 1938.
STAGE AND FILM DECOR. R. Myerscough-Walker. *Pitman*, London and New York, 1939.
THEATRE SCENECRAFT. Vern Adix. *The Children's Theatre Press*, Anchorage, Ky, U.S.A., 1956.
THE ENGLISH HOME. Doreen Yarwood. *B. T. Batsford*, London, and *Verry*, U.S.A., 1956.
STAGE DESIGN THROUGHOUT THE WORLD SINCE 1935. Edited by R. Hainaux. *Harrap*, London, and *Theatre Arts Books*, New York, 1956.
STAGE DESIGN THROUGHOUT THE WORLD SINCE 1950. Edited by R. Hainaux. *Harrap*, London, and *Theatre Arts Books*, New York, 1964.
STAGE SCENERY: ITS CONSTRUCTION AND RIGGING. A. S. Gillette. *Harper and Row*, New York, 1959.
SCENE DESIGN AND STAGE LIGHTING. W. Oren Parker and Harvey K. Smith. *Holt Rinehart and Winston*, New York, 1963.
SCENE PAINTING AND DESIGN. Stephen Joseph. *Pitman*, London and New York, 1964.

THE CRAFT OF COMEDY. Athene Seyler and Stephen Haggard *Garnet Miller*, London and *Theatre Arts*, New York

ADAPTABLE STAGE COSTUME FOR WOMEN. Elizabeth Russell *Garnet Miller*, London 1974 and *Theatre Arts*, New York 1974

PLAYING PERIOD PLAYS. Lynn Oxenford *Garnet Miller*, London 1958 and *Coach Horse Press*, Chicago 1958

STAGE FIGHTS: A HANDBOOK OF TECHNIQUE. Gilbert Gordon *Garnet Miller*, London 1973 and *Theatre Arts*, New York 1973

MAKE-UP: THE DRAMATIC STUDENT'S APPROACH. Charles Thomas *Garnet Miller*, London 1951 and *Theatre Arts*, New York